I0808338

Cavalry Divisions

Cavalry Divisions

of the

Waffen-SS

Rolf Michaelis

Schiffer Military History
Atglen, PA

Book translation by David Johnston

Book Design by Ian Robertson.

Copyright © 2010 by Schiffer Publishing.
Library of Congress Control Number: 2010931403

All rights reserved. No part of this work may be reproduced or used in any forms or by any means – graphic, electronic or mechanical, including photocopying or information storage and retrieval systems – without written permission from the copyright holder.

Printed in China.
ISBN: 978-0-7643-3661-4

This book was originally published in German under the title
Die Kavallerie Divisionen der Waffen-SS by Michaelis-Verlag

We are interested in hearing from authors with book ideas on related topics.

Published by Schiffer Publishing Ltd.
4880 Lower Valley Road
Atglen, PA 19310
Phone: (610) 593-1777
FAX: (610) 593-2002
E-mail: Info@schifferbooks.com.
Visit our web site at: www.schifferbooks.com
Please write for a free catalog.
This book may be purchased from the publisher.
Please include $5.00 postage.
Try your bookstore first.

In Europe, Schiffer books are distributed by:
Bushwood Books
6 Marksbury Avenue
Kew Gardens
Surrey TW9 4JF, England
Phone: 44 (0) 20 8392-8585
FAX: 44 (0) 20 8392-9876
E-mail: Info@bushwoodbooks.co.uk.
Visit our website at: www.bushwoodbooks.co.uk

Contents

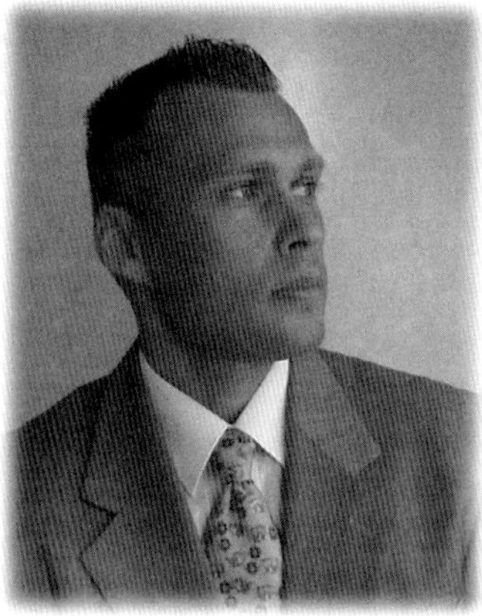

Foreword

There were three cavalry divisions in the *Waffen-SS*, all created for different purposes. The first, the 8th SS Cavalry Division "Florian Geyer," was made up of members of the reinforced SS Death's Head Regiments and ethnic Germans, and was mainly employed to guard the rear areas in the eastern territories. The second, the 22nd SS Volunteer Cavalry Division, was also made up of ethnic Germans, but despite shortages of vehicles and fuel it was meant to be a front line division. The last—created in 1945 from the remnants of the first two—was the 37th SS Volunteer Cavalry Division, which was also envisaged as a front line division. In addition two Cossack divisions, initially part of the army, were transferred to the Waffen-SS at the end of 1944-beginning of 1945 with approximately 25,000 men.

This book is intended to document these SS divisions and bring them to life through eyewitness accounts, photographs, and documents. The reader should not forget the suffering caused by this war. Physical and psychological injuries, death, and loss of property and possessions affected millions of people. It is all the more important to keep this in mind as these apocalyptic events recede farther into the past.

My thanks to all those whose assistance made this publication possible.

Berlin, June 2007
Rolf Michaelis

The 8th SS Cavalry Division "Florian Geyer"

(*8. SS-Kavallerie-Division "Florian Geyer"*)

The SS Death's Head Cavalry Regiments (*SS-Totenkopf-Reiter-Standarten*)

At the end of 1934 the chief of the army command (*Heeresleitung*) recorded that the leadership of the SS had been given permission to form a so-called "police reinforcement" of up to 25,000 men from the ranks of the General SS (*Allgemeine-SS*). The personnel were to have completed their military service and be between 35 and 45 years of age. While the SS men were members of this police reinforcement, the *Wehrmacht*'s right of disposal in the event of mobilization was suspended—meaning that the men could not be called up by the army.

Under the pretext of police-related duties during mobilization, the SS thus had the capability of forming a reserve with the strength of at least a division. As there were already plans to incorporate this potential—at least in part—into the fighting units of the SS at a later date, in 1938 the age requirement was lowered to 25 to 35 years of age. Hitler declared:

"The reinforcement of the SS Death's Head units is a police unit which is to be activated and armed by my order in case of need, but automatically in the event of mobilization.

Its strength will be determined by the Reichsführer-SS and the Chief of German Police within the total strength of all police units that I will fix for the Reich territory.

Organization, distribution of forces, arms, and training of the SS Death's Head units' reinforcement will be determined solely by the police tasks that will fall to it. The Reichsführer-SS and the Chief of German Police will be responsible for full operational capability in this respect and are to make appropriate recommendations to me— after consultation with the Wehrmacht High Command with respect to armaments and equipment.

Training of the SS Death's Head units' reinforcement envisaged for the case of war, age 25 to 35 years, is to be conducted in peacetime by the replacement training units of the SS Death's Head units."

With the expansion of the fighting SS units, in 1939 Hitler authorized the recruitment of volunteers **with no prior service** for the reinforced SS Death's Head Regiments. As these were officially designated police reinforcements, they did not affect the armed SS units' personnel quota imposed by the *Wehrmacht*.[1] On 19 September 1939 a press release declared:

"The SS Death's Head Regiments are conducting a one-time recruitment of a limited number of volunteers from the 1921 and 1922 age classes. Conditions: full SS suitability, minimum height 168 cm, age 17 years, 12-year service commitment.

The recruits cannot be poached from the Wehrmacht and cannot be in possession of a Wehrmacht volunteer acceptance certificate. If qualified, they can opt for an officer career path. They can later enter the police service (including the Secret State Police), middle or upper civil service, or become a defense construction worker."

In the course of this expansion, on 15 September 1939 orders were issued for the creation of a mounted battalion for the SS Death's Head units' reinforcement. The framework of the unit—mainly members of the General SS—was established in just six weeks. Under the command of *SS-Standartenführer* Fegelein, it was sent to the *Generalgouvernement* (Poland) for occupation duties as the reinforced

(1st) SS Death's Head Cavalry Regiment

((1.) SS-Totenkopf-Reiter-Standarte).

Under the Senior SS and Police Commander "East," eight cavalry troops (with the 4th and 8th designated heavy troops) were to be established along with two batteries of horse artillery. A 9th (Replacement) Troop was located in Munich at the Central Riding School of the General SS.

The regiment was deployed as an occupation unit in the Warsaw – Cracow – Chelm area (approx. 200 x 250 km), with single troops stationed in various places. Its reported strength on 28 July 1940 was:

Officers	NCOs	Enlisted Men	Total
54	190	1,585	1,829
3%	10.4%	86.6%	100%

A 2nd **SS Death's Head Cavalry Regiment** was formed in Lublin in the spring of 1940—also mainly with reservists of the General SS. On 28 July 1940 its reported strength was:

Officers	NCOs	Enlisted Men	Total
31	114	1,366	1,511
2.1%	7.5%	90.4%	100%

In addition to training and the general guarding of the area against so-called "looters," the units were also used to guard Polish prisoners of war and to carry out special operations at the behest of the Senior SS and Police Commander "East." In the course of one such action, on 14 January 1940 elements of the (1st) SS Death's Head Cavalry Regiment shot approximately 600 Polish prisoners of war.

On 1 August 1940 Hitler's and Himmler's original intention to use the reinforced SS Death's Head Regiments to enlarge the armed SS was revealed when these units were incorporated into the *Waffen-SS*. Renamed SS Death's Head Cavalry Regiments 1 and 2 (*SS-Totenkopf-Reiter-Regimenter*), the units were organized as follows:

I Battalion	(1st – 5th Troops)
II Battalion	6th Troop
	7th Horse Artillery Battery
	8th (Reconnaissance Troop)
	9th (Infantry Gun) Troop

On 25 February 1941 the former "*reinforced SS Death's Head Regiments*" were incorporated into the *Waffen-SS*. Outwardly this was marked by the removal of the Death's Head collar patches in favor of patches bearing the double *Sig-Runen*. At the same time, the titles of the cavalry units were changed to:

SS Cavalry Regiments 1 and 2

(*SS-Kavallerie-Regimenter 1 und 2*).

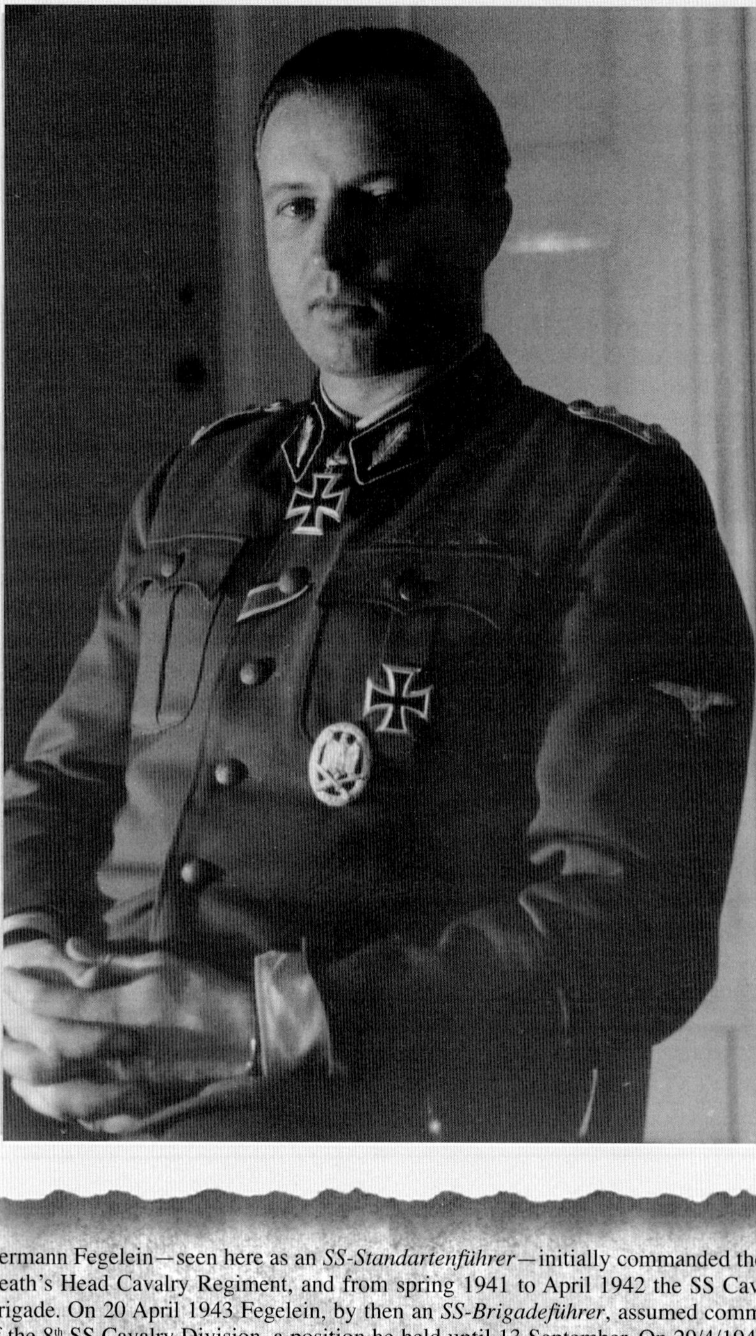

Hermann Fegelein—seen here as an *SS-Standartenführer*—initially commanded the SS Death's Head Cavalry Regiment, and from spring 1941 to April 1942 the SS Cavalry Brigade. On 20 April 1943 Fegelein, by then an *SS-Brigadeführer*, assumed command of the 8th SS Cavalry Division, a position he held until 13 September. On 29/4/1945 he was shot on Hitler's order for treason and desertion.

The SS Cavalry Brigade
(*Die SS-Kavallerie-Brigade*)

In anticipation of the war against the Soviet Union, on 24 February 1941 Himmler issued orders for the two SS cavalry regiments on security duties in the *Generalgouvernement* to be combined into an SS cavalry brigade. On 9 April, with no reorganization, the units were placed under the newly-created Operations Staff *Reichsführer-SS*[2] and moved into the Lyck area in East Prussia. From there the operations staff temporarily attached SS Cavalry Regiment 1 to the 87th Infantry Division to guard its flank. The units saw no further action, however, and the order to create the SS Cavalry Brigade was not realized until the summer of 1941. On 19 July 1941 the operations staff declared:

"*By order of the RFSS, SS Cavalry Regiments 1 and 2 are being committed in and around Baranovice. SS Cavalry Regiment 2 has been placed under Standartenführer Fegelein, commander of SS Cavalry Regiment 1. On crossing the Reich border, tactically and for supply purposes, the SS cavalry unit will fall under the command of the Senior SS and Police Commander attached to the commander of Army Group Center's rear area.*"

The units were reorganized in preparation for this deployment. New units were created from the existing 18 troops with no changes in strength. The brigade was organized as follows:

- Brigade Headquarters with military police, dispatch rider, and music platoons
- SS Cavalry Regiment 1 with
  - I Battalion
    - 1st – 4th Troops
    - 5th (Heavy) Troop
- SS Cavalry Regiment 2 with
  - I Battalion
    - 1st – 4th Troops
    - 5th (Heavy) Troop
- SS Bicycle Reconnaissance Battalion with 3 troops
- SS Artillery Battalion with 2 batteries[3]

In keeping with its original role, the Senior SS and Police Commander "Russia Center" assigned the SS Cavalry Brigade, along with his Police Regiment "Center," the task of "*pacifying*" the conquered areas. In addition to engaging regular Soviet troops trapped behind the lines, "pacification" included shooting undesirable elements of the population: in particular communists, Jews, and Gypsies. As the initial area of operations consisted mainly of forests and swamps, on 28 July 1941 the Operations Staff "*Reichsführer-SS*" issued "Guidelines for Combing Swampy Areas":

"I. Capabilities of Cavalry Units

(1) It is to be taken into consideration that, on average, mounted units cover less ground per day than infantry without baggage. Average daily march distance of 40 – 60 km is the upper limit for the cavalry.

(2) For this reason, actions must always be planned in such a way that no unnecessary roads (which would not be used by the motorized forces) must be used.

(3) Patrolling and combing, meaning an advance with combat actions and searching of villages, imposes an upper limit of 20 – 30 km per day.

II. Participation of the Police

(1) As a rule, the security police are to be involved in actions from the very outset. Their reports and intelligence are essential in planning the operations.

(2) Provided they are equipped appropriately and have forces available, Order Police units will take part in the actions, including patrolling.

(3) Motorized units of the Order Police, advancing in step with the forces in the interior of the swampy region, are to screen and secure the lateral boundary lines and military and other roads. Remember that an enemy wanting to break out across the military road will not come directly from the side, but instead will first flee straight ahead for a distance and then attempt to break out before the area that can be driven through in one day. Patrols on the roads are the only means of guarding the entire segment, which can perhaps be searched in four days. Stronger forces are to be massed only at intervals equivalent to two days travel (i.e. 60 km).

III. Operational Planning

(1) Each clearance action is to be prepared with care. It must be preceded by thorough reconnaissance and scouting by patrols and aerial reconnaissance (if necessary by Fieseler Storch). The population is to receive appropriate notification through air-dropped leaflets and be warned against offering support to marauders.

(2) Efforts are to be made to limit the size of the area to be patrolled in order to maintain an overall picture.

(3) Patrolling without securing the boundaries of the area being patrolled is pointless.

(4) Guarding and screening the boundary lines are the responsibility of the motorized and wheeled elements of the cavalry units. Security is to take the form of small hedgehog positions, as the [boundary] line is to be guarded both in the direction of the area being searched and towards the rear. Also to be guarded are the roads and pathways coming out of the swampy area.

(5) Dead and living booty (cattle) must be taken to safety.

(6) In the event of major resistance in the villages, the air force is to be summoned in order to minimize casualties.

(7) All signals assets are to be used to ensure flawless communications, so that command is always in the picture. The danger that the unit becomes split up and lost in the swampy area must be eliminated at all costs.

IV. Treatment of the Population

(1) We must be clear that the villages in the swampy area are either strongpoints for us or strongpoints for the enemy. They can only be strongpoints for us if their population is not made up of criminals, but, from a racial point of view, consists of Ukrainians—or otherwise consists of a minority population which is well-disposed towards us and ill-disposed towards the Russians or the Poles. If this is the case, then we must see to it that these villages can defend themselves against marauders and entirely become strongpoints for us. We must appoint and confirm village leaders. The Security Police, which is to take part in these actions, is to employ trusted persons at all times. As well, the population is to be armed to a limited

degree, for otherwise they will be overrun, no matter how supportive they are, and become supply bases for the enemy. When villages are occupied, it is best to post notices instructing the population how to behave. Furthermore, they should be promised a share of the booty from captured partisans and marauders. Their share can be a portion (but not all) of the horses, of foodstuffs, wagons, and other things not needed by the troops themselves.

(2) If the population is generally hostile, racially inferior, or even, as is very often the case in swampy areas, made up of escaped prisoners, then all those suspected of aiding the partisans are to be shot; women and children are to be transported elsewhere. Cattle and foodstuffs are to be confiscated and taken to safety. The villages are to be burned to the ground.

(3) Either the villages and settlements are a net of strongpoints whose inhabitants automatically kill every partisan and marauder and report everything to us, or they cease to exist. We cannot allow any hostile elements to find support and subsistence in this area."

After the release of these guidelines, the SS Cavalry Brigade began combing the Pripyat Marshes between *Rollbahn 1* and the Pripyat River. After the operation, which lasted until 11 August 1941, *SS-Standartenführer* Fegelein reported just two fatal casualties, while the number of persons shot by his men totaled 13,788. Entire villages were liquidated and some burned down.[4] Even allowing for the fact that the SS officers—*SS-Standartenführer* Fegelein[5] especially—boastfully exaggerated the numbers, the operation was unbelievably harsh. SS Cavalry Regiment 2's final report provides an insight into the nature of its actions:

"*Combat Impressions: None*

Population: Mainly Ukrainian, in second place White Russians, in third place Poles and Russians, with very few of the latter. Jews are mainly in the larger towns, but there they form a high percentage of the population, in some cases 50 – 80%, but in others just 25%.

The Ukrainian and White Russian population is very cooperative. This they demonstrated, in particular, by reporting partisan bands that had operated in the area a short or long time ago. Only rarely, however, were these found and ferreted out so that they could be shot.

They showed further proof of their good will by bringing milk, eggs, and all kinds of food to the troops as soon as they arrived. These they gave of their own volition with no request for payment.

Poles and Russians were silent and taciturn; however, they welcomed the presence of German soldiers and declared that they were happy that Bolshevism had been driven out.

In many cases, when the troops arrived the Ukrainians set out a table with a white tablecloth, on which there was bread and salt, which was offered to the unit officers. In one case there was even a band waiting to welcome the troops.

Worth noting is the large number of children present in every village. It is not unusual for families to have 10 to 12 members.

From a racial standpoint the Ukrainians make a good impression, even if short, but they are all of a uniform build and shape with a clear facial expression. The same can be said of the White Russians, though not so markedly. As there were only a few Poles and Russians no record was made of their characteristics.

Terrain Conditions: The entire area consists of large areas of swampy terrain interspersed with a few sandy sections; consequently, the ground is not very firm. Even if it was better in some places, it was all the worse in others.

The area is crisscrossed by numerous canals and streams, whose flow is for the most part unregulated. Between them are large areas of forest, consisting mainly of birches, alders, and pines.

The most common crops are rye, oats, and potatoes. Hemp and flax grows everywhere else; also a great deal of millet, which is an important food source. Hemp and flax are cultivated to meet the local demand for materials. One almost always sees spun and woven clothing. Among the Ukrainian population this is adorned with embroidery.

The road conditions are extremely poor, in part sandy, in part muddy, often causing the troop trains to lag two days' march behind the troops.

Supply: Keeping the troops supplied with food and hay was very difficult on account of the road conditions. The food shortage was made good through voluntary donations from the inhabitants. The only thing that could not be found anywhere was oats for the horses. Hay was also impossible to procure, and so the horses had to be fed grass almost exclusively. One disadvantage of the poor deliveries of rations and fodder was that the area assigned to the mounted battalion for pacification was too large. In some cases the troops formed trains of 20 to 25 panye wagons so as to be able to transport with them everything they needed. Worst off in terms of supply was the 3rd Troop, which was deployed in the southern areas, south of the Pripyat.

Condition of the Troops: The health of the troops was excellent throughout the entire operation. Only a very small percentage of the men had to be sent to hospital, and they were able to return to their units after a few days. The morale of the troops was consistently very good. There were no casualties.

Condition of the Horses: The condition of the horses suffered on account of inadequate supplies of oats and the strenuous marches that had to be covered each day. If, for example, an area 30 kilometers deep had to be pacified in one day, that meant about 60 kilometers or even more for horse and rider. In this way a large number of horses were disabled through lameness or sores, draft horses through sores on the withers and chafing. Some of the horses had to be replaced with farm horses. Long marches were made on foot to take the strain off the horses. The 2nd and 4th Troops suffered the heaviest attrition in horses.

Pacification: Pacification took the form of the unit or platoon leader contacting the mayor of the affected town and discussing all matters affecting the population. The mayors were questioned as to the number and composition of the inhabitants, whether they were Ukrainian, Russian, etc. They were also asked if there were still communists in the village or disguised Red Army men, or anyone else who had been involved in bolshevism. Usually members of the population then came forward, having claimed to have seen partisan bands or other suspicious persons. If still in the village, such elements were arrested and, after a brief interrogation, were either released or shot. Where there was no organization for the maintenance of public order such an organization was established, based on the number of inhabitants and taking into consideration the racial makeup in the villages. In the smaller villages the mayor was made responsible for maintaining order. He was forbidden to engage in any kind of political activity.

Jewish looters were shot. Only a few manual laborers, who were employed in Wehrmacht repair shops, were left behind. Driving women and children into the swamps failed to achieve the desired effect, for the swamps were not deep enough for them to become submerged. In most cases, after a depth of 1 meter they usually struck firm ground (probably sand), making it impossible to submerge.

No communists were encountered. Usually it was persons who had been involved in communist activities. Reports about partisan bands were usually exaggerated. Most investigations proved fruitless. In one case a Polish clergyman was shot for spreading Polish propaganda and encouraging the population to hold out: Poland would rise again. Leaflets bearing a similar message were dropped in the area of Kamien Koscyrsko.

Ukrainian clergymen were very eager to help and offered their assistance in every operation. It was also remarkable that the population for the most part spoke favorably about the Jewish element of the population. They did, however, willingly help in the rounding up of the Jews.

The total number of looters etc. shot by the mounted battalion was 6,526 persons.

About 10 prisoners were brought in. 1 Russian agent is still being held by battalion headquarters in Luniniec.

Summing up, it can be said that the action was a success."

From 15 to 30 August 1941 the brigade searched the area south of the Pripyat between Turov and Mozyr. From there the SS Cavalry Brigade marched into the triangular area between the Pripyat in the southwest, the Dniepr in the east, and the Mozyr – Gomel rail line in the north. The Senior SS and Police Commander "Russia Center" noted in his war diary:

"*...a vast area, in which there have been no German troops to date. [...] I flew over SS Cavalry Regiment 2's columns on the move between Bobruisk and*

Mozyr. The troops waved enthusiastically, as they always do when I fly over them. […] After transmitting a radio message from Rechitsa to the commander (of the army rear area) concerning my observations, I flew back to Choiniki. By then the headquarters and the reconnaissance battalion had arrived there. Fegelein, with the help of men and women recruited locally, had spruced up the quarters fantastically for the conditions and had procured the makings for an excellent supper. I lived with Fegelein and his staff in the party building, a wooden house beneath old oak trees, situated next to a stream where the wild geese cackled. The 10th of September was filled with officer conferences, drafting of orders for the pacification action and reconnaissance patrols against the forest complex between Choiniki and Rechitsa. The subsequent issuing of orders in the evening hours in front of the party building, while the SS men sang soldier's songs around their campfires as if on maneuvers, was even recorded on records from the propaganda company's radio truck. […] In order to set a good example, and because only one man—Fegelein—could lead, I armed myself with a submachine-gun and thus equipped took part in the action on the front line. The operation was a success, especially in the village of Torny. I personally succeeded in arresting 1 commissar, 2 leading partisans, 6 other partisans, and 13 Russian soldiers. Drumhead court-martials were at once convened and all of those who had been found with weapons were immediately shot."

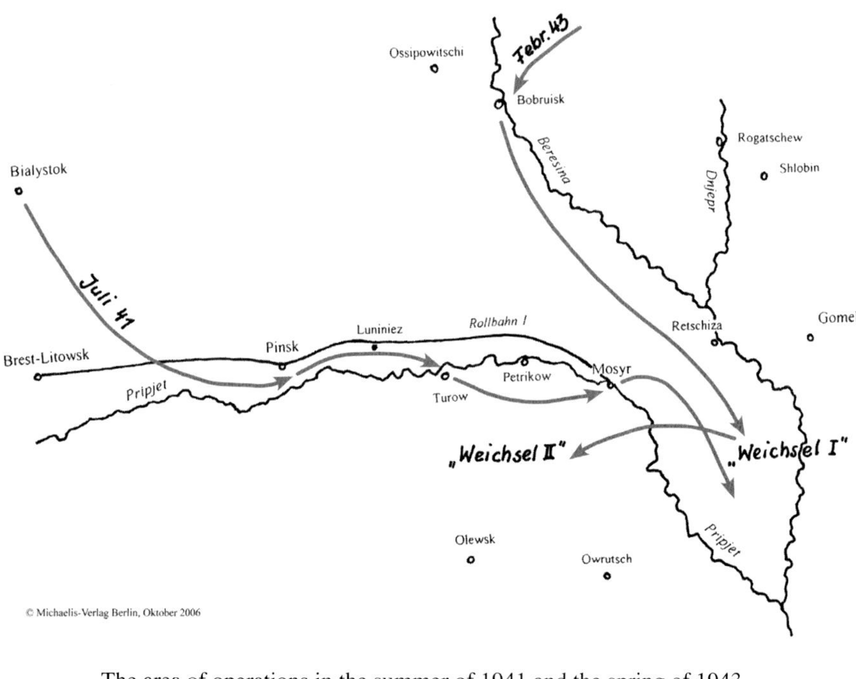

The area of operations in the summer of 1941 and the spring of 1943.

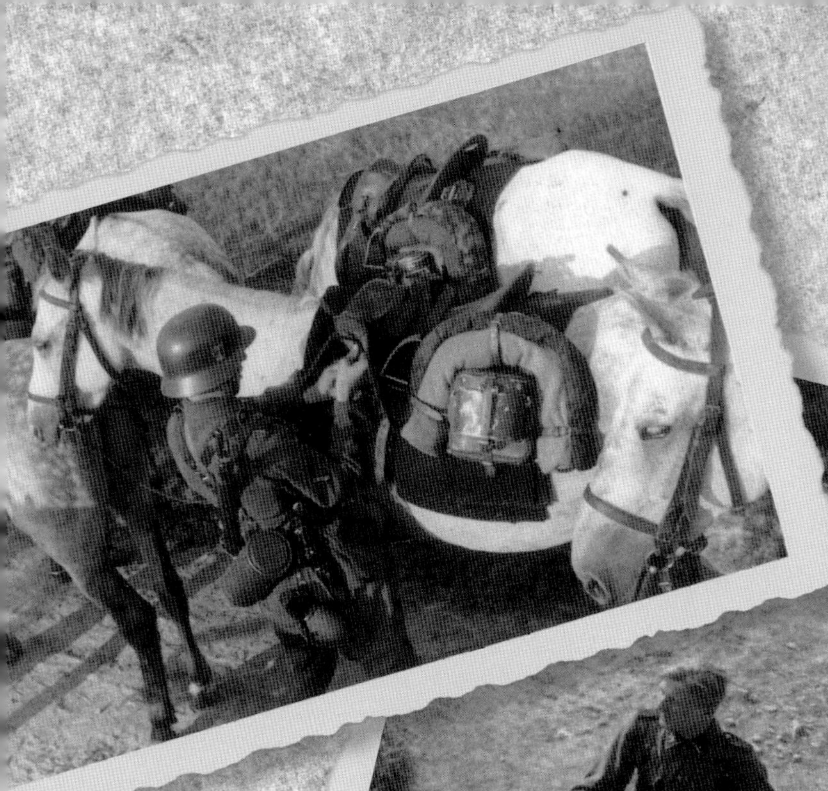

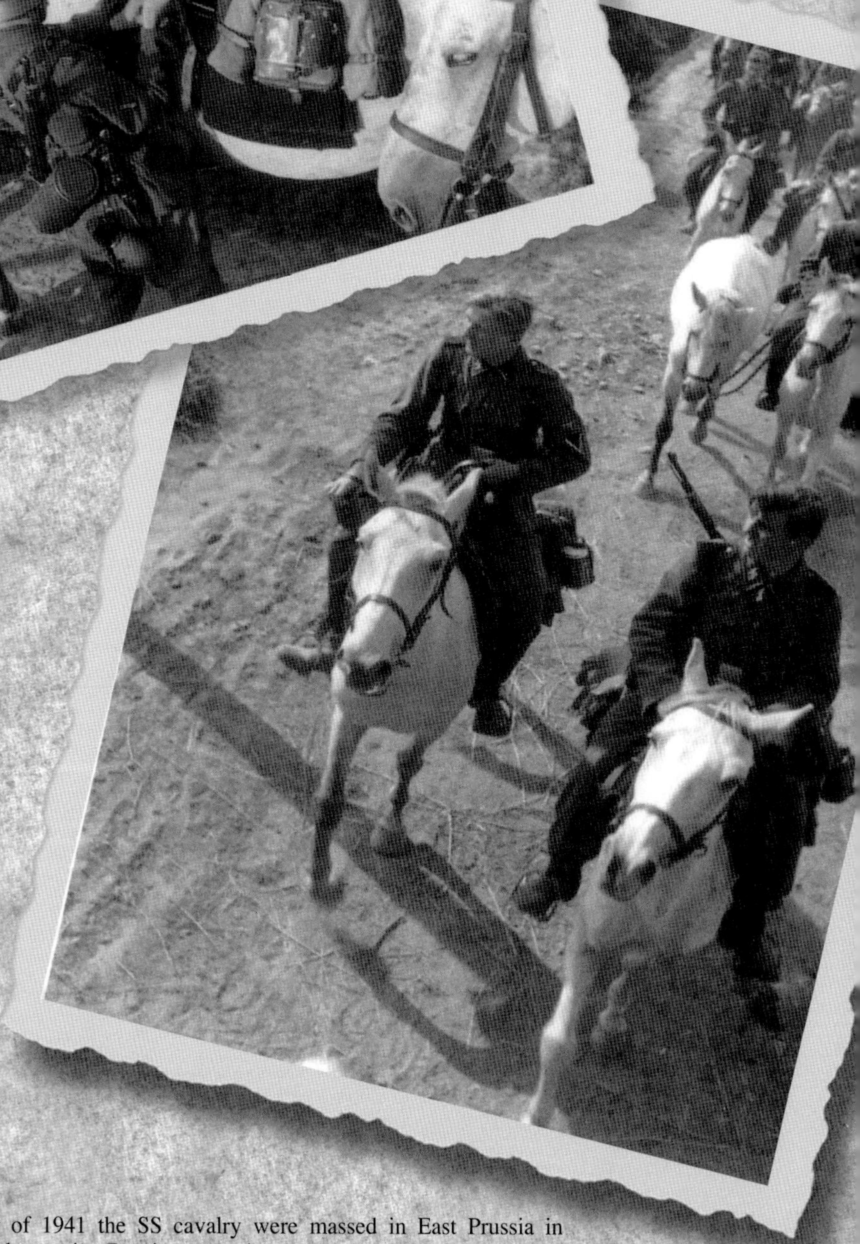

In the summer of 1941 the SS cavalry were massed in East Prussia in preparation for the coming Russian campaign.

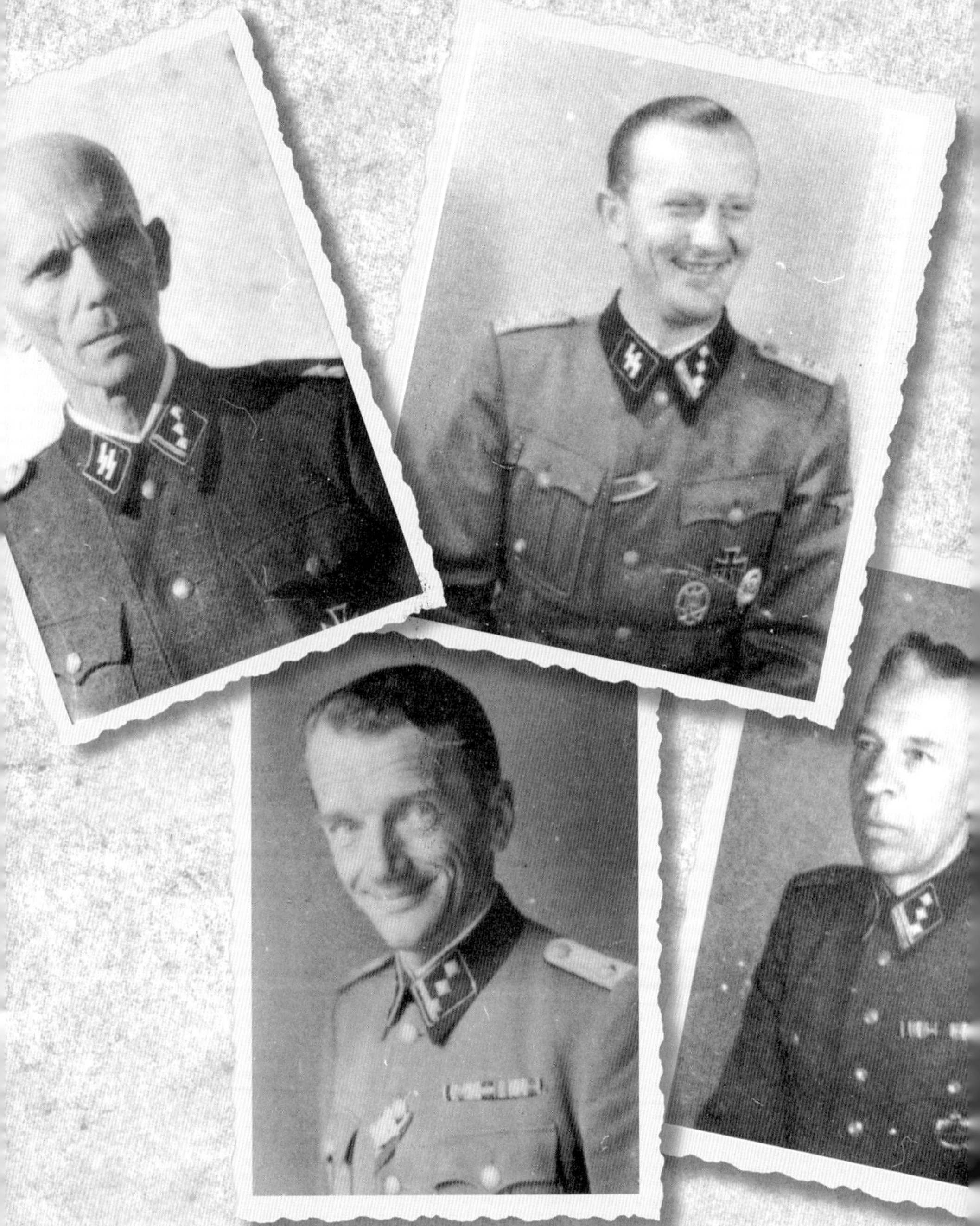

In the beginning, the officer corps of the SS Cavalry Brigade was largely made up of members of the General SS, most of whom were veterans of the First World War.

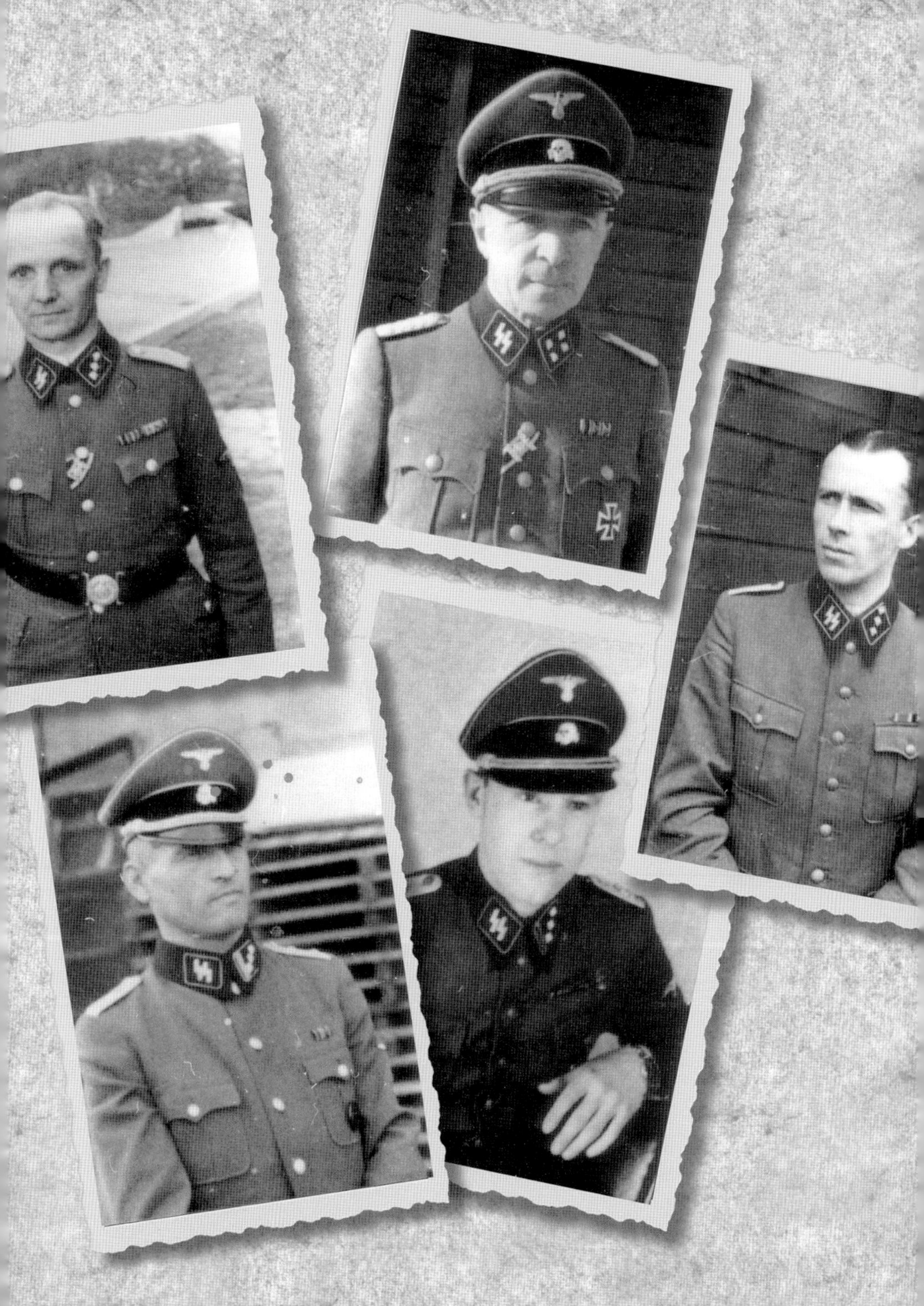

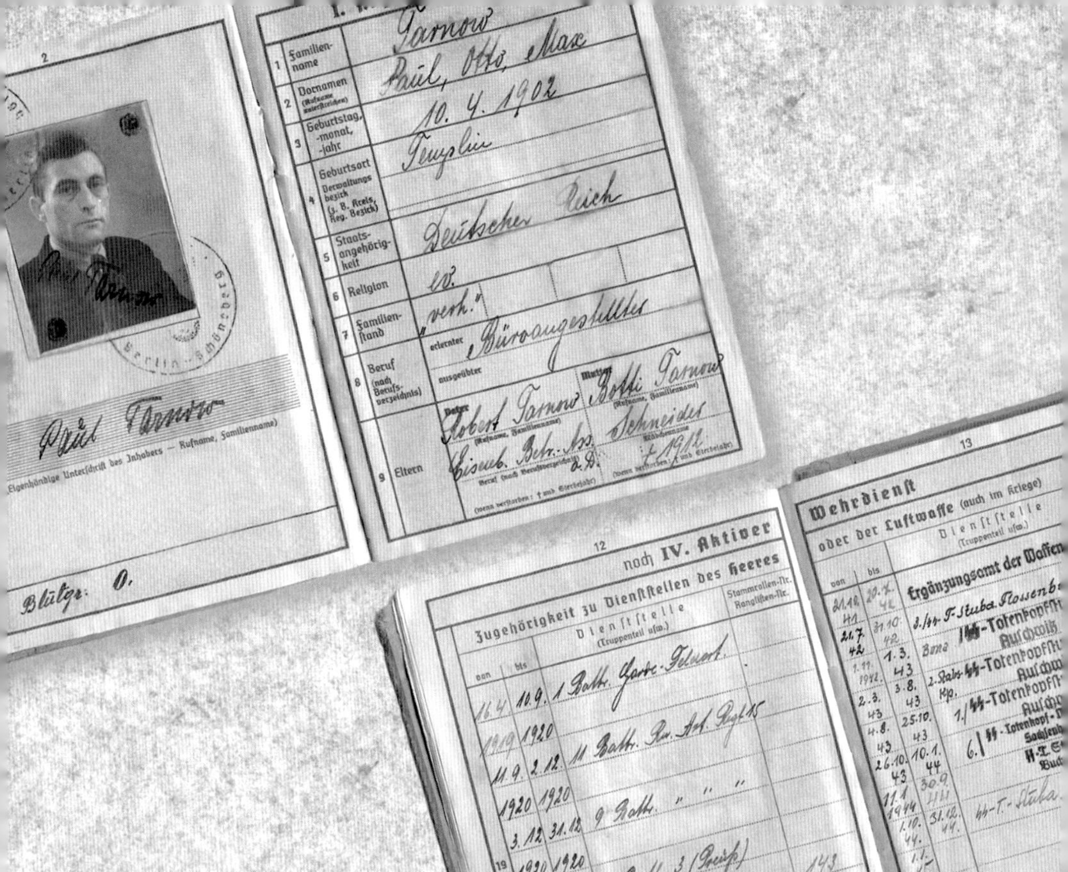

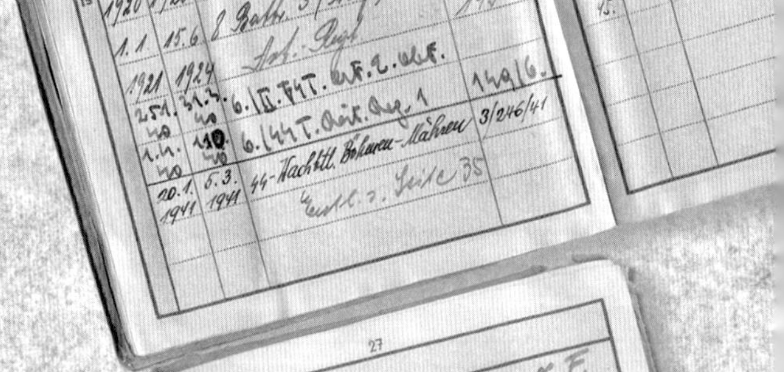

A member of the General SS, Paul Tarnow joined the SS Death's Head Artillery Replacement Battalion on 25/1/40 and subsequently served with the 6th Company of SS Death's Head Cavalry Regiment 1 from 1/4 – 1/10/40. Briefly employed as a guard at the Theresienstadt ghetto, from 21/7/41 until the end of the war Tarnow served in various concentration camps.

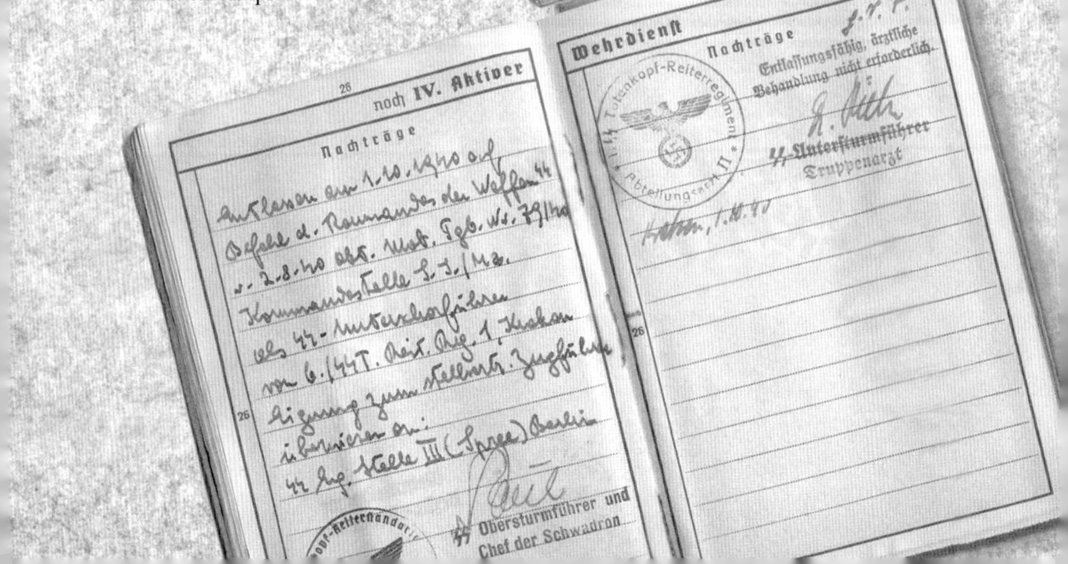

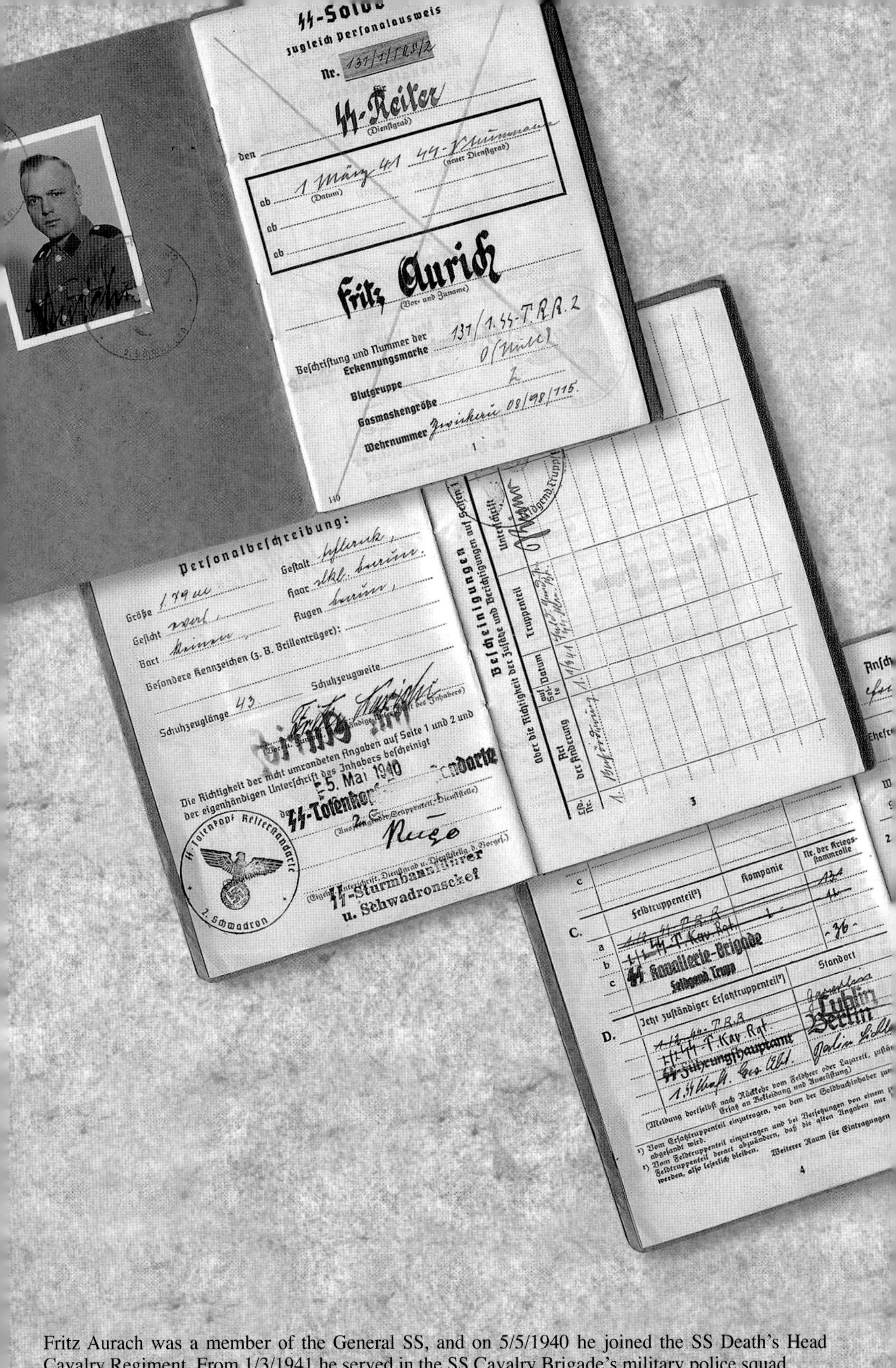

Fritz Aurach was a member of the General SS, and on 5/5/1940 he joined the SS Death's Head Cavalry Regiment. From 1/3/1941 he served in the SS Cavalry Brigade's military police squad.

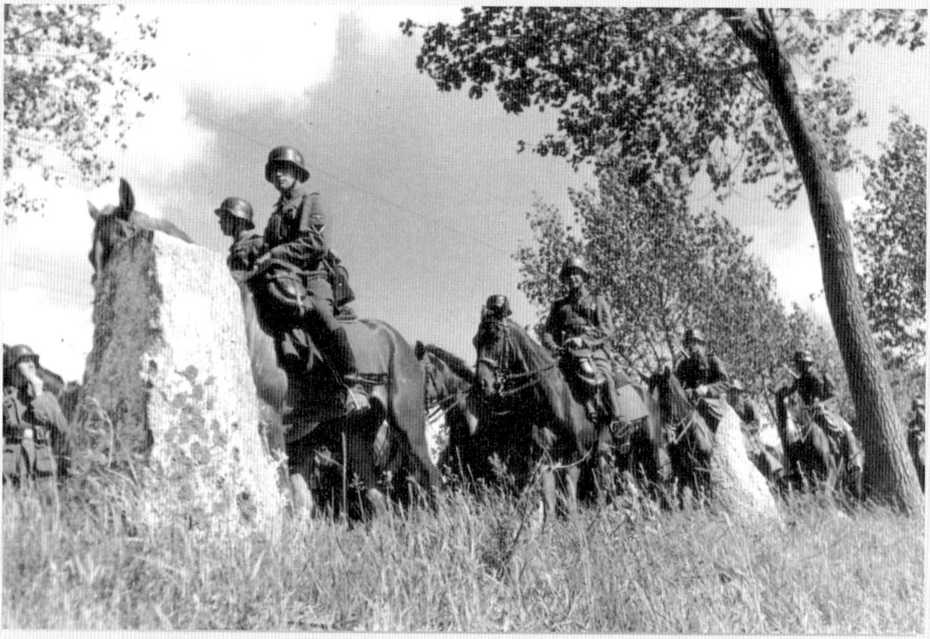

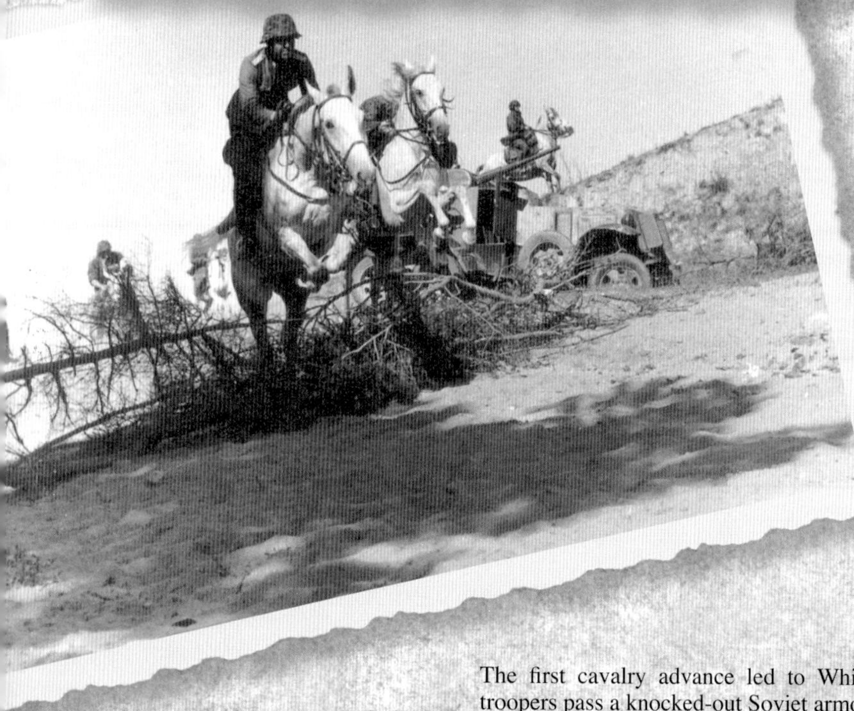

The first cavalry advance led to White Russia—here troopers pass a knocked-out Soviet armored car.

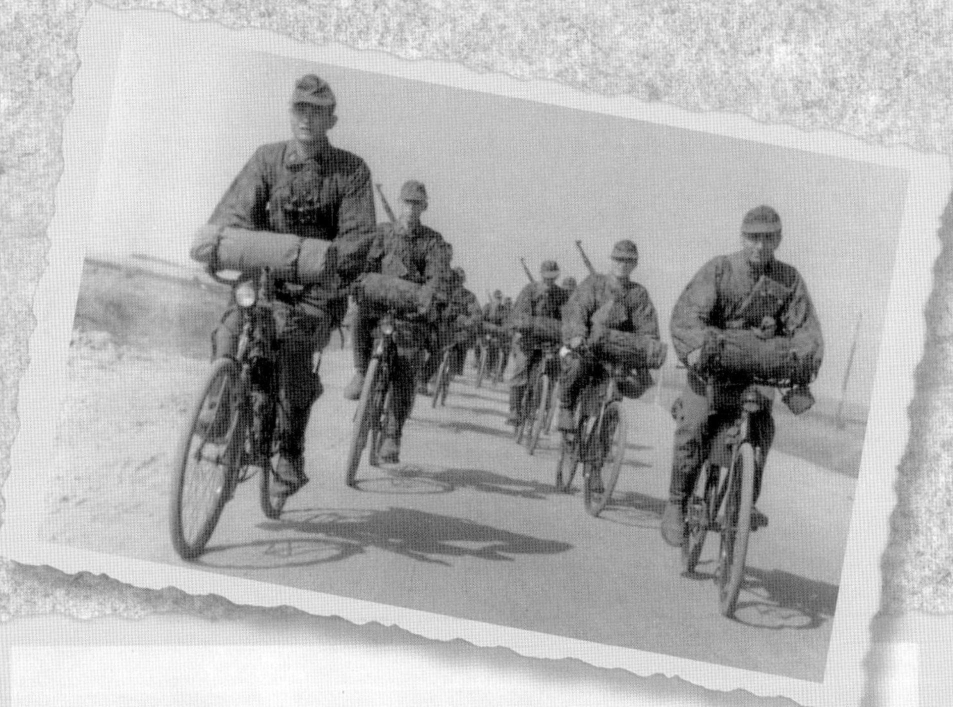

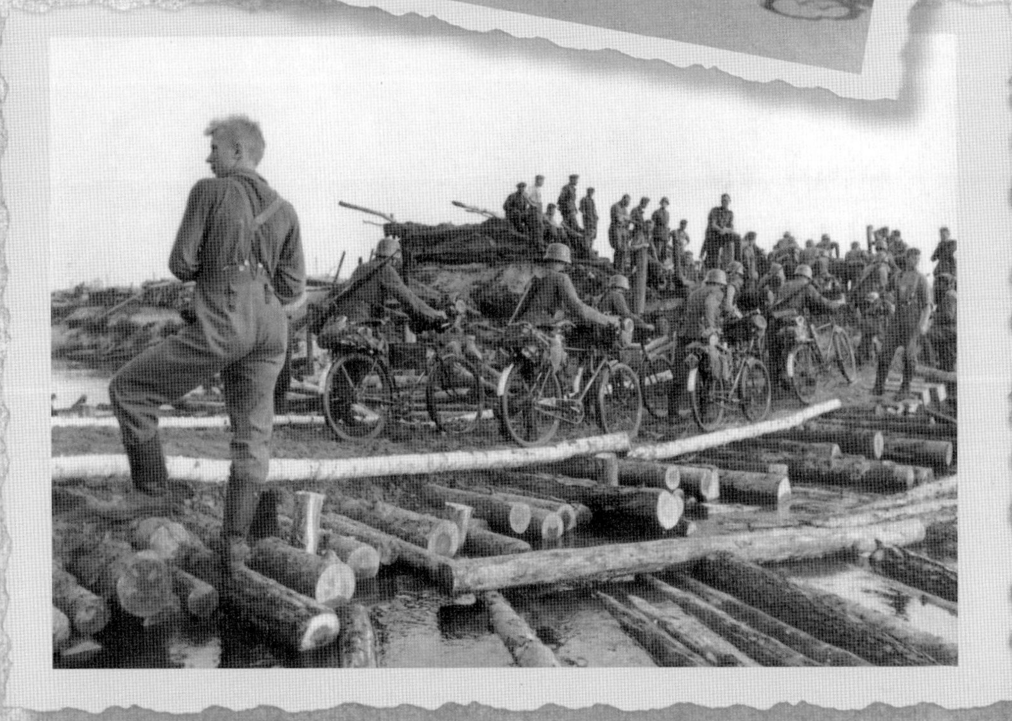

The SS Bicycle Reconnaissance Battalion on the move—summer 1941.

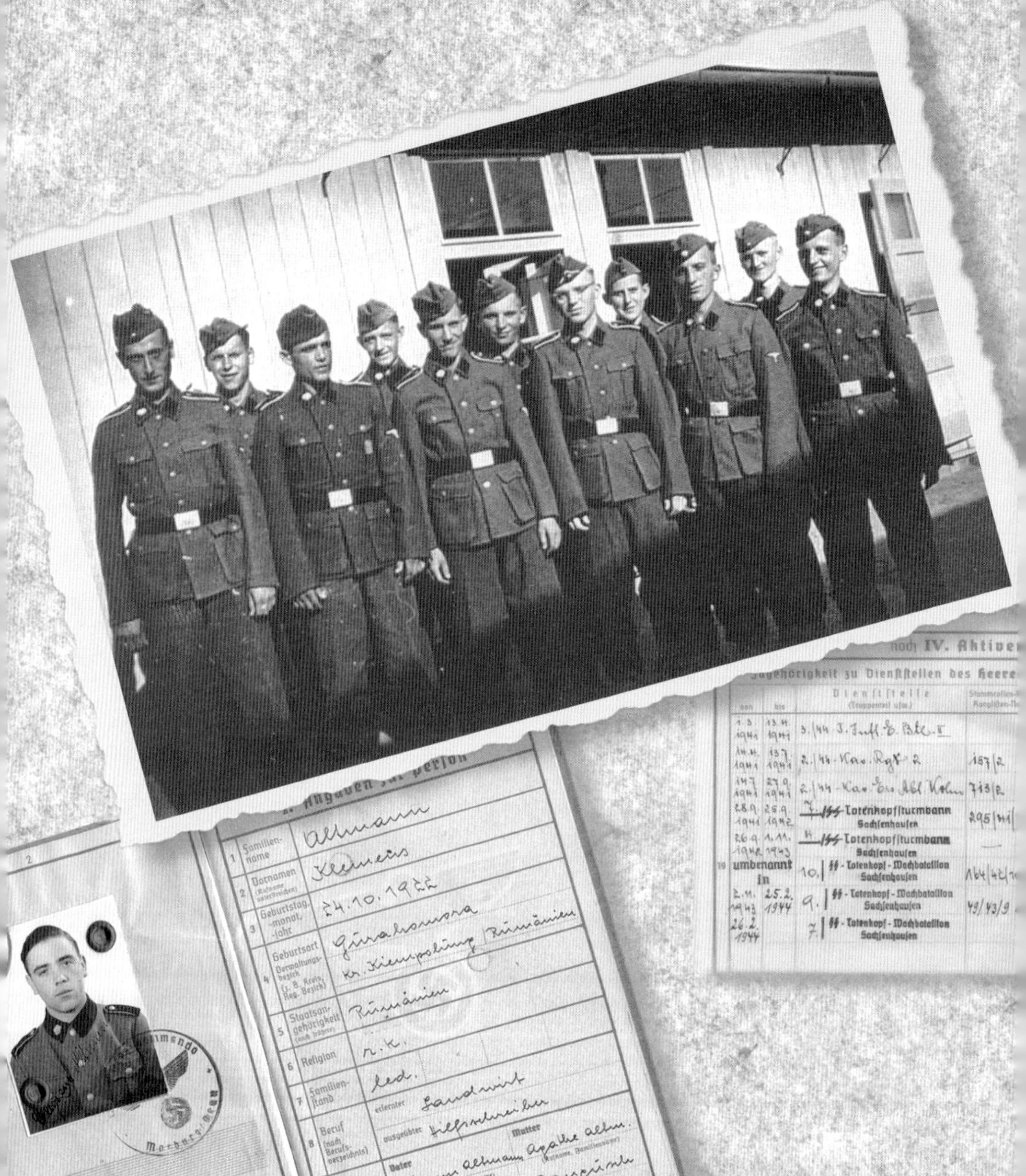

Klemens Altmann, an ethnic German from Rumania, joined the Waffen-SS in March 1941 and served as an SS cavalryman from 14/4 to 27/9/41. From then until the end of the war he served as a guard at the Sachsenhausen concentration camp.

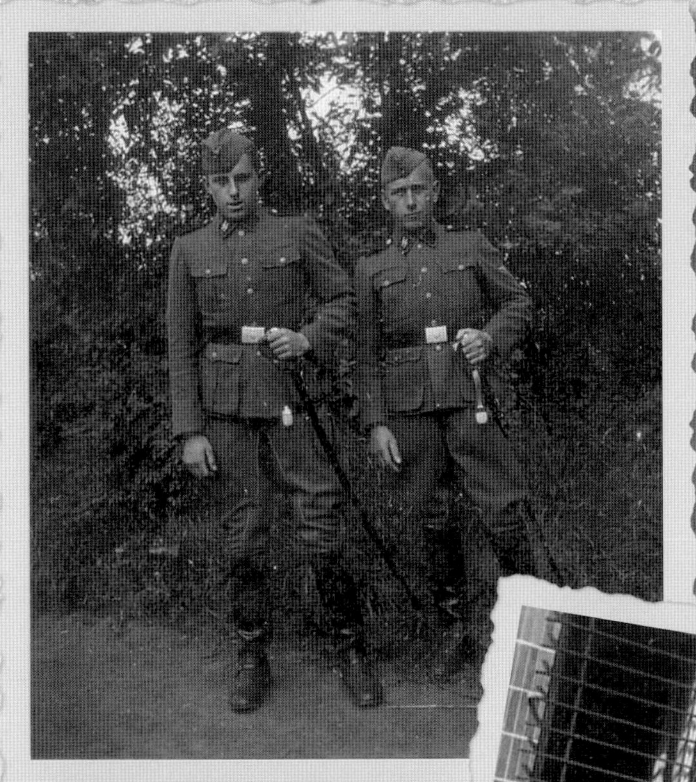

Note the different-colored troop sword knots worn by these two SS troopers.

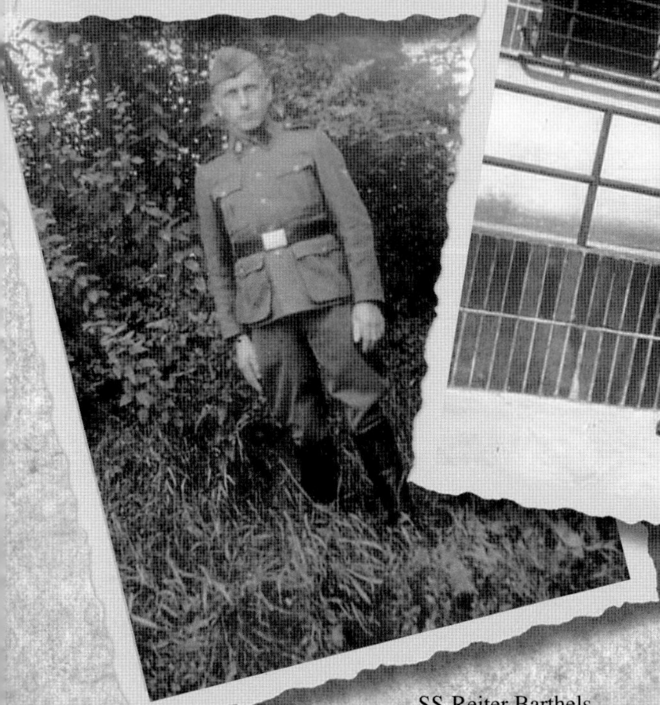

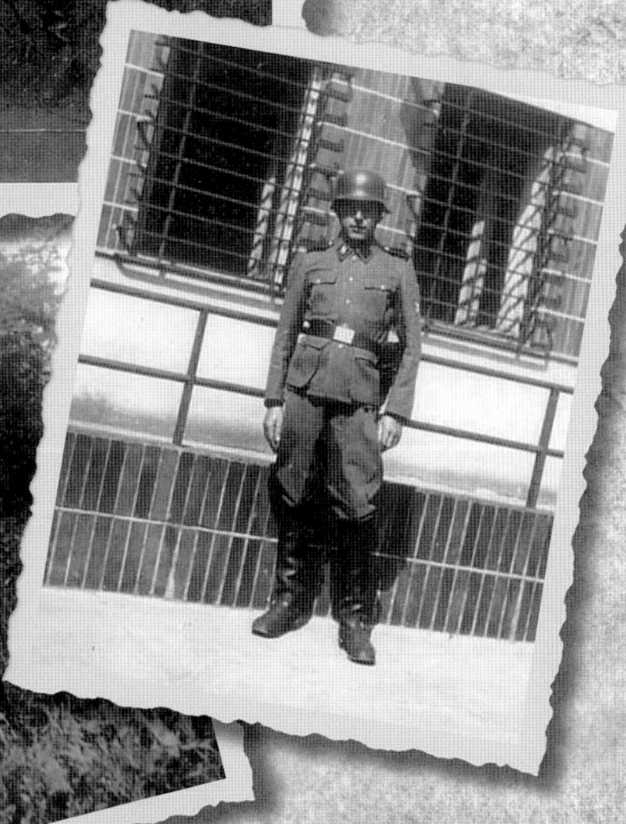

SS-Reiter Barthels.

Action in the Rzhev Area

At the beginning of October 1941 the SS Cavalry Brigade was ordered into the Toropets – Kholm area, approximately 500 kilometers to the north, and placed under the Commander of Rear Army Area Center (H.Q. Mogilev). On 18 October 1941 SS Cavalry Regiment 1 was committed to a pacification operation along the Velikiye Luki – Rzhev railway line. There were numerous small-scale actions, including one in which a forest camp was taken after a brief fire fight. Located 22 km north of Semtzy (approx. 140 km east of Velikiye Luki), it was found to contain 227 hand grenades and 18,000 rounds of rifle-caliber ammunition. In mid-November SS horsemen discovered an ammunition depot whose contents included 400 kg of explosives, several crates of detonators, 950,000 rounds of small arms ammunition, and 1,200 heavy rocket projectiles. During the month of October 1941 the brigade reached its authorized strength through the addition of:

1 pioneer company
1 signals company
1 flak battery
1 veterinary company
1 medical company

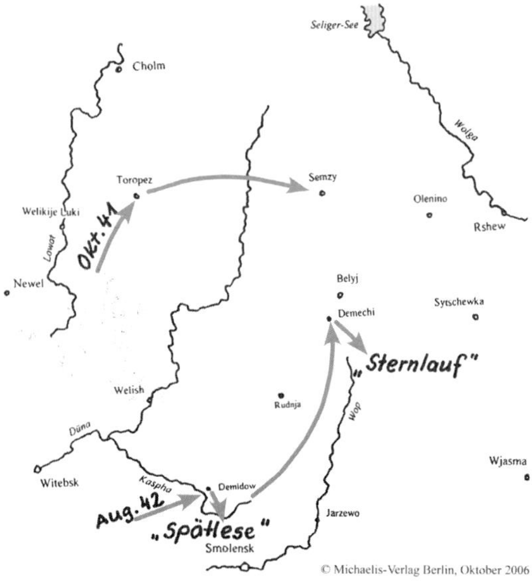

The area of operations autumn-winter 1941/42 and summer-winter 1942/43.

In the course of the Soviet winter offensive, which began on 5 December 1941, forces of the Red Army crossed the Volga between Lake Seliger and the area north of Rzhev, placing the German units of the 9th Army in a critical situation. The German XXIII Army Corps was encircled west of Olenino. With no winter clothing, special lubricants for weapons and equipment, and no deliveries of food or ammunition, in temperatures as low as minus 40 degrees the German troops were able to offer little resistance.

To reinforce the hard-pressed units, the SS Cavalry Brigade was ultimately sent in the direction of Rzhev to bolster the front. On 14 December 1941 the SS Bicycle Reconnaissance Battalion was ordered into the combat zone of the 253rd Infantry Division. At the end of December the two cavalry regiments followed into XXIII Army Corps' sector, where they were attached to the 206th Infantry Division. On 11 January 1942 the enemy pressure abated temporarily. Powerful enemy forces continued driving towards the southwest, however, reaching the area northwest of Vyazma. The German counter-operation began the next day, restoring the front and pinching off the enemy point units. Four days later *Generalleutnant* Höfl, commander of the 206th Infantry Division, wrote of the operation:

"*Dear Fegelein!*

The recognition accorded the officers and men of the division in the special order of the day of 23 January 1942 also extends to the cavalry brigade, as one of the units tactically attached to the division during the fighting.

But I would also like express my personal thanks and appreciation to you and your brave troops. By simultaneously guarding the supply base in Olenino and conducting a series of attacks with your usual vigor, covering the division's right flank, you made a significant contribution to the success of this difficult operation.

Your devoted Höfl."

From then on the cut-off Soviet troops made repeated attempts to break out of the pocket, while the German side strove to crush it as quickly as possible. The attack began on 29 January 1942. On 5 February the spearheads of the 1st Panzer Division and the SS Cavalry Brigade linked up near Cherdino, significantly reducing the size of the pocket. By 18 February 1942, after fierce and costly fighting, the encircled enemy forces had been destroyed. The enemy's losses were 187 tanks, 343 guns, and 26,647 killed. The fighting, the cold, and the inadequate rations had reduced the SS Cavalry Brigade's combat strengths by up to 80%. *General der Infanterie* Schubert, commanding general of XXIII Army Corps, praised the SS Cavalry Brigade's performance:[6]

"[...] In the difficult, sometimes costly, but vigorously-prosecuted fighting, the brigade not only frustrated every enemy attempt [to break out], but also carried out the main attacks in the subsequent encirclement and destruction of enemy elements southwest of Rzhev."

During the same period, the SS Bicycle Reconnaissance Battalion was deployed with the 253rd Infantry Division in Selizharovo, on the Volga (approx. 45 km SE of Lake Seliger), separate from the SS Cavalry Brigade. On 13 January 1942 the battalion reported that it already suffered 75% casualties in killed, frostbitten, and wounded. The SS men were forced to withdraw towards Toropets, where they were incorporated into the weak defenses. The Red Army was just 10 kilometers from the city, which it occupied two days later. This left no continuous German front in the more than 100-kilometer-wide area between Velikiye Luki and Rzhev, and a panicked retreat in the direction of Vitebsk followed. On 22 January 1942 the approximately 50 members of the SS Bicycle Reconnaissance Battalion were attached to the 89th Infantry Division. The survivors of the Heavy Troop fought in the village of Nelidova, which lay on the Velikiye Luki – Zemtsy – Olenino – Rzhev rail line and was viewed by the SS Cavalry Brigade as a rear strong point between the headquarters and supply units in Toropets and the front. Nelidova had to be abandoned on 24 January 1942. Men from the 1st Mountain Division were picked up near Dobrina.

After the Soviet winter offensive came to an end the SS Cavalry Brigade remained in its positions west of Rzhev, and was employed sporadically against fragmented enemy units. The unit was pulled out of the front in mid-April 1942 so that it could be sent to SS Training Camp "Heidelager" to be expanded into a division.

A battalion-strength battle group under the command of *SS-Sturmbannführer* Zehender initially remained in the main line of resistance. This consisted of:

1st Troop (members of SS Cavalry Regiment 1)
2nd Troop (members of SS Cavalry Regiment 2)
3rd Troop (pioneer company)
4th Troop (members of the brigade)
flak battery
artillery battery
signals company

At the end of June 1942 the so-called "Battle Group Zehender" followed to Debica. *SS-Unterscharführer* Rudolf Hüholt remembered:

"On 5 July 1941 I was called up and assigned to the 1st Battery of SS Flak Battalion "Operations Staff RF-SS" in Weimar-Buchenwald. A total of four 20-mm anti-aircraft batteries were formed there. After we had completed training and received our equipment we were moved to Berlin. We were quartered in the Friederichstrasse for 14 days and subsequently in Oranienburg. At the end of October 1941 we boarded trains at the Berlin-Tempelhof freight depot and set off for Eydtkau. From there we continued by vehicle through Kovno, Vilnius, Minsk, Orsha, Vitebsk, Velikiye Luki, and Toropets to Nelidovo, where we arrived at the end of November 1941. Our area of operations was located there with the command post of the SS Cavalry Brigade, to which we were attached as a flak battery. At the beginning of 1942 we saw action in the Olenino area, southwest of Rzhev. The great winter battle was fought there following the retreat from Kalinin. In Nelidovo we went from being a motorized unit to a horse-drawn one, meaning our vehicles were sent back to Toropets, where they later fell into the hands of the Russians. The 20-mm guns were mounted on panye sleighs, each of which was pulled by four horses. In the spring of 1942 we again received a few vehicles, and the SS Cavalry Brigade was supposed to be pulled out of the combat zone

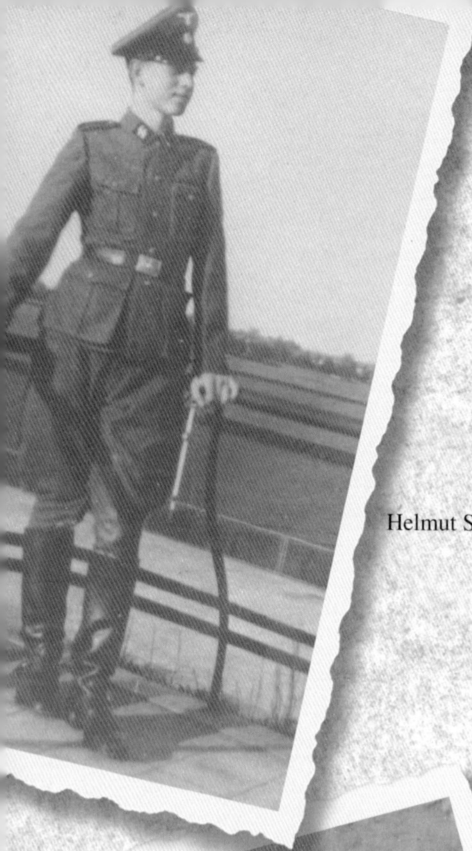

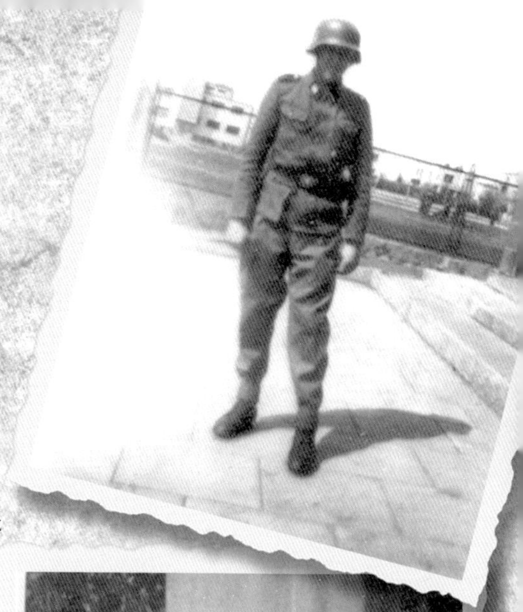

Helmut Schwarz

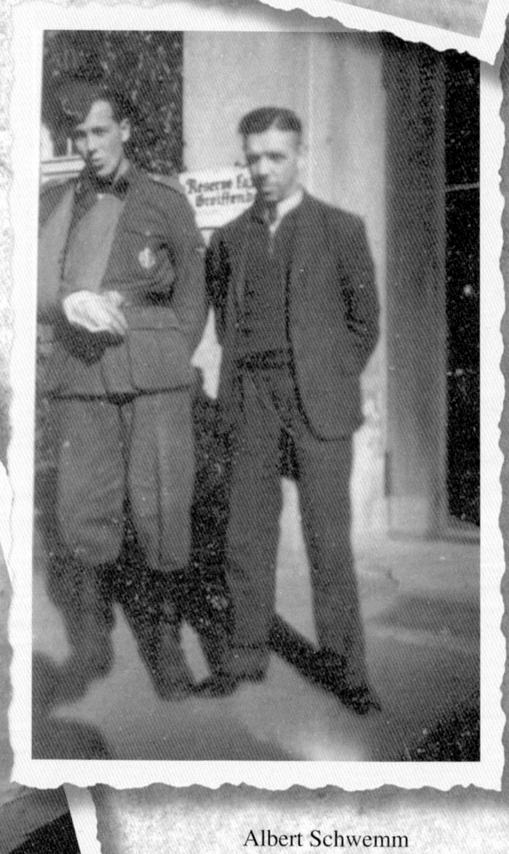

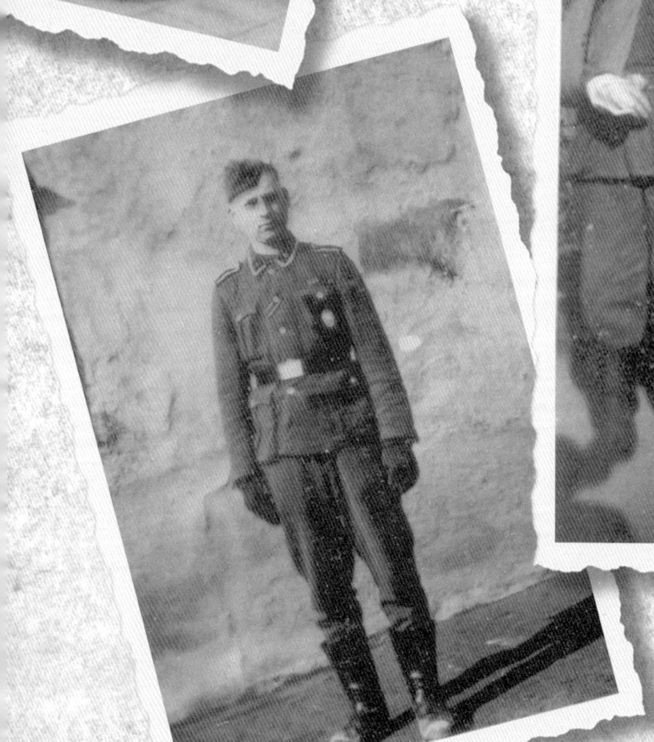

Albert Schwemm

Rudolf Hüholt

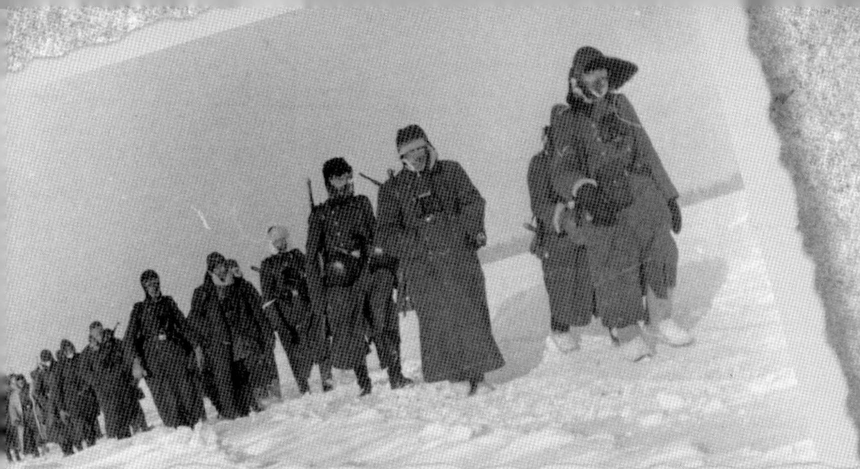

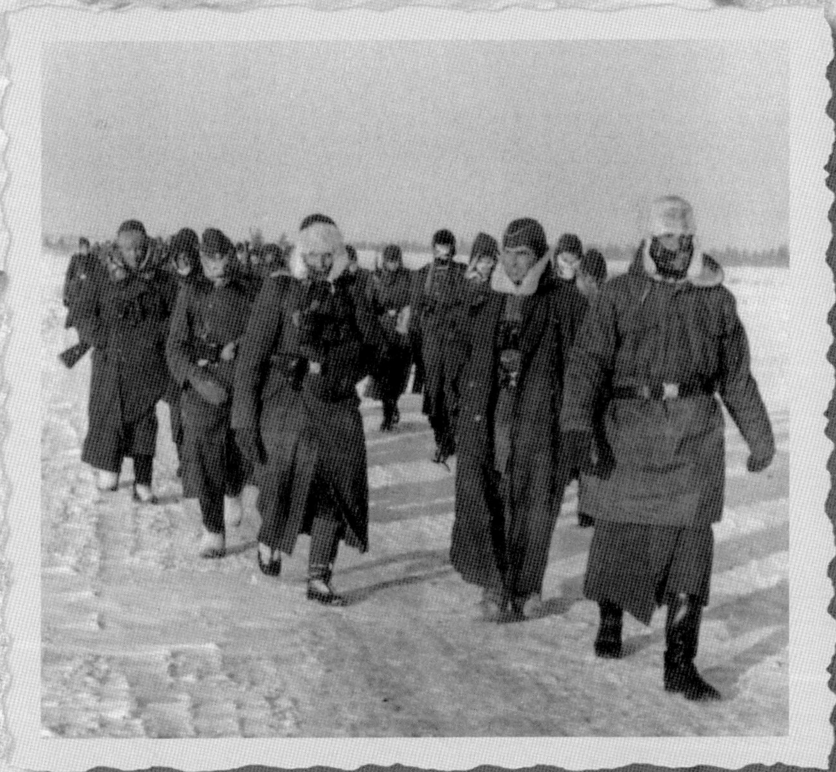

Action in the Rzhev area, winter 1941/42.

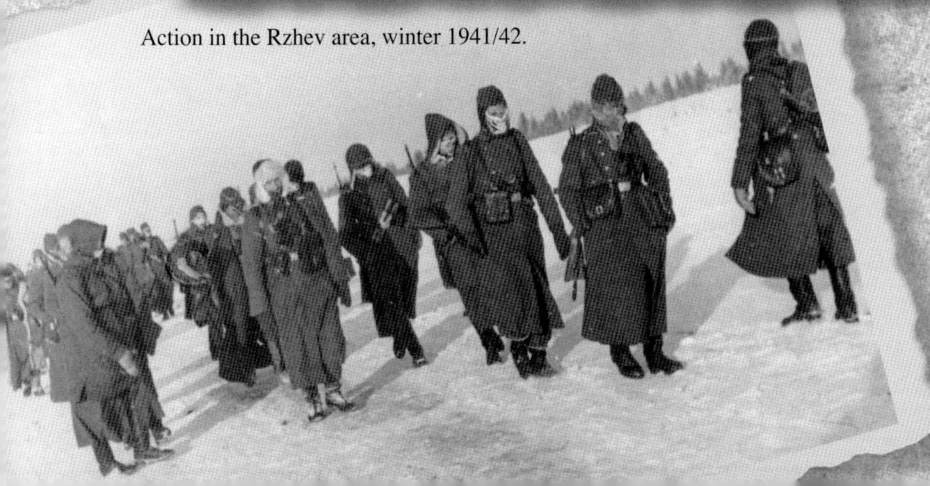

ϟϟ-Reiter im Ring bei Toropez

PK-BILDBERICHT VON ϟϟ-KRIEGSBERICHTER BÜTHEL (PBZ)

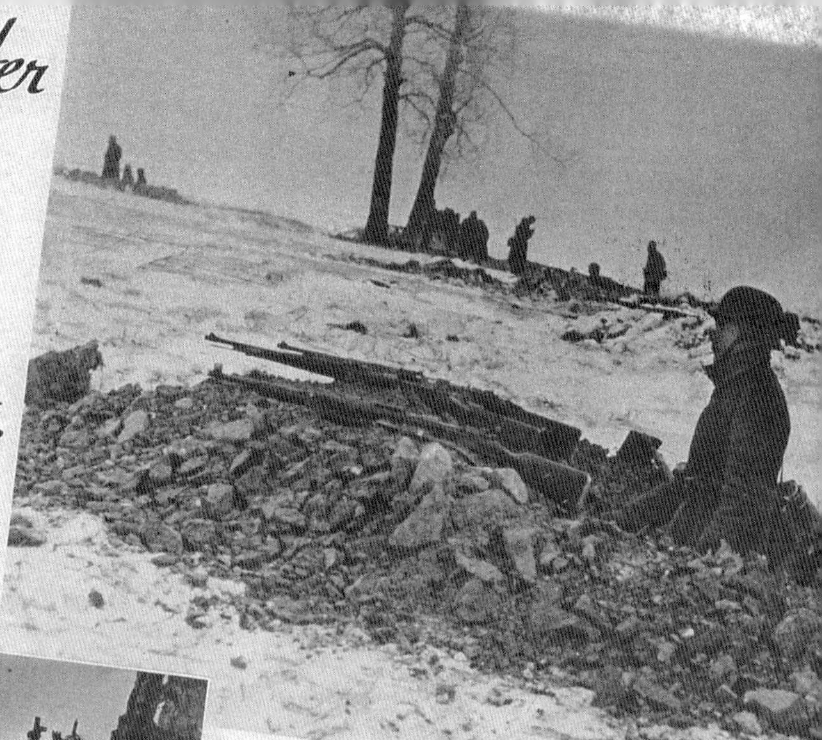

Der Boden in diesem Kampfabschnitt ist flach wie ein Brett. Stein für Stein muß von den ϟϟ-Reitern aus d hartgefrorenen Boden herausgebrochen werden, um sich ein Schützenloch graben zu können ◆ Unten: MG. Feuerstellung

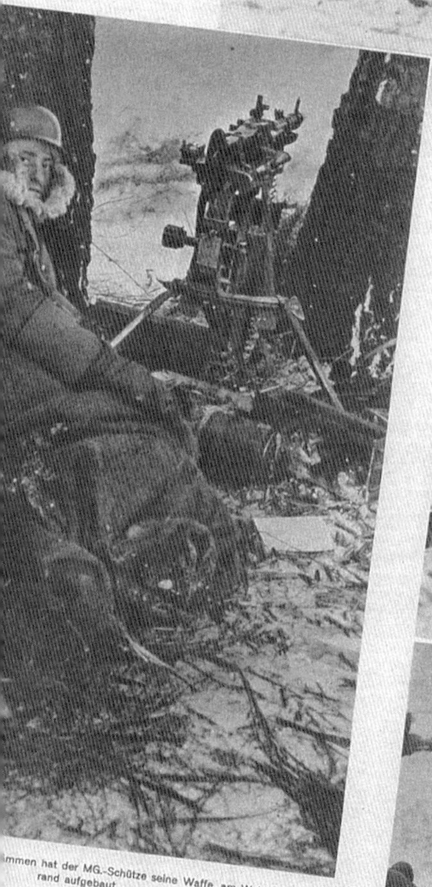

mmen hat der MG.-Schütze seine Waffe am Waldrand aufgebaut

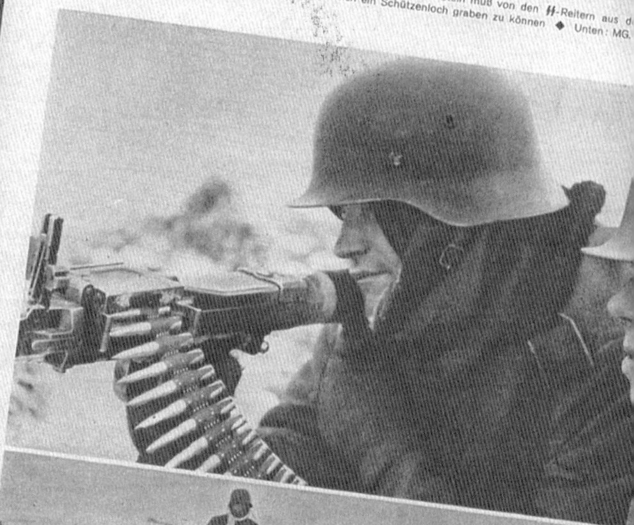

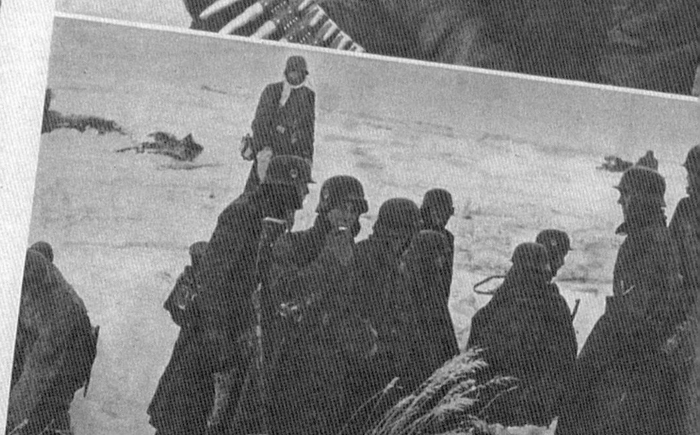

chts: Wieder ist ein Ausbruchsversuch der stur anrennenden schewisten abgeschlagen. Während der Kampfpause wird im eitstellungsraum rasch eine kleine Stärkung eingenommen

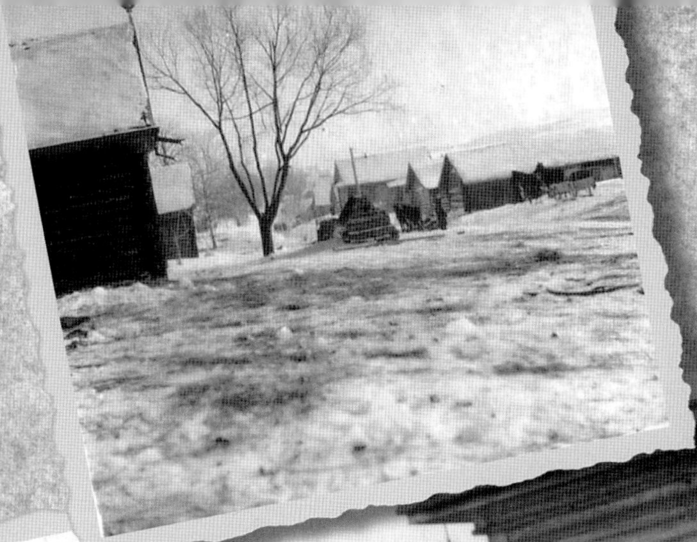

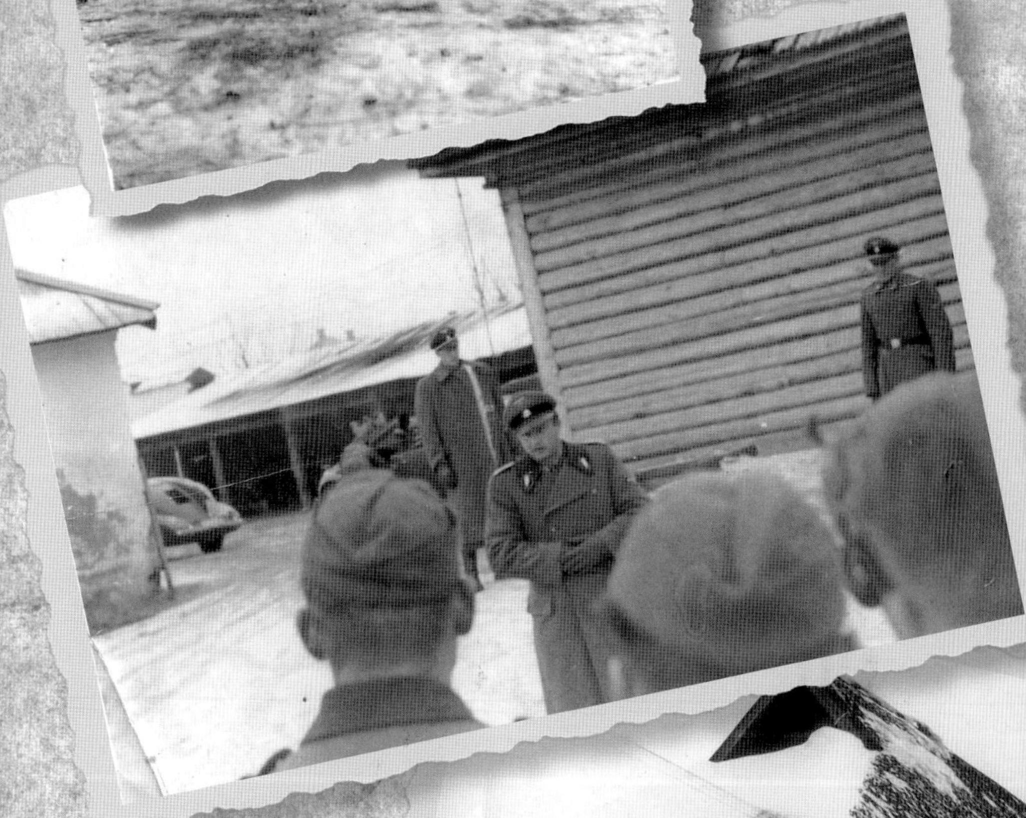

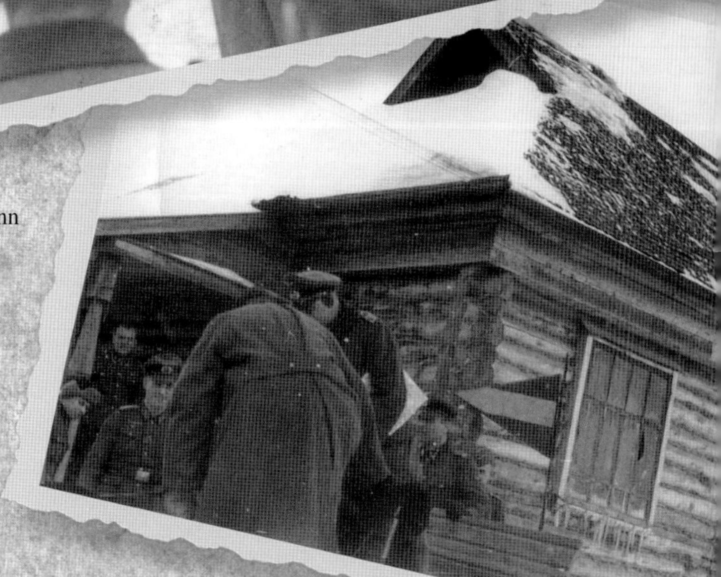

SS-Standartenführer Hermann Fegelein, winter 1941/42.

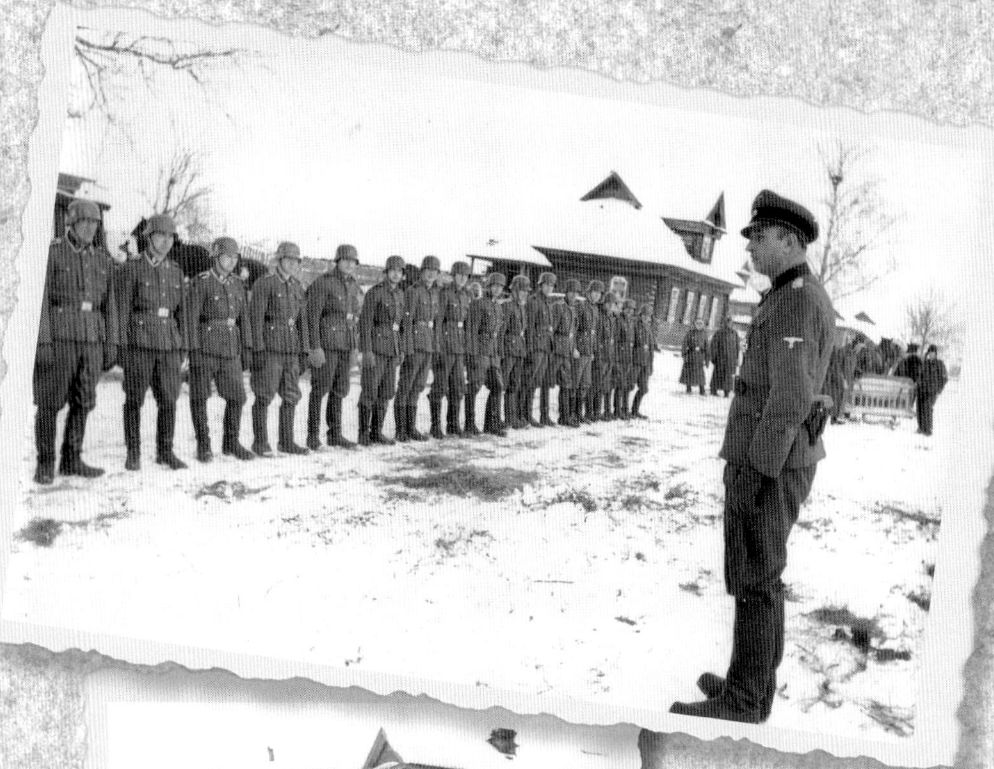

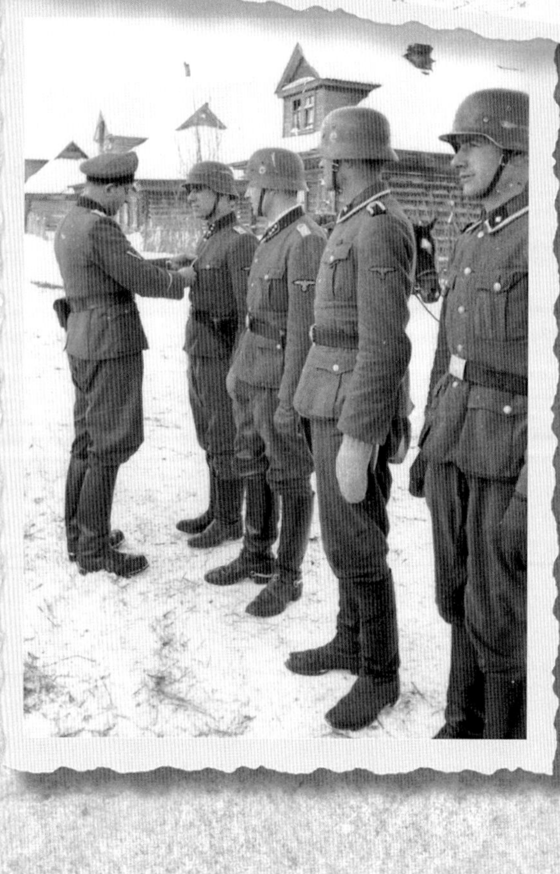

Spring 1942: *SS-Standartenführer* Hermann Fegelein decorates deserving members of his SS Cavalry Brigade with the Iron Cross, Second Class after the fierce winter fighting at Rzhev.

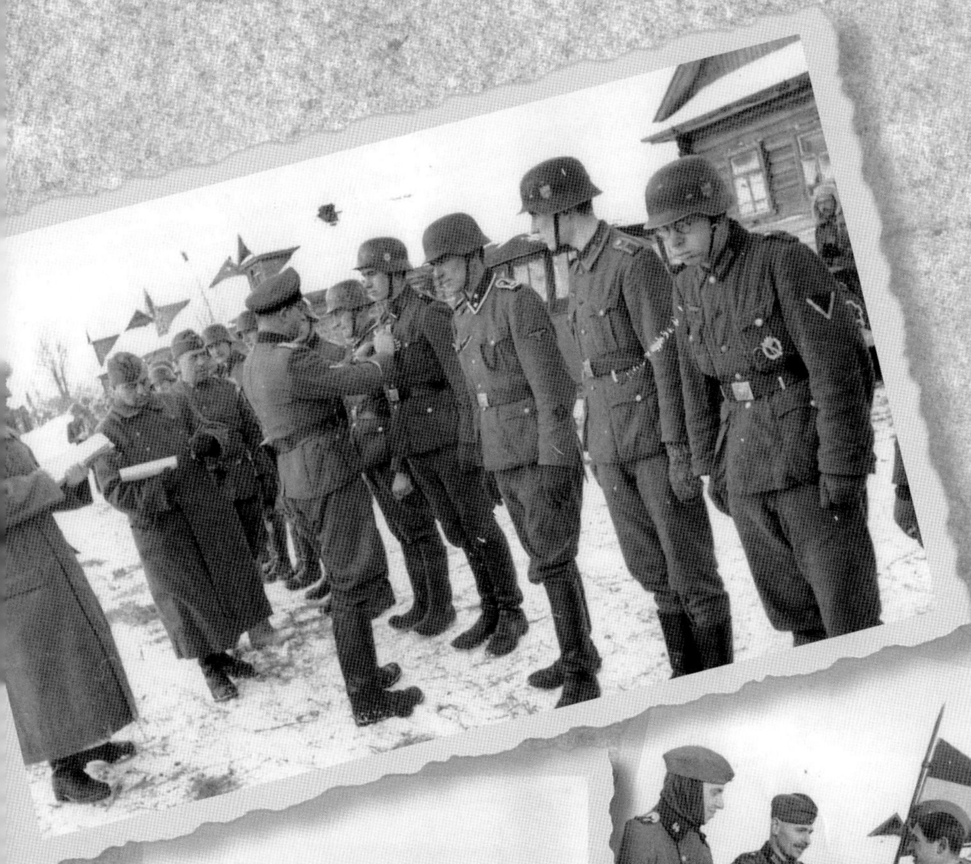

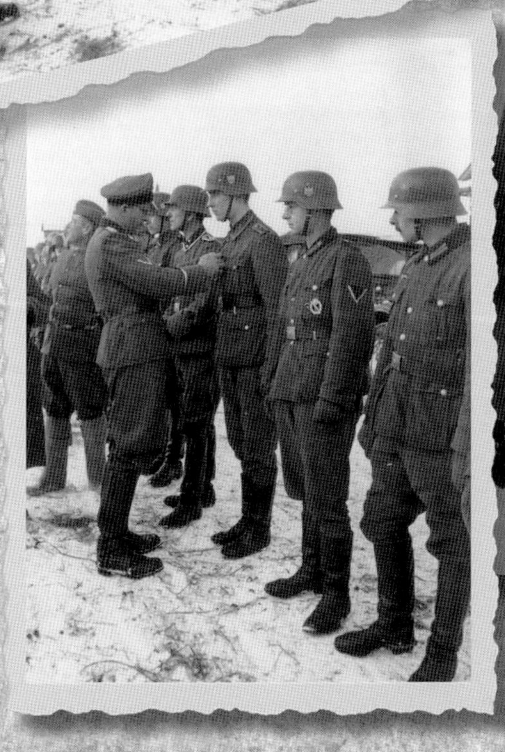

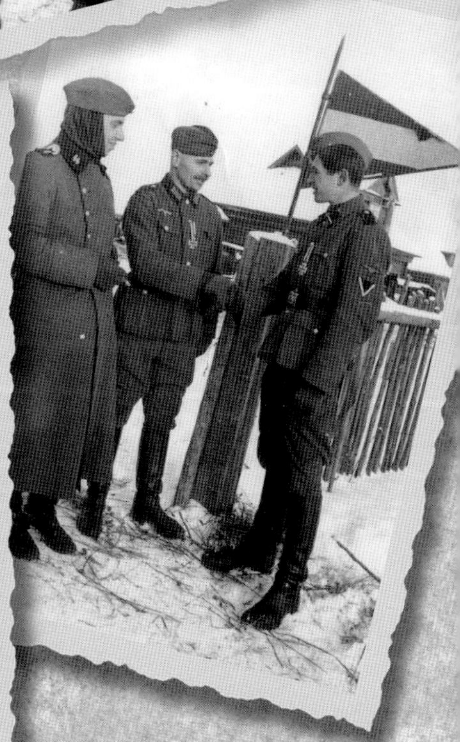

and sent back to SS Training Camp "Debica" for expansion into a division. We stayed behind in Russia and saw action in the area east of Smolensk – Yarzevo. Then, in June 1942 we also arrived at SS Training Camp "Debica." Only 68 of our original 236 men were left. The rest were dead, missing, or wounded. We had lost 9 of our 12 guns, plus 4 60-mm searchlights and all our vehicles. From Debica we were all sent on a 14-day leave. A leave train took almost the entire brigade from Debica to Berlin-Tempelhof and later back to Debica. Meanwhile, SS Flak Battalion "East" had also arrived in Debica from its area of operations on the Volkhov and had also gone on leave. There were a few changes in Debica. Our 1st Battery became 3rd Battery, SS Flak Battalion "East," which in turn became the SS Cavalry Division's flak battalion. After the division was formed at Debica, at the end of August-beginning of September 1942 we were transported by rail to the Beloye area, north of Smolensk."

Formation of the Division

As the result of an agreement with Hungary concerning the recruitment of ethnic Germans for the Waffen-SS, in the spring of 1942 the force found itself with 16,000 replacements. These enabled SS Operational Headquarters to make good the losses suffered during the winter of 1941-42, for which there were insufficient Reich Germans, and also expand the SS Cavalry Brigade into the SS Cavalry Division. Gradually, the brigade's remaining approximately 3,000 men were joined by a total of about 9,000 ethnic Germans from Hungary. The former *SS-Unterscharführer* Albert Schwenn remembered:

"*The SS Cavalry Division was a regular band of gypsies. There was scarcely a corner of eastern and southeastern Europe that was not represented. The 5th Troop had two lads who had supposedly lived as Germans in Russia. One had the amusing name of Amann, the other Zucker. Neither of them spoke more than a few words of German and they traipsed along behind everyone. There was no shortage of ethnic Germans of every category and, while not wanting to offend these comrades, one must say that they were mainly employed within the mounted battalions. For the most part, those who were over 25 years of age had served in the Serbian military or had been soldiers in Hungary and Rumania, meaning they had served in armies where the officer was everything and the man—which included the sergeants—was absolutely nothing. Beatings and other forms of physical abuse were still very common. The older ones had told the young ones about this, and one day these lads found themselves standing in the barracks square before an NCO who wore a stern look but was secretly grinning. There were no "floggings" there. One stood straight and looked obediently at the superior. This pleased the instructors from the Reich—finally their stripes and silver braid were getting the respect they deserved. We Reich German recruits were different, having been prepared by the Hitler Youth and Reich Labor Service…*

In our troop we also had an ethnic German by the name of Franz Kappel. Franz was undoubtedly a genius when it came to scrounging, cooking, and brawling, but after four months of training and two months of supplementary training he still hadn't caught on to how a rifle was stripped and reassembled. Later he rescued a comrade from a cornfield under heavy artillery fire. We thought he was crazy, but he simply said: "Well, what would I do if mother asked, Franzl, why didn't you rescue your comrade?""

Formed at SS Training Camp "Heidelager" in Debica (*Generalgouvernement*), the SS Cavalry Division was organized as follows:

Headquarters
SS Cavalry Regiment[7] 1 with 6 troops
SS Cavalry Regiment 2 with 6 troops
SS Cavalry Regiment 3 with 6 troops
SS Artillery Regiment with 2 battalions
SS Bicycle Reconnaissance Battalion with 3 troops
SS Pioneer Battalion
SS Anti-Tank Battalion
SS Assault Gun Battalion
SS Signals Battalion
SS Flak Battalion
SS Veterinary Company
SS Medical Battalion
SS Economic Battalion

The former *SS-Unterscharführer* Ludwig Mückl recalled:

"*On arriving in Debica we were housed in barracks and, as we in the signals battalion also had a mounted platoon, the stables were not far away. The same could be said of the flies. There were swarms of them, and the toilets in the quarters didn't help. The training base consisted of a single huge forest camp. Our duties were light, for we were sent on leave a few days after our arrival. Our leave began in Berlin, and we had to have our leave passes stamped there going and coming.*

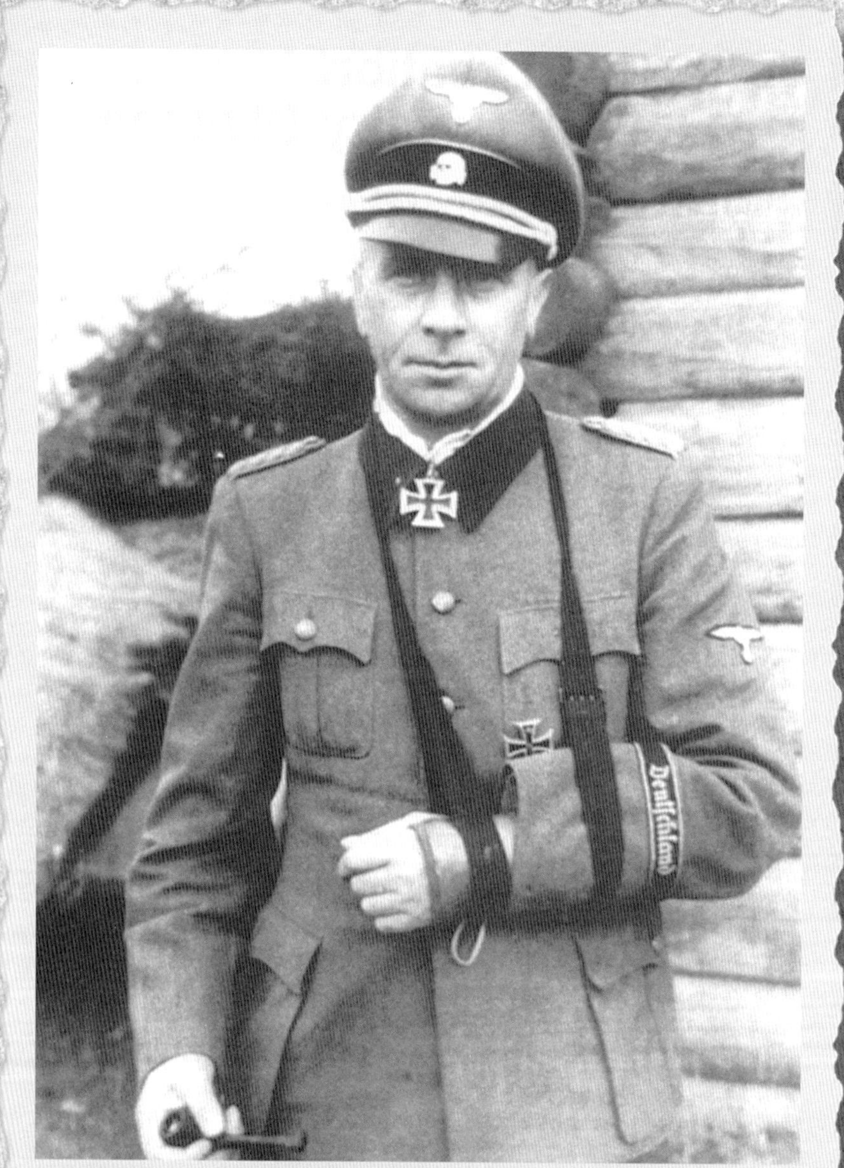

SS-Brigadeführer Bittrich led the SS Cavalry Division from May 1942 to January 1943.

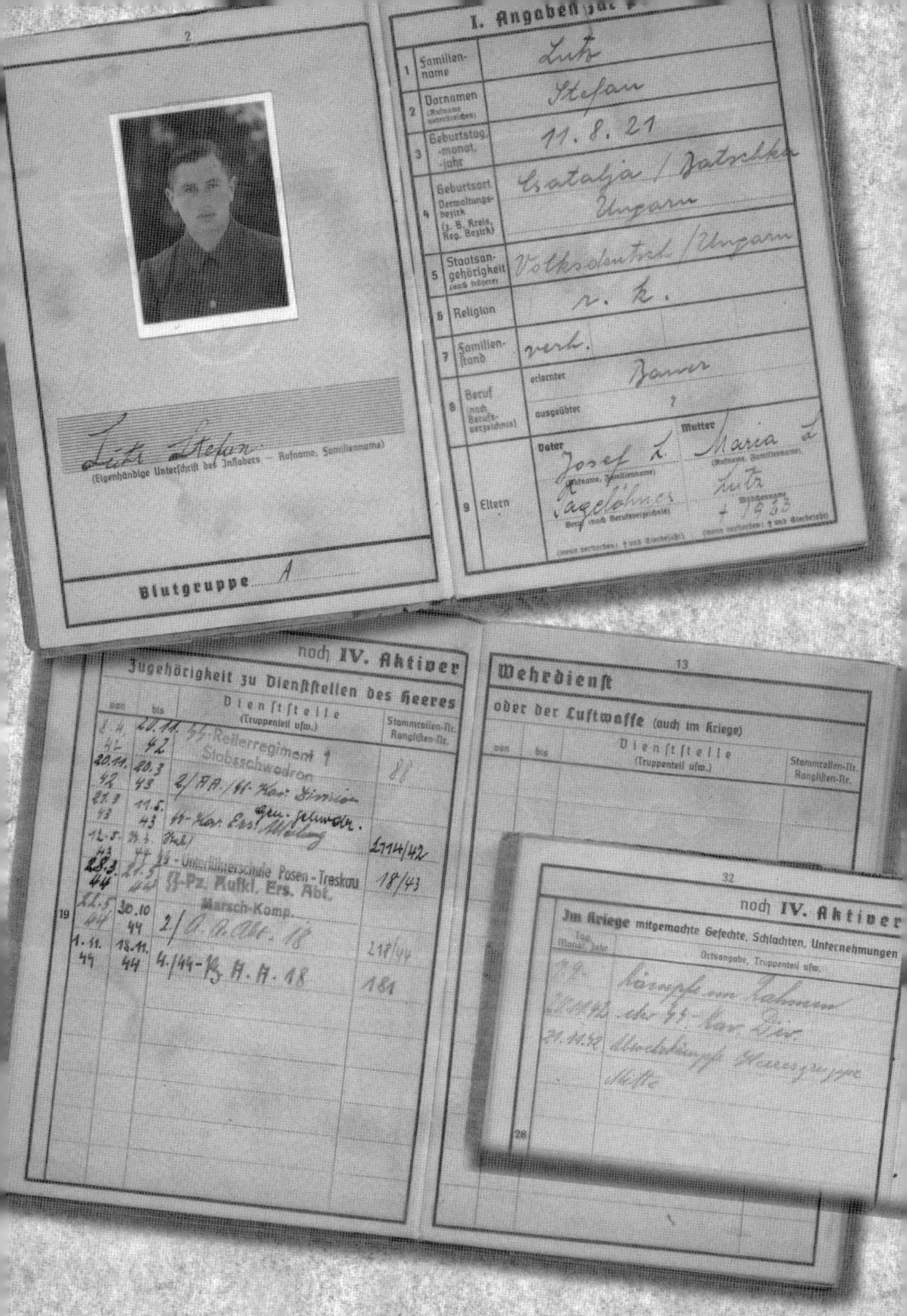

2

Lutz Stefan
(Eigenhändige Unterschrift des Inhabers — Rufname, Familienname)

Blutgruppe A

I. Angaben zur P…

1	Familienname	Lutz
2	Vornamen (Rufname unterstreichen)	Stefan
3	Geburtstag, -monat, -jahr	11. 8. 21
4	Geburtsort Verwaltungsbezirk (z. B. Kreis, Reg. Bezirk)	Csatalja / Batschka Ungarn
5	Staatsangehörigkeit (auch frühere)	Volksdeutsch / Ungarn
6	Religion	r. k.
7	Familienstand	verh.
8	Beruf (nach Berufsverzeichnis)	erlernter: Bauer; ausgeübter: ?
9	Eltern	Vater: Josef L. (Rufname, Familienname), Tagelöhner (Beruf (nach Berufsverzeichnis)); Mutter: Maria L. (Rufname, Familienname), Lutz (Mädchenname), † 1933

noch IV. Aktiver Wehrdienst

Zugehörigkeit zu Dienststellen des Heeres oder der Luftwaffe (auch im Kriege)

von	bis	Dienststelle (Truppenteil usw.)	Stammrollen-Nr. Ranglisten-Nr.
8.4.42	20.11.42	SS-Reiterregiment 1 Stabsschwadron	88
20.11.42	20.3.43	2/ A.A. / SS-Kav. Division	
21.3.43	11.5.43	SS-Kav. Ers. Abteilung	
12.5.43	24.3.44	SS-Unterführerschule Posen-Treskau	2714/42
25.3.44	21.5.44	SS-Pz. Aufkl. Ers. Abt. Marsch-Komp.	18/43
22.5.44	30.10.44	2./ A. A. Abt. 18	218/44
1.11.44	13.11.44	4./SS-Pz. A. A. 18	181

13

32

noch IV. Aktiver

Im Kriege mitgemachte Gefechte, Schlachten, Unternehmungen

Tag, Monat, Jahr	Ortsangabe, Truppenteil usw.
28.11.42	Kämpfe im Rahmen der SS-Kav. Div.
21.11.42	Abwehrkämpfe Heeresgruppe Mitte

Stefan Lutz, an ethnic German from Hungary, joined the SS Cavalry Division, then in the formation process, on 1 April 1942.

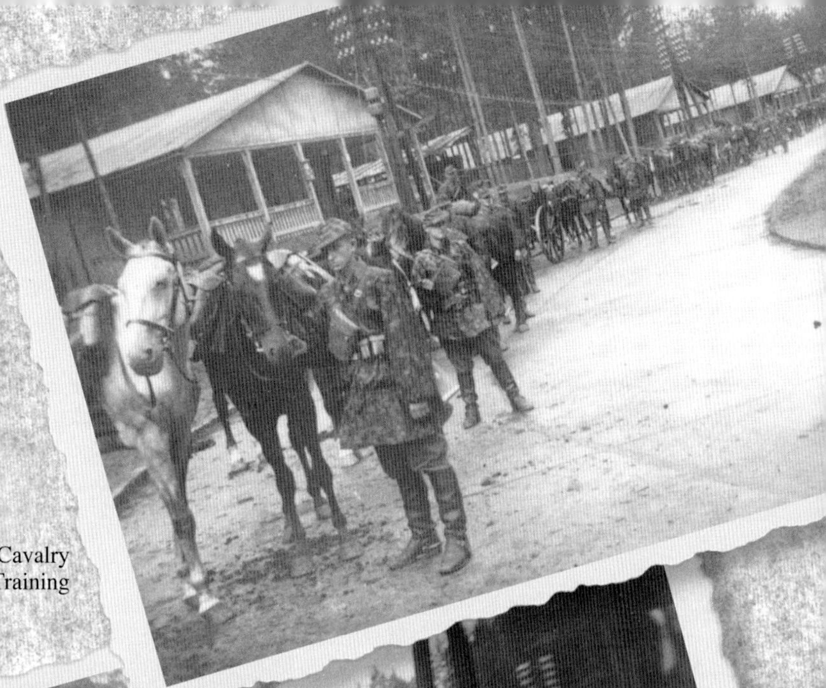

Formation of the SS Cavalry Division at the SS Training Camp in Debica.

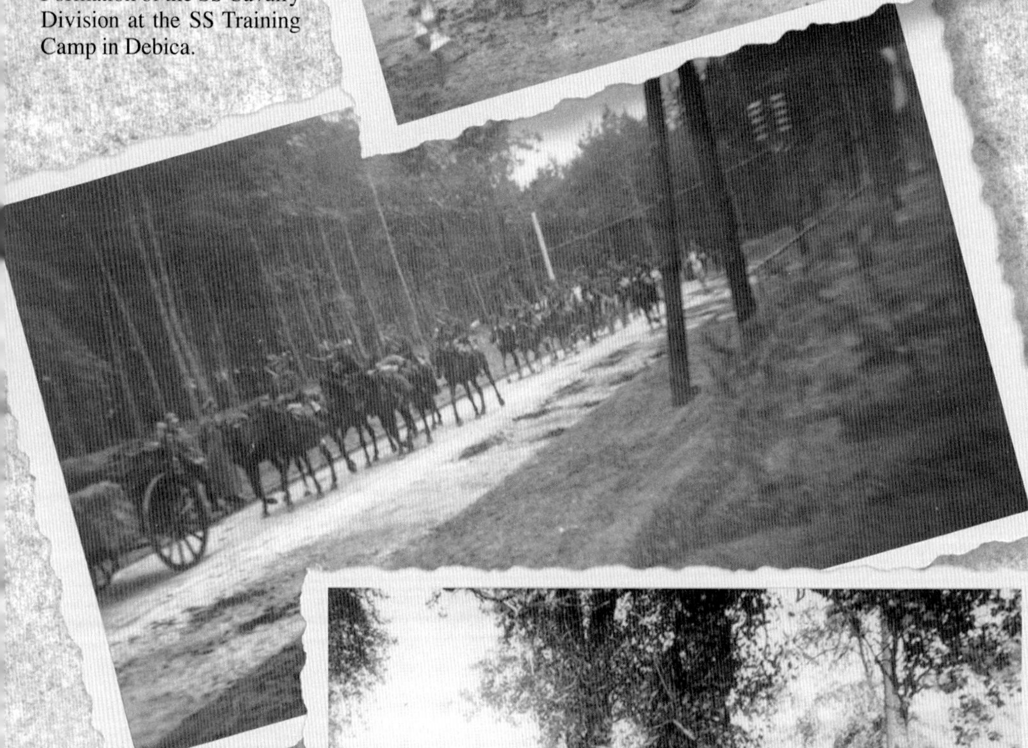

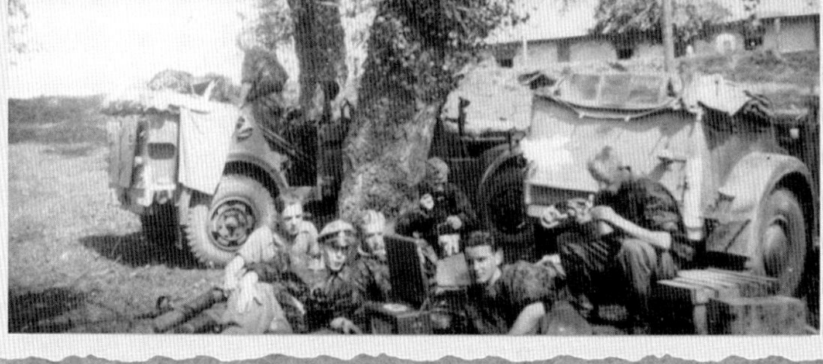

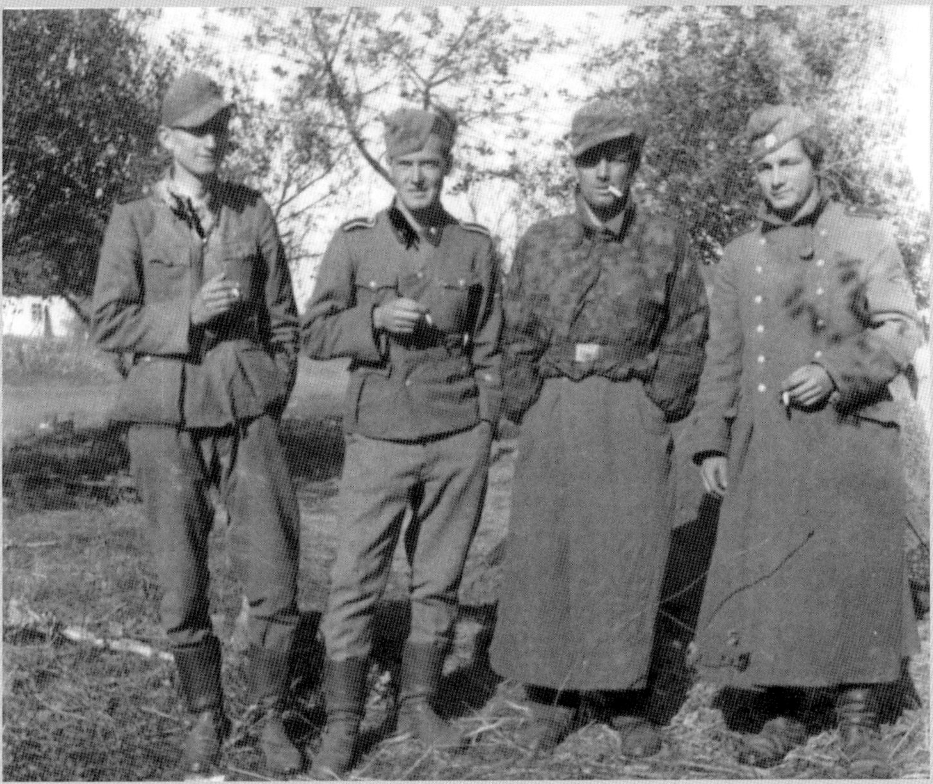

Ludwig Mückl.

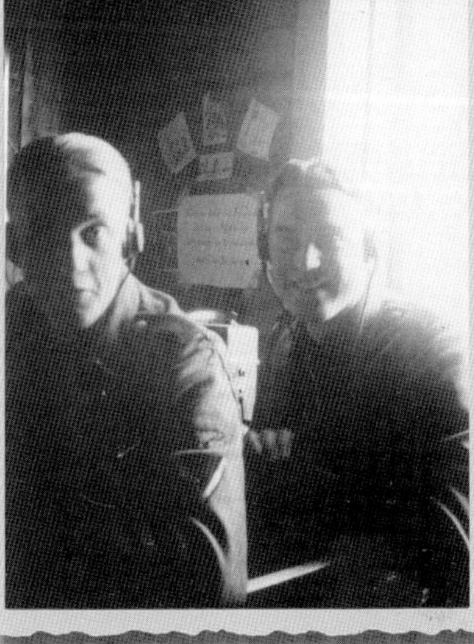

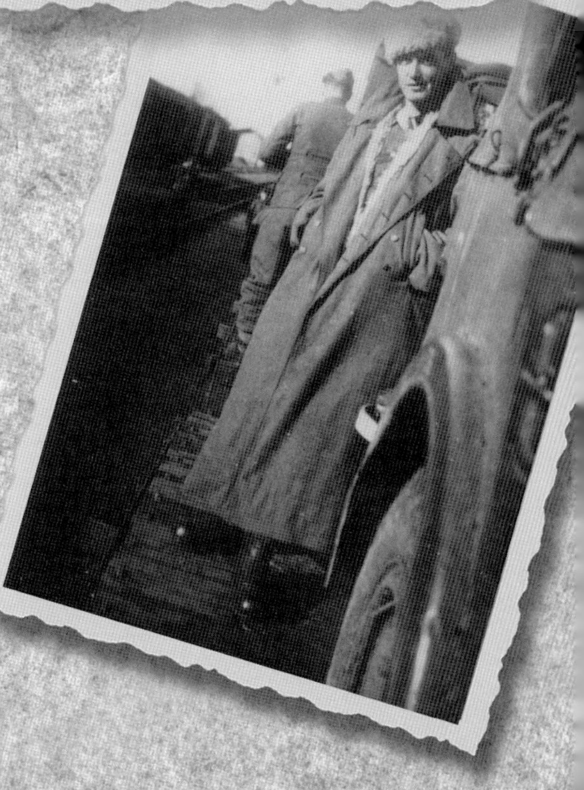

On the way back to Debica I stopped in Berlin again and had a look around: the Brandenburg Gate, Unter den Linden, Ku'damm, and the Reich Chancellery with the snappy guards standing outside. The brigade was increased in size to that of a division and we also got replacements from the Reich and ethnic Germans from the Batchka—the 18-year-olds were fine fellows."

Action in the Vitebsk – Vyazma – Rzhev Area

After *SS-Standartenführer* Fegelein was assigned to Führer Headquarters as liaison officer, *SS-Brigadeführer* Bittrich assumed command of the new division. While some of the newly-formed units—mainly those created using ethnic Germans recruits—stayed at the SS training camp (SS Cavalry Regiment 3, SS Flak Battalion, and the SS Pioneer Battalion), in mid-August 1942 the division command received orders to move operational elements back to the 9th Army. *SS-Brigadeführer* Bittrich subsequently formed two battle groups:

SS Battle Group "Lombard" with:
- SS Cavalry Regiment 1
- SS Veterinary Company

SS Battle Group "Zehender" with:
- SS Cavalry Regiment 2
- SS Bicycle Reconnaissance Battalion
- I Battalion, SS Artillery Regiment

Attached to the 330th Infantry Division within LIX Army Corps, the units participated in "Operation Spätlese," which began on 20 September 1942. The target of the operation was Red Army stragglers and partisans in the area of forests and swamps west of Yarzevo. When it was over, the two battle groups moved to the front and occupied positions between the 197th and 330th Infantry Divisions at the junction of XXIII and LIX Army Corps in the Demetshi area.

In mid-October 1942 the units still at Debica were sent to the front. By then the recruits, mainly ethnic Germans, had about six months of training behind them, which was considered sufficient. On 21 October 1942 SS Cavalry Regiment 2 and the SS Bicycle Reconnaissance Battalion were among the units that carried out an anti-partisan operation in the area of the Gobsa Valley between Burdukova and Demidov. The SS cavalry were in action until the end of the month alongside the 20th Panzer Division, Light Infantry Battalions 4 and 8, Police Regiment 13, and the 7th Luftwaffe Field Division. On 26 October 1942 *SS-Brigadeführer* Bittrich reported a battle strength (*Gefechtsstärke*) of:

Officers	NCOs	Enlisted Men	Total
161	677	5,471	6,309
2.6%	10.7%	86.7%	100%

Combat strength (*Kampfstärke*) at that time was about 9,000 men and rations strength about 12,000 men, thus the division was roughly at authorized strength.

At the beginning of November 1942 SS Cavalry Regiment 1, bolstered by an anti-tank platoon and a platoon of 20-mm anti-aircraft guns, was in the area Kurotsha – Novo Pokrovskoyino – Padsaytsevo area with orders to scout the Losmyanka River line and guard VI Army Corps' right flank.

SS Cavalry Regiment 2 was assigned to Parachute Regiment 4 in the Osotkya sector. SS Cavalry Regiment 3 (still on foot), which had just arrived from the *Generalgouvernement*, was supposed to make contact with the 197th Infantry Division in the Kletki – Rasinkova area; operationally, however, it was under the direct command of VI Army Corps. The SS Bicycle Reconnaissance Battalion occupied the Stary Dvor area, while the SS Pioneer Battalion fortified positions in the Nikala – Yedrevichi – Velyushino area. The SS Signals Battalion took up quarters in Nekuyudova and laid field telephone lines between the various units of the SS Cavalry Division.

Elements of SS Cavalry Regiment 1 carried out "Operation Vodnevka," which began on 9 November 1942. The operation's objective was to clear partisans from the area around the village of Vodnevka. Two days later VI Army Corps directed the units under its command to form winter-mobile formations. The SS Cavalry Division subsequently established a ski battalion from the SS Bicycle Reconnaissance Battalion. The battalion consisted of three ski companies, a heavy ski company, a light battery (four Type 16 light field howitzers), a pioneer platoon, and a signals section. On 21 November 1942 the division reported that formation of the battalion was complete, and its reported strength was 16 officers, 90 non-commissioned officers, and 628 enlisted men. The very next day a ski patrol rescued two soldiers of the 2nd Luftwaffe Field Division who had been captured by the Russians.

On 25 November 1942 the Red Army took the offensive in four places: northwest of Sychevka – west of Rzhev – north and south of Belyje. By about 14:00 hours enemy troops had taken Toropino (10 km SE of Belyje), Yemelyanoca, Petrushina, and Zyguni, and were advancing down the road to Demechi. SS Cavalry Regiment 1 was subsequently moved into the Belousovo area (19 km SW of Belyje) as army reserve, and in the evening was moved forward to Belyje. The Soviet troops advanced to Demechi, where they were stopped. The next day the enemy succeeded in establishing himself in Selishche, between the 2nd Luftwaffe Field Division and the 197th Infantry Division. Although the village was retaken, the enemy was able to extend his penetration to a depth of 20 km. On 28 November 1942 *SS-Brigadeführer* Bittrich issued operational orders for the reinforced SS Cavalry Regiments 1 and 2. XXX Army Corps under *General der Artillerie* Fretter-Pico was transferred from Army Group North and positioned in the threatened sector. The next day the SS Cavalry Division was attached to XXX Army Corps.

The German counterattack began on 7 December 1942. The 20th Infantry Division, the 19th Panzer Division, and the SS Cavalry Division attacked from the north, while elements of the 1st Panzer Division and the Fusilier Regiment "Großdeutschland" struck from the south. During the fighting the SS Cavalry Division's fighting strength was just:

SS Cavalry Regiment 1: 454 men
SS Cavalry Regiment 2: 533 men
Ski Battalion: 407 men

The fighting units had sustained losses of about 50% in one month. In spite of this, contact with XXXXI Panzer Corps (*General der Panzertruppe* Harpe) was established on 10 December 1942: the 1st and 19th Panzer Divisions linked up, trapping a large number of enemy troops, including the:

19th Motorized Brigade
37th Motorized Brigade
74th Stalin Brigade
75th Stalin Brigade
78th Stalin Brigade
17th Guards Division

The destruction of these units began on 11 December 1942. Four days later the fighting ended and the reinforced Ski Battalion was disbanded back into its original units. One week later the SS Cavalry Division, with a strength of 310 officers and 10,569 other ranks, was attached to XXXXI Panzer Corps. SS Cavalry Regiments 1 and 3 were pulled out of the front and moved to rest areas. SS Cavalry Regiment 2, together with the SS Bicycle Reconnaissance Battalion and the SS Artillery Regiment, remained in action with elements of the 20th Panzer Division, engaging partisans and Red Army stragglers from the recent battles in the Nefedova – Lykino and Demechi areas. On 23 December the SS Bicycle Reconnaissance Battalion discovered three parachute units in a wooded area southeast of Soino. The enemy units, which had a combined strength of about 3,000 men, even had their own airfield. At the end of the year *SS-Brigadeführer* Bittrich wrote in an order of the day:

"*My SS men! The year 1942 is drawing to an end, a new year of battle is beginning! Looking back at the tough battles fought by the SS Cavalry Division, which were of vital importance to the decisions made by the supreme command, obliges me to express my utmost appreciation and heartfelt thanks to you, my soldiers, for what you have achieved. We bow with the deepest respect before the division's dead, who must remain with us in spirit so that we will be able to face the coming battles with the same strength and fortitude. Our dead shall be the division's sacred and constant admonishers for us to carry on with courage and willingness to fight.*"

On 4 January 1943 XXXXI Army Corps ordered the pacification of the area north and south of the road to Nikitinka. SS Cavalry Regiment 3 and the SS Bicycle Reconnaissance Battalion were initially given reconnaissance assignments. The area (about 300 km^2) consisted almost entirely of swampy old-growth forest. It was home to a number of partisan groups, including the Chapayev, Yakovlev, Korevsky, Morgov, Vorodpokov, and Voroshilov Brigades.

At this time *SS-Brigadeführer* Bittrich handed command of the division over to *SS-Standartenführer* Freitag. Before leaving for France to oversee formation of the SS Panzer Grenadier Division "Hohenstaufen," Bittrich bade his men farewell:

"My comrades! An order from the RF-SS has given me a new mission. This means bidding farewell to the battle-tested SS Cavalry Division, from all of you, who under my command have fulfilled your duty as soldiers to the point of self-sacrifice. But the division's old and new glory, and that of every one of you, is also the glory of the brave men who now lie beneath the soil of Russia.

As I say goodbye, my heart is filled with pride and gratitude. The shared experience of these fierce winter battles will always unite us, even though we are separated. In these decisive battles we will continue to swear in memory of our fallen comrades: our entire strength, our lives for Germany's freedom!"

Under the command of *SS-Standartenführer* Freitag, approximately 3,000 SS cavalrymen took part in "Operation Sternlauf," which was carried out in the area of the Vop River from 27 January to 8 February 1943. *General der Panzertruppen* Harpe and *Generaloberst* Model both helped plan the operation, which was supposed to lead to the encirclement and destruction of the partisans in the forest south of Tatyanka. On 24 January 1943, prior to the start of the operation, the SS Cavalry Division's strength stood at:

97 officers, 265 non-commissioned officers, and 2,327 enlisted men

"Operation Sternlauf" began the next day. Heavy snow, blown bridges, and fuel shortages hampered the operation. A panzer company with five 38-ton tanks was attached to the division for the operation. After fierce fighting the enemy fled to the south. The action demonstrated that without winter-mobile units, operations in persistent drifting snow and difficult terrain were scarcely possible. The partisan-held area south of Timoshino was systematically encircled, with the SS cavalry deployed in the north, the Krohn Regiment in the west, troops of the rear corps area in the south, and the Richter Regiment in the east. The operation in the Vop sector was halted on 7 February 1943. It was reported that 1,067 partisans and Red Army troops had been captured and 1,882 killed.

On 14 February 1943 the SS Cavalry Division left XXXXI Panzer Corps, was ordered into the Bobruisk area just under 400 kilometers away, and was attached to the Senior SS and Police Commander Russia Center.[8] That same month Albert Schwenn joined 5th Company, SS Cavalry Regiment 15:

"In 1940 I volunteered for the Waffen-SS and was mustered. Of about 50 young men, just eight were accepted. All of the others failed to meet the entrance criteria then in force—how drastically this later changed, when we received ethnic German comrades who were only 1.6 meters tall! When the long-awaited call-up order finally came, my initial disappointment was great. Instead of being assigned to the tanks or motorcycle troops as I had hoped, I was sent to the cavalry. My father, who loved everything about horses and who had no concept of the difference between civilian and military riding, was as delighted as I was disappointed. In October 1942 I became an SS-Reiter in the SS Cavalry Replacement Battalion. The training did not exactly instill us young boys with enthusiasm for military life. Throughout our entire training period we were hungry, so hungry that we stole turnips from the stores and ate them raw.

In February 1943 we were sent to the field unit. We were quartered in a former Russian cavalry barracks in Lapichi, near Osipovichi. We got up at 04:00 and at 05:00 rode off to hunt partisans. After three kilometers we dismounted and then walked five kilometers—the horses had to be spared. At 09:00 we were overtaken by the motorized units which had departed later. The crews sat comfortably leaned-back in their Kfz 15s and waved patronizingly at us grooms."

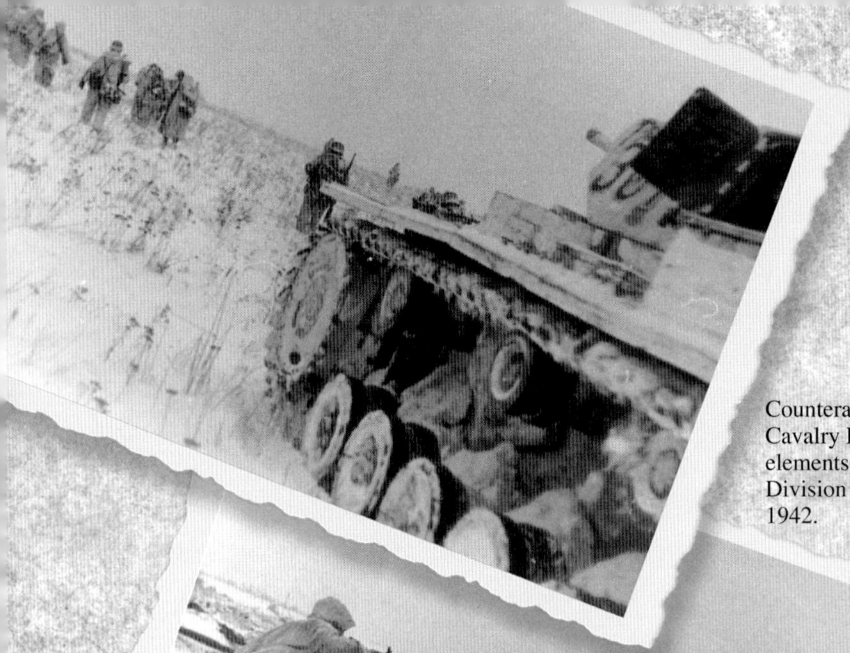

Counterattack by the SS Cavalry Division and elements of the 20th Panzer Division in the winter of 1942.

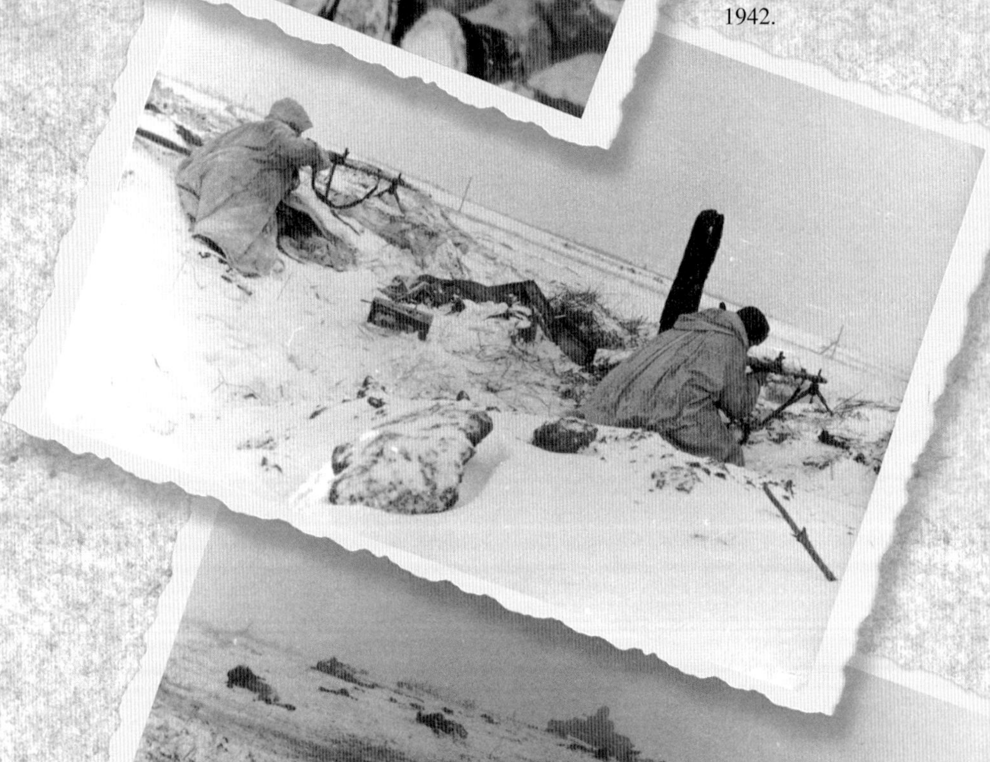

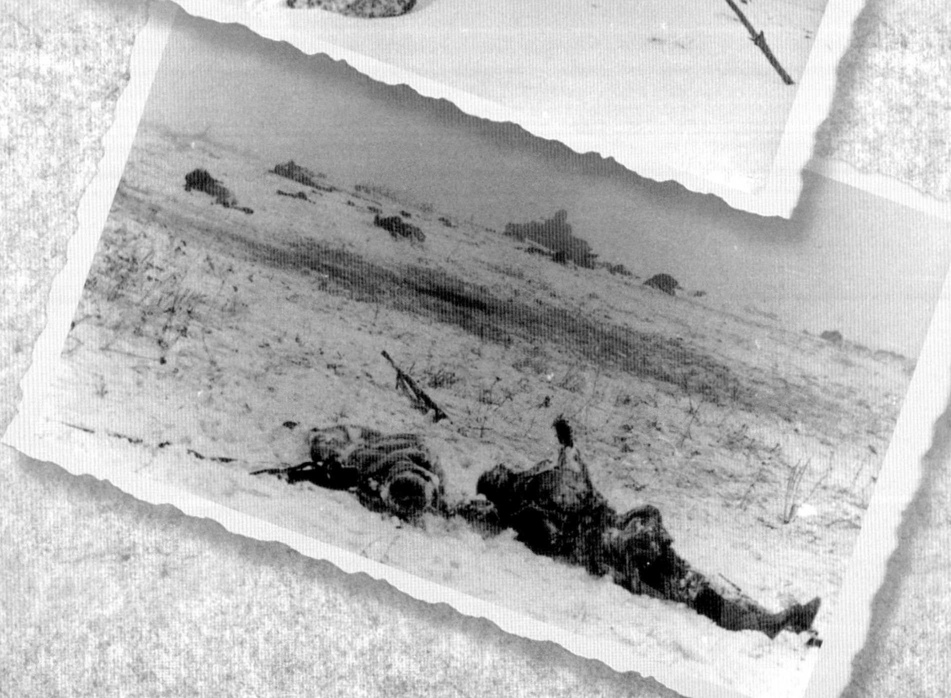

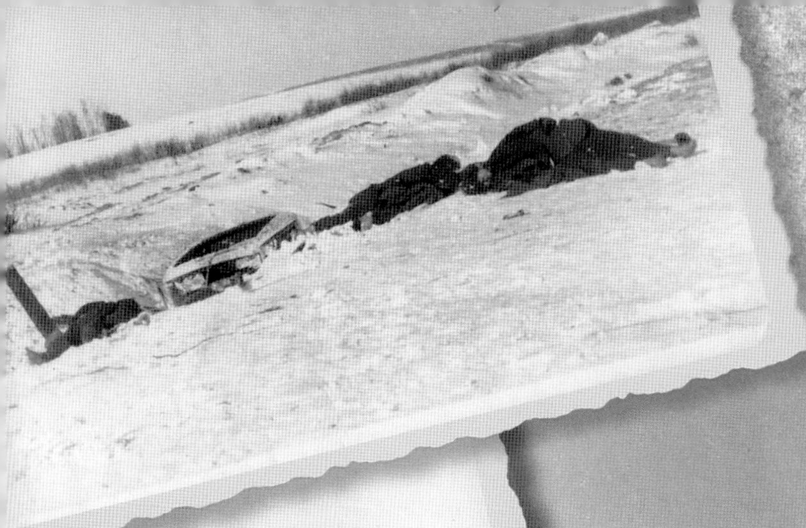

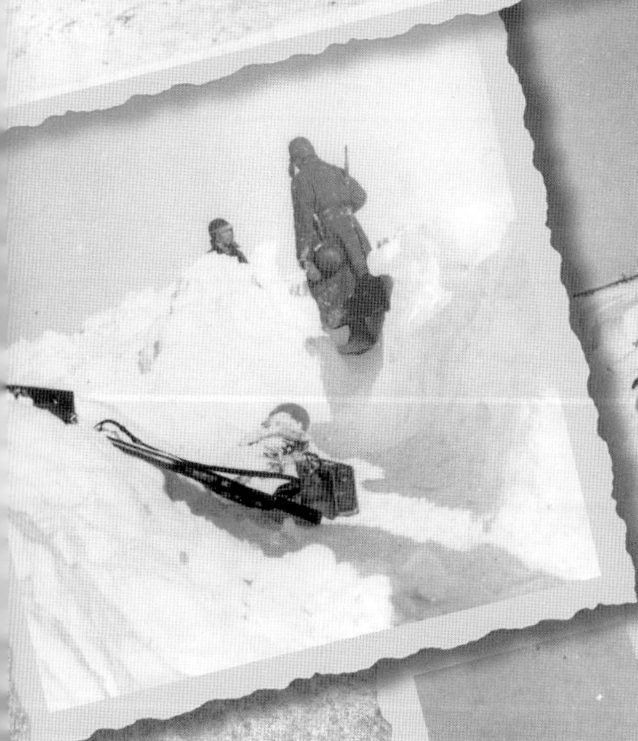

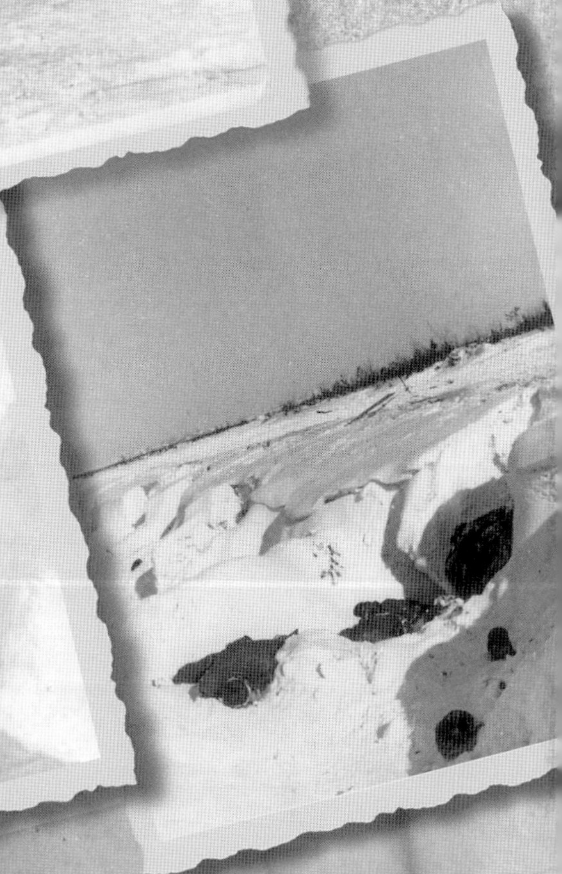

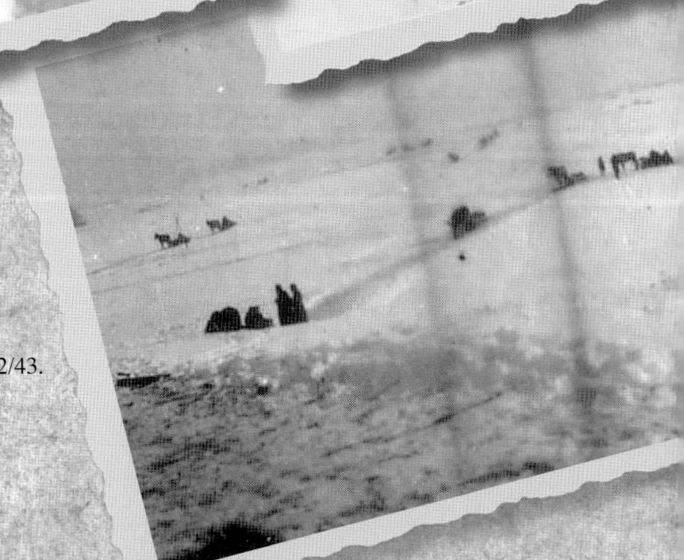

Winter warfare 1942/43.

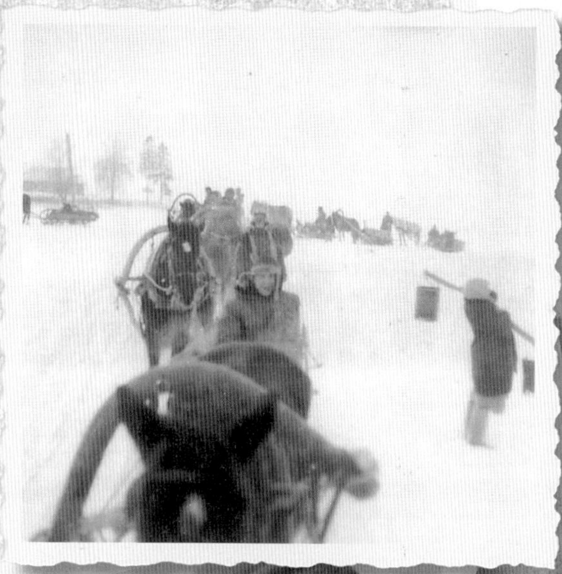
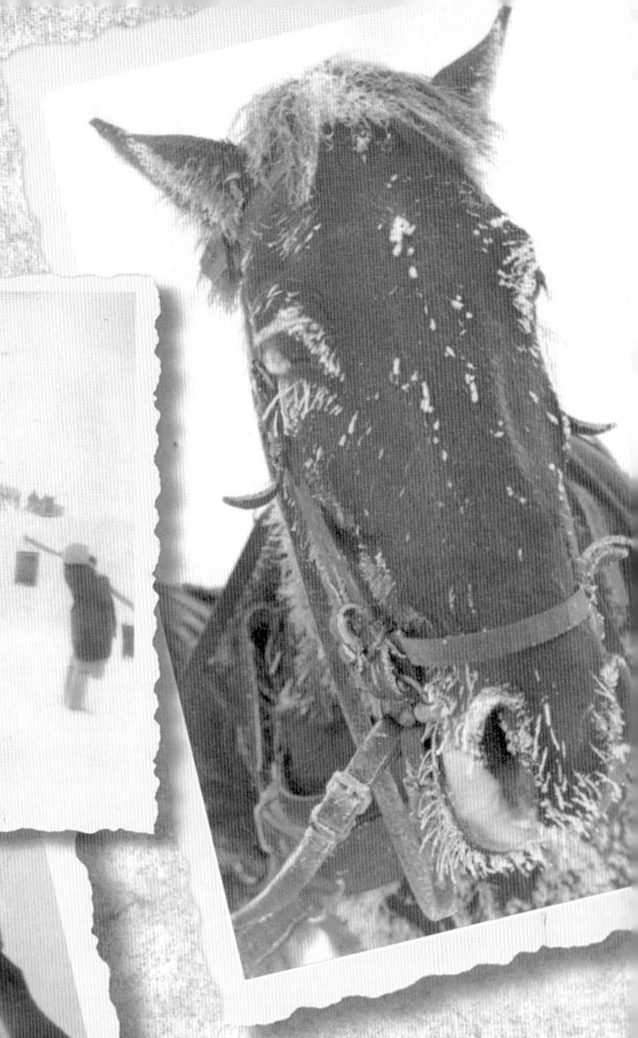
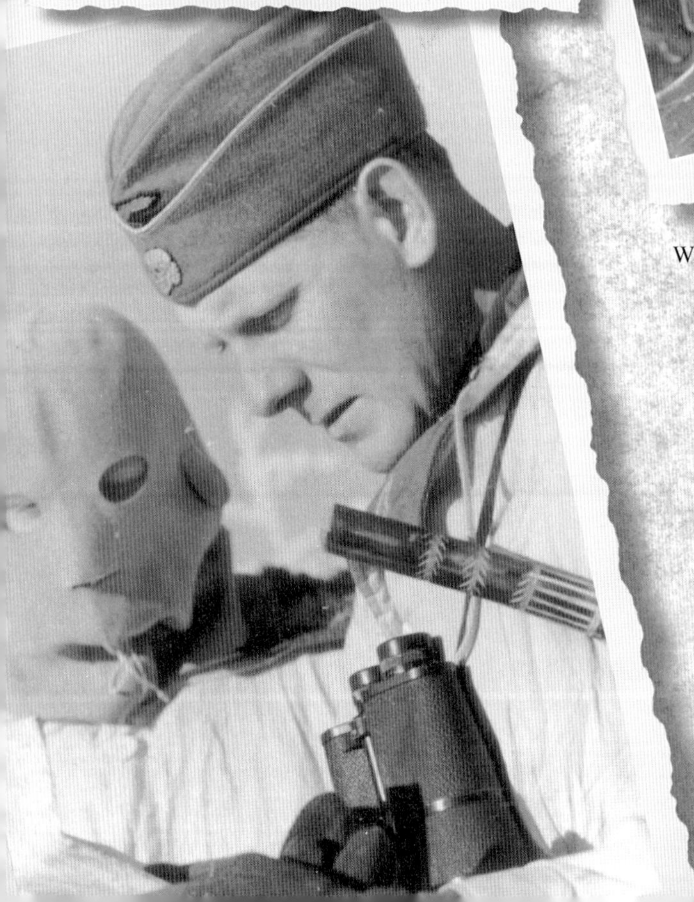

Winter 1942/43.

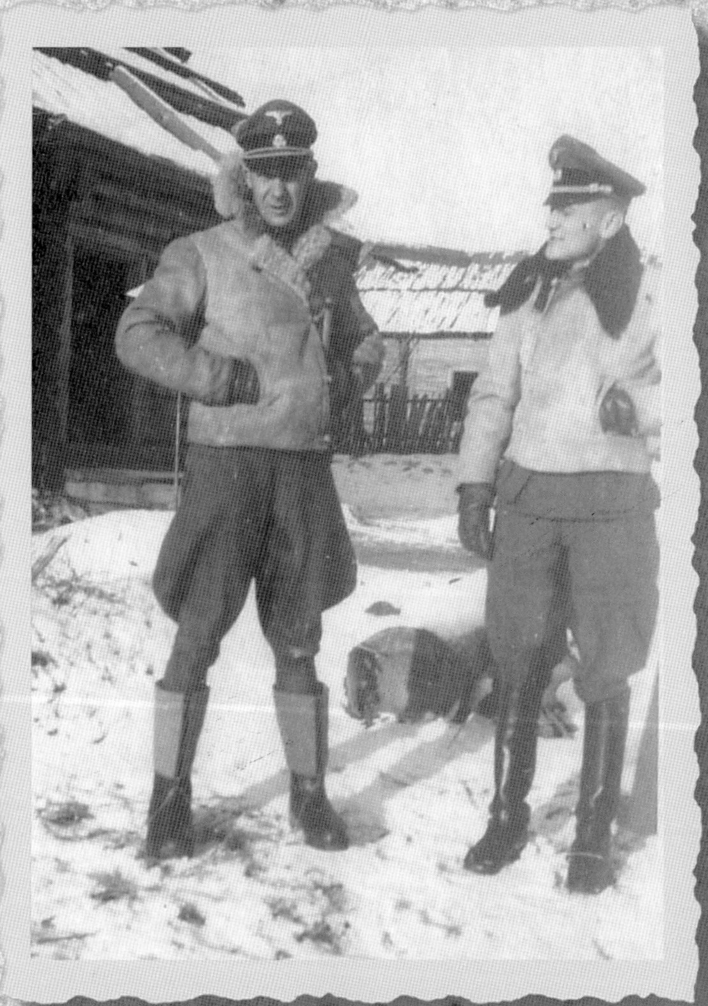

Officers of the SS Cavalry Division in spring 1943.

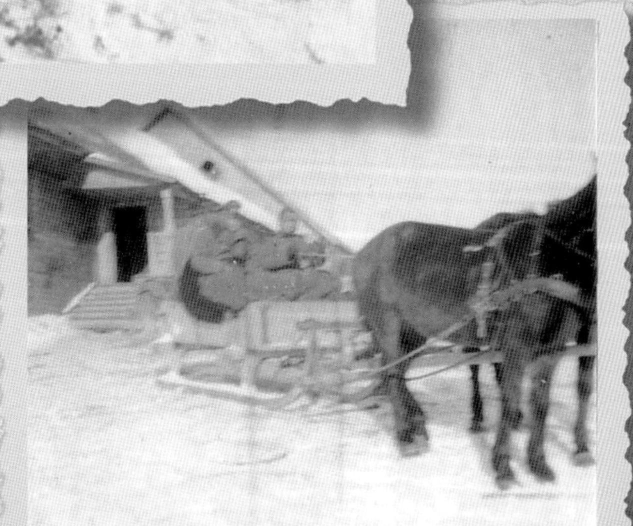

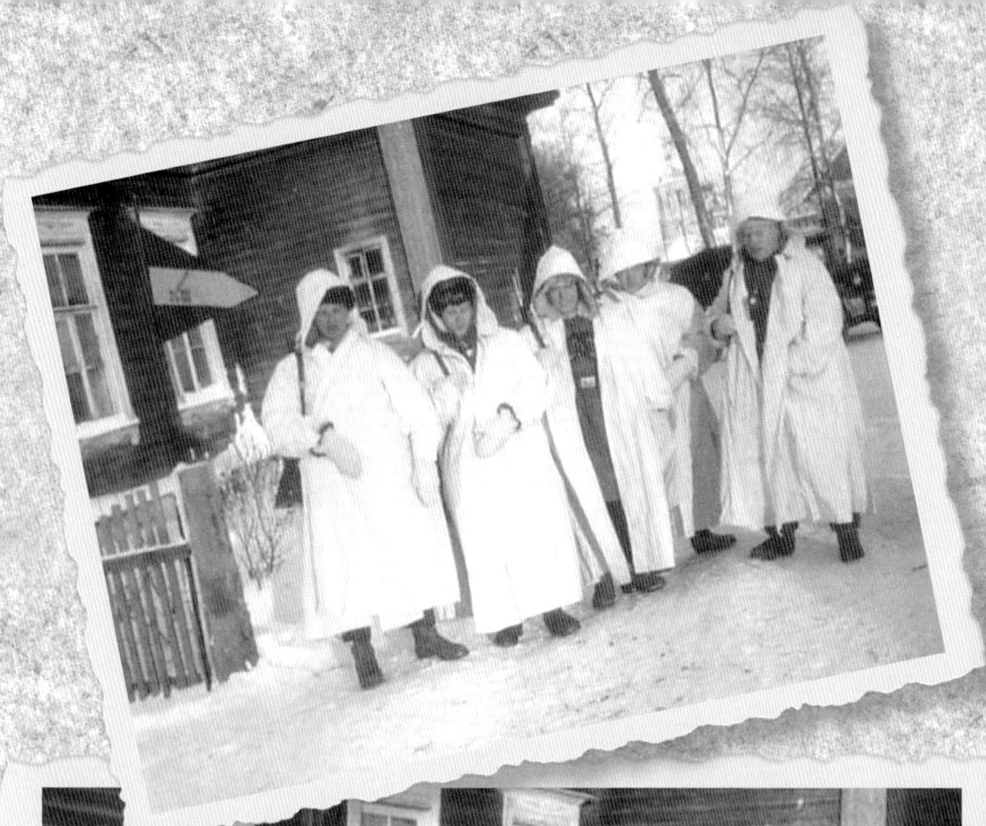

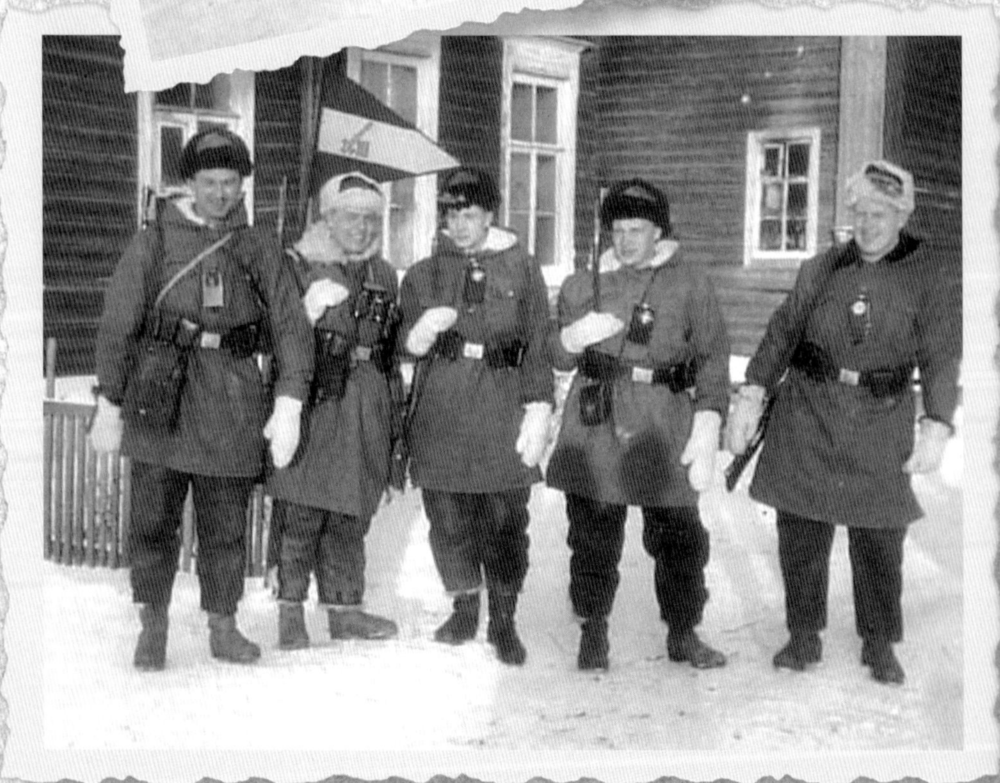

1943: members of the SS Cavalry Division show off their winter clothing.

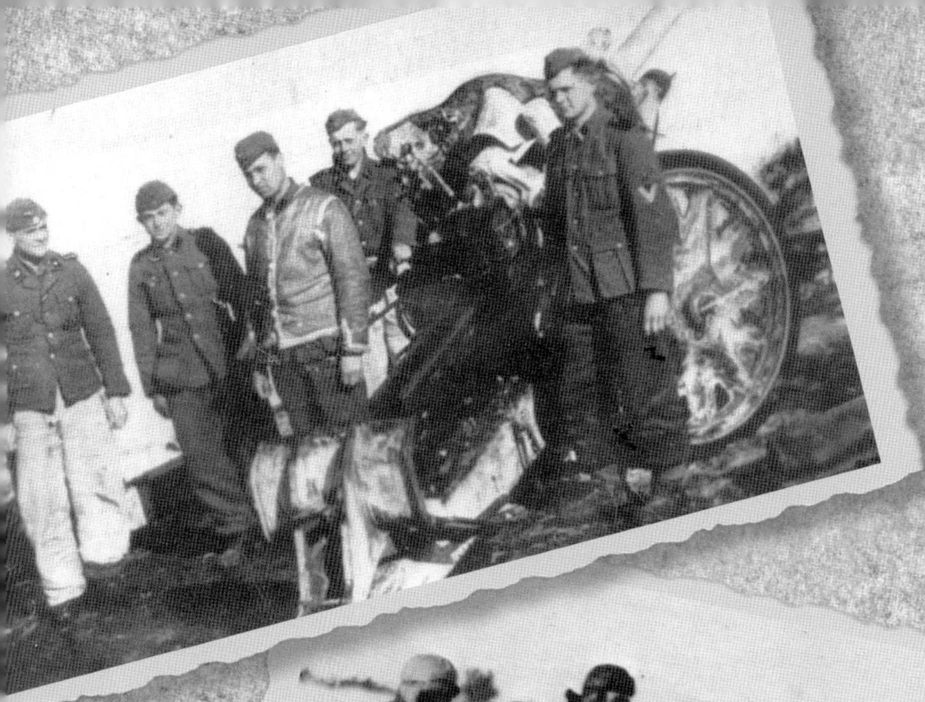

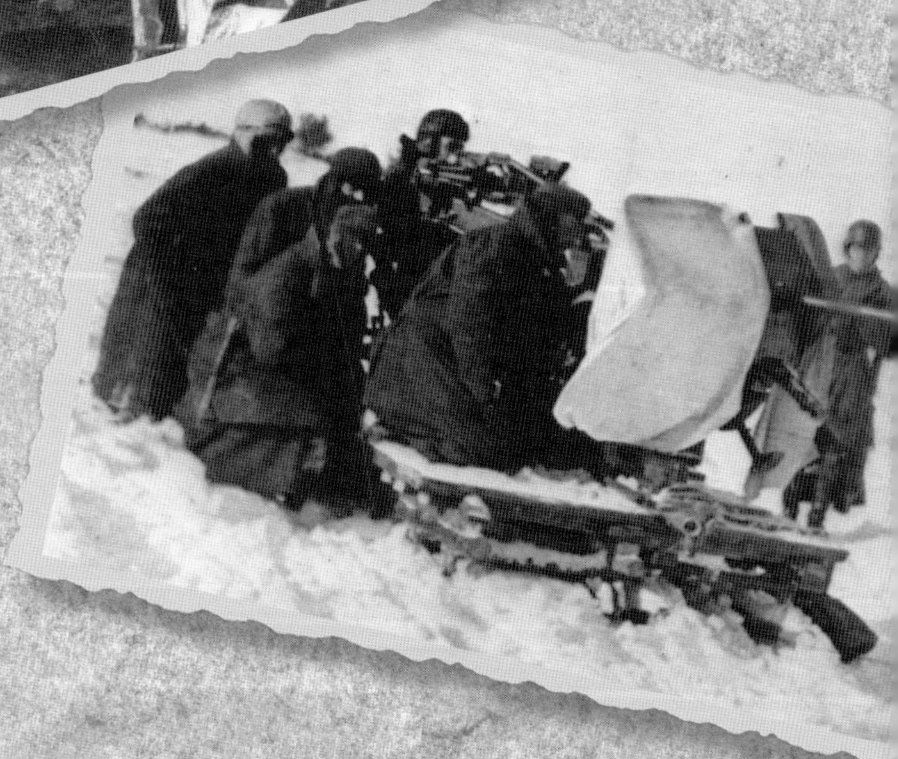

Members of the SS Artillery Regiment and the SS Flak Battalion, winter 1942.

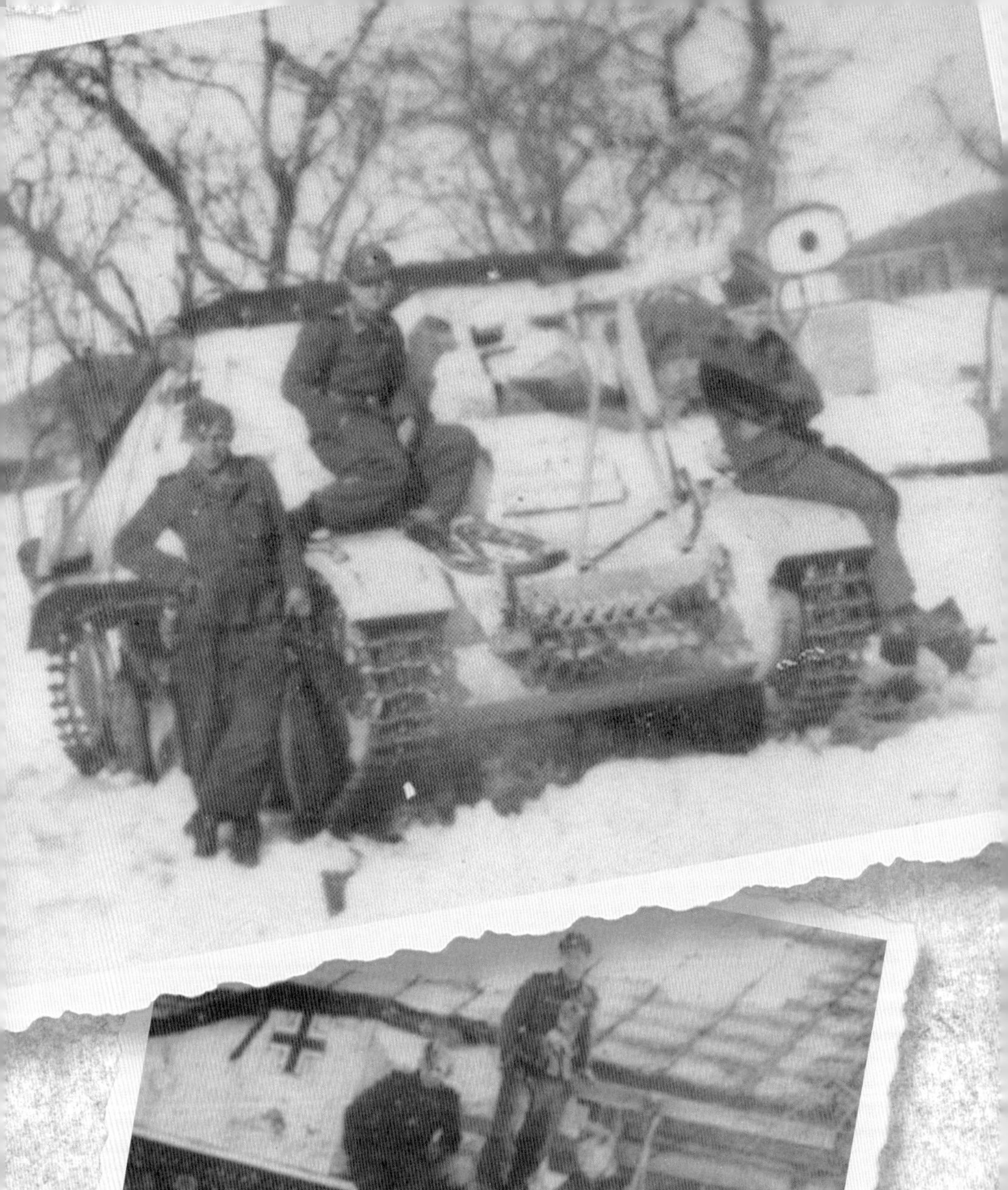

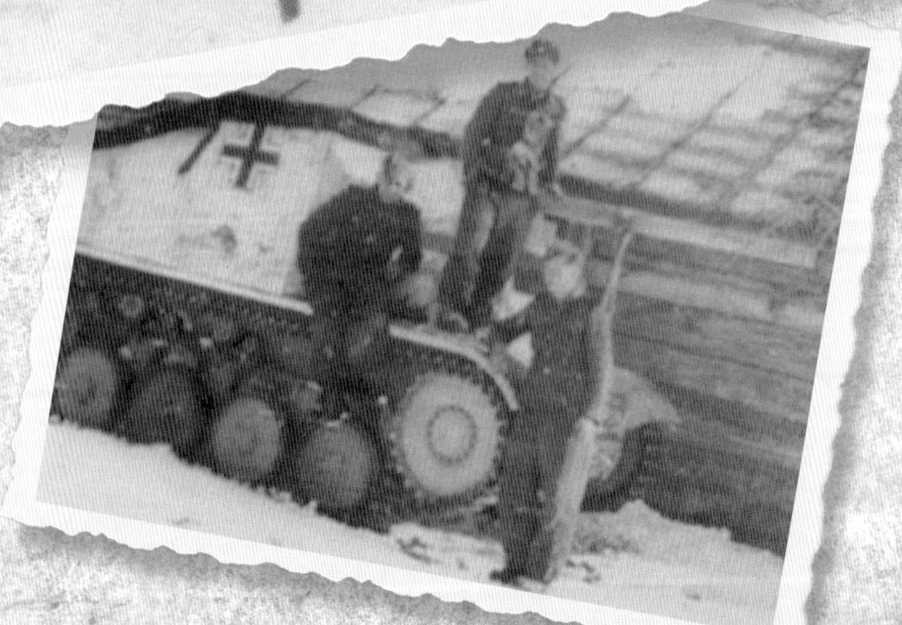

Self-propelled guns of SS Artillery Regiment 8.

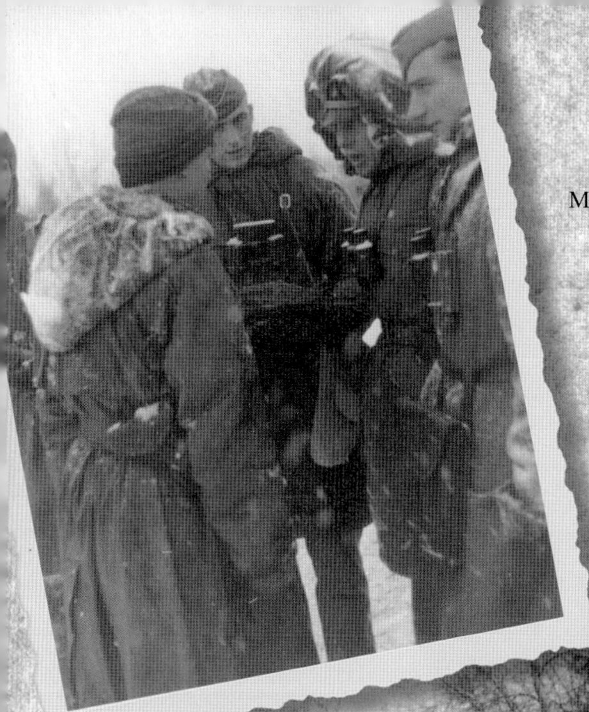

Mission briefing.

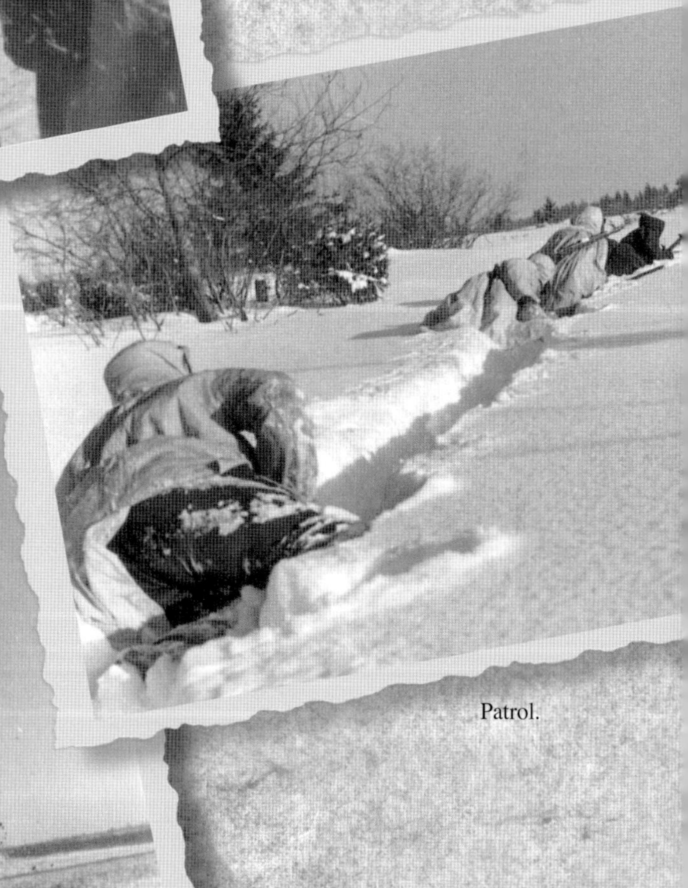

Patrol.

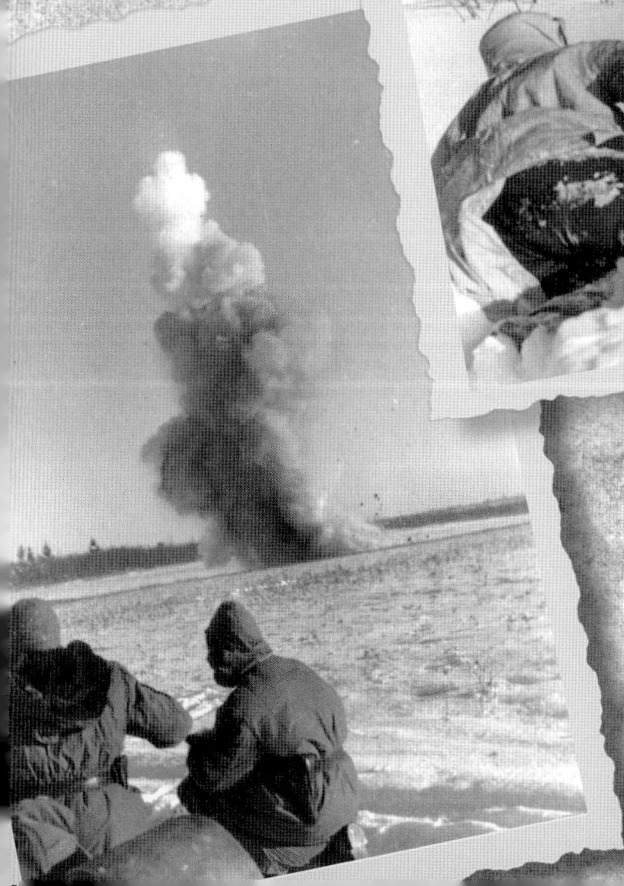

Exploding mortar shell.

The Winter Battle at Dmitrovsk

On 16 February 1943 the division was ordered to form a regiment-size battle group which was to be deployed in the area of Dmitrovsk (approx. 90 km SW of Orel) with XXXXVII Panzer Corps. The Red Army's winter offensive had placed the 2nd Panzer Army in a difficult situation there. Dubbed SS Battle Group Zehender, the unit was made up of elements of:

SS Cavalry Regiment 2
SS Artillery Regiment
SS Flak Battalion
1 anti-tank company
1 pioneer company
1 motor transport column
1 medical company
1 ambulance platoon

The battle group marched to Komarichi (SW of Dmitrovsk), which was the scene of fierce fighting that went on until the middle of March 1943. On 24 March Headquarters, 2nd Panzer Army issued orders for the engagement of partisans, now reinforced by Red Army troops, in the forests south of Briansk – Navlya (approx. 40 km NW of Dmitrovsk). On 5 April SS Battle Group Zehender was ordered back to Lapichi (NW of Bobruisk). The former *SS-Unterscharführer* Ludwig Mückl recalled:

"At the start of February 1943 our division suddenly began to move—to where no one knew. But the Russians knew, for the next morning—we had moved out during the night—aircraft circled overhead and dropped leaflets on which was printed: "See you in Orel!" What kind of war was this, in which the enemy always knew what we were going to do! And, sure enough, we moved through Smolensk, Roslavl, and Briansk to Karachev, west of Orel. In the ice and snow it took us three days and nights to cover 400 kilometers, for the most part at a walking pace. We took turns sleeping in the vehicles for a few hours. A gap had to be filled resulting from the loss of the 6th Army. Day after day we looked to the east across the endless expanses and hoped and hoped, but no one came back. The Soviets also employed loudspeakers: "German soldiers come over to us. Thousands of naked women are

waiting for you in Moscow. Don't forget your mess kit cover, there's pudding too!" I don't know if anyone fell for it. Our division communications center was set up in Orel. There were permanent stone houses, which were whitewashed—as they were almost everywhere in the Ukraine. We were relieved and sent to Karachev. There I was ordered to attend a course for non-commissioned officers. They probably needed replacements because of losses. They often worked us until we were at the point of exhaustion, and this just a few kilometers from the front. They chased us through ice, snow, and mud—by then the thaw had set in. SS-Oberscharführer Thoma, a butcher from Nuremberg, was the worst; his carotid artery was always swollen from screaming at the top of his lungs. In Karachev we were billeted with civilians in the houses. As it was winter, they had their sheep, goats, and a few chickens in the house—all in one room. We had it relatively easy, as we only had to go outside when we were used to look for breaks in the lines."

On 20 April 1943 Himmler relieved *SS-Standartenführer* Freitag because of his incompetence and made *SS-Oberführer* Fegelein, former commander of the SS Cavalry Brigade, temporary commanding officer. At the same time, the enlisted men of SS Cavalry Regiment 3 were divided among the other two cavalry regiments and a formation cadre was transferred to SS Training Camp "Heidelager" in Debica. The SS Bicycle Reconnaissance Battalion was renamed the SS Reconnaissance Battalion.

Anti-Partisan Warfare in the Ukraine

About two weeks later there followed an action in the area between the Pripyat in the southwest, the Dniepr in the east, and the Mozyr – Gomel rail line in the north. The SS cavalry had previously been deployed in this mainly marshy area from 15 to 30 August 1941. Following discussions with the Commander of the Rear Army Area, *General der Infanterie* von Schenkendorf, and the *Reichsführer-SS*' Plenipotentiary for Anti-Partisan Warfare, *SS-Obergruppenführer* von dem Bach, on 9 May 1943 orders were issued for the SS Cavalry Division to take part in "Operation Vistula I." The division was attached to Police Battle Group Schimana, which consisted of elements of the:

SS Cavalry Division
SS Police Regiments 10 and 11
SS Police Assault Battalion South

The units were to advance southwards and clear the suspected powerful partisan units from the area as far as the Choiniki – Bragin road. The division was organized as follows for the operation:

reinforced SS Cavalry Regiment 1 with:
- 1 battery from II Battalion, SS Artillery Regiment
- 1 platoon from 3rd Company, SS Flak Battalion
- 1 platoon from the SS Assault Gun Battery

reinforced SS Cavalry Regiment 2 with:
- 1 battery from I Battalion, SS Artillery Regiment
- 1 battery from II Battalion, SS Artillery Regiment
- 1 platoon from 3rd Company, SS Flak Battalion
- 1 platoon from the SS Assault Gun Battery

reinforced SS Reconnaissance Battalion with:
- 1 battery from I Battalion, SS Artillery Regiment
- 1 platoon from 3rd Company, SS Flak Battalion
- 1 platoon (50-mm Pak) from the SS Anti-Tank Battalion

The following partisan groups were suspected to be present in the so-called "wet triangle":

- elements of the Kolpak main group, with headquarters in Grebenovo, fortified camp in Lesnoye, main camp in Omelkovshchin, strength approx. 600 men
- Sanyukhov Group, headquarters in Raysk (25 km S of Saspa), recruited mainly from regular troops of the Soviet 44th Rifle Regiment. The group's strength was approximately 500 men, who had in their possession German uniforms, mainly air force.
- Kolpak Group, strength of up to 10,000 men (!), operating south of the line Lotsha (95 km S of Rechitsa), Savichi, Babtshin, Tulgovichi (20 km SW of Choiniki). Supply battalion and an airfield in the forests west of Drunki. Partisan headquarters in Novy – Radin.
- Filipenko Group, headquarters in Stepanov, in the south of the "west triangle."

During the initial scouting operations, on 12 May 1943 the SS Reconnaissance Battalion became involved with a group of about 600 partisans. The next day 500 partisan vehicles were captured in a wood.

Two days later *SS-Oberführer* Fegelein issued the following order of the day addressing the operation and his assumption of command over the SS Cavalry Division:

"The tasks now facing the division were ordered by the Führer, because they will contribute to the stabilization and strengthening of the entire front in the east. It is an honor for our unit to be given the opportunity to prove that we are capable, through superiority in command and stubborn determination—both in march and battle performance—to destroy the dangerous enemy facing us. Our will to destroy must be merciless, without quarter or compassion. Any weakness means a lengthening of the war. With the same vigor and drive and the same determination with which I once led the first cavalry unit of the Schutzstaffel, I assume command of the only cavalry unit in the Greater German Army. Long live the Führer!"

Hampered by the complex terrain of forests and swamps, the operation failed to achieve the desired success, however. On 10 June the SS Cavalry Division returned to its starting positions. The operation did produce one useful result, as large numbers of farm animals were requisitioned in the operational area:

5,676 cows
1,073 calves
1,233 horses
3,153 sheep
1,398 pigs

After the operation, the SS Cavalry Division moved from Army Group Center's sector to that of Army Group South, and thus also left the area of the Senior SS and Police Commander Russia Center for that of the Senior SS and Police Commander Russia South, *SS-Obergruppenführer* Prützmann, based in Kiev.

The division was moved south so that it could take part in "Operation Vistula II" in the second third of June 1943. The objective was to destroy the approximately 20,000 partisans believed to be in the area bounded by Ovruch – Mozyr – Petrikov – Leltshitsy – Olovsk – Belekurichi – Ovruch. Mobile forces of the SS Cavalry Division would cross the Pripyat between Skyrgalova and Petrikov and attack along the Ubort River. Police Battle Group Schimana (without the SS Cavalry Division) was to march into the target area from Ovelak. The Royal Hungarian VII Army Corps and the SS Grenadier Replacement Battalion "East" were deployed around Ovruch to prevent the partisans from breaking out to the south and east.

On 19 July 1943 the SS Cavalry Division encircled and crushed a large group of partisans. Total partisan losses in this operation were 1,256 killed and 206 captured. The SS cavalry lost one officer, seven NCOs, and 14 enlisted men killed and 56 men wounded. The relationship between the casualty figures suggests that most of the enemy dead must have been unarmed civilians!

In the days that followed the units were used mainly to guard the grain harvest. Skirmishes with national-Ukrainian partisans showed that, unlike the communist-oriented partisans, they preferred to strike economic targets rather than taking direct action against the German occupation forces. While these actions were going on replacements were trained and integrated into the units. Ludwig Mückl recalled:

"From Karachev we drove past Briansk in the direction of Gomel. Through the endless forests we moved to Reshitsa on the Dniepr. The operation in the swamps was seriously hampered by heavy rain and unbearable plagues of mosquitoes. Smoking was of some help against the pests, but not much, especially as I was a non-smoker. We were issued mosquito nets that we could pull over our steel helmets. But they weren't of much use either, for the beasts could crawl through the tiniest hole—it was horrible.

Our division communications center was set up in Reshitsa in the "wet triangle." It even had a direct line to Führer Headquarters in the Wolf's Lair in East Prussia. We advanced deeper into the Pripyat Marshes, and I was assigned the task of setting up a telephone central on a road in the forest. Ten men were assigned to accompany me. We lived well there. Each day we went to the nearby villages to procure eggs (jeikas). We soon became so cheeky that on arriving at the outskirts of the village we fired into the air three times and simply passed by the houses to collect the jeikas. The division Headquarters moved from Mozyr to Lutsk, because Ukrainian and Polish partisans were raising proper hell there in Volhynia in the area between Kovel, Dubno, Rovno, and Volynsk. Intensive operations destroyed several partisan bands.

One partisan was captured. The man was sentenced to death by hanging. Strict orders were issued for the entire company to assemble and watch the execution. I was sitting comfortably with some of my comrades when the time came. A whistle blew and everyone went to the place, some even cheerfully – "Man, I'm excited!" One comrade and I remained where we were—luckily no one came and got us. I didn't want to see or hear anything, and visions of the Middle Ages appeared before my eyes."

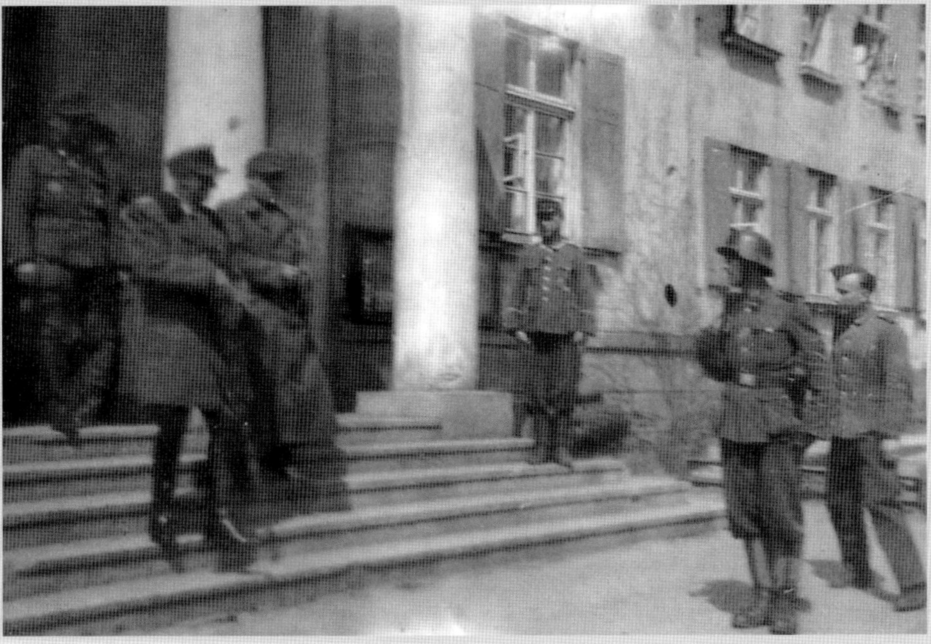

In the spring of 1943 the SS Cavalry Division was attached to the Army Group Center Rear Area Commander, *General der Infanterie* von Schenkendorff.

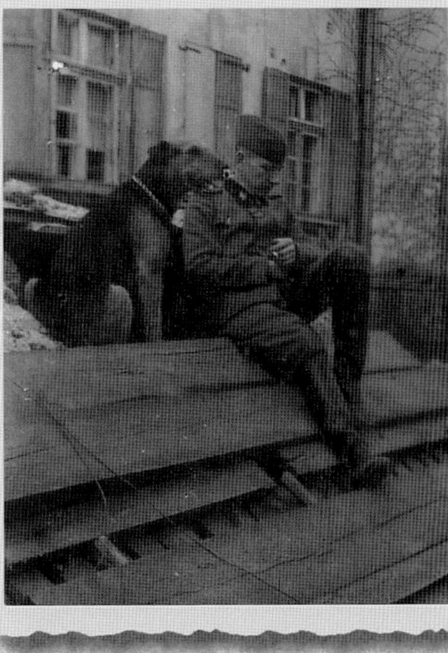

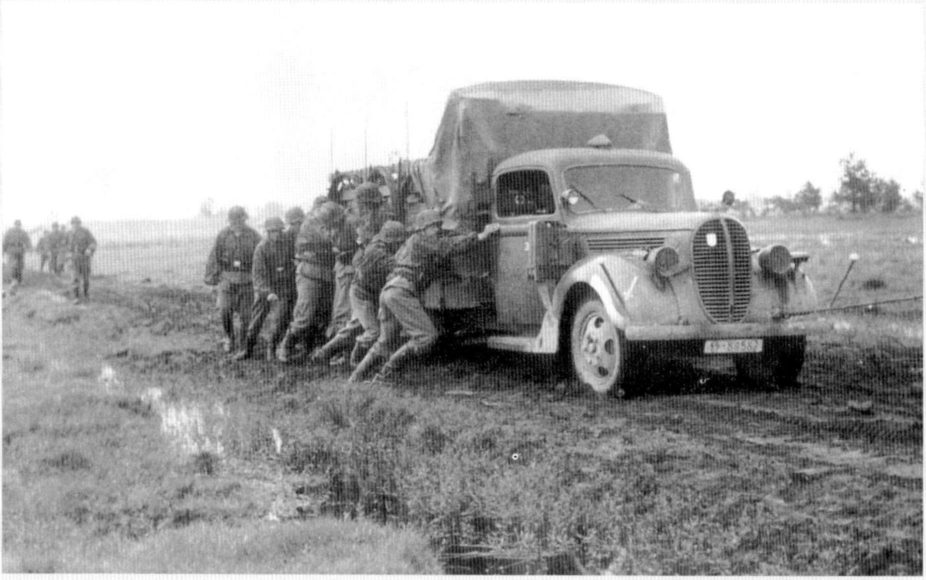

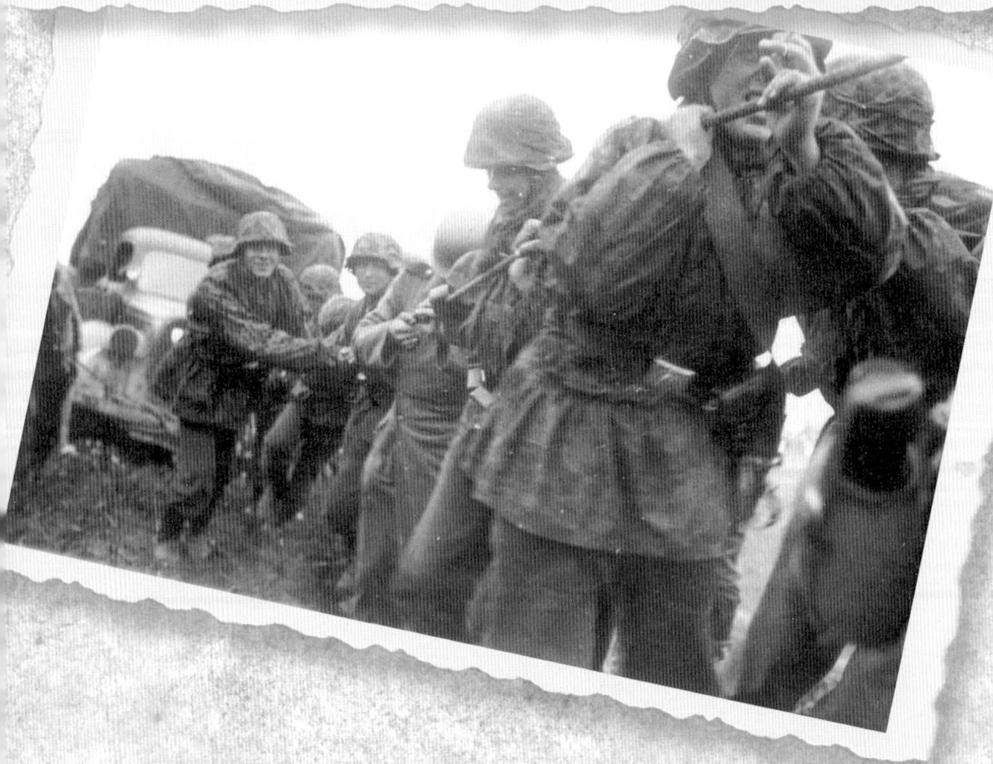

Action during "Operations Vistula I and II" in the marshes between Ovruch and Gomel, May to July 1943.

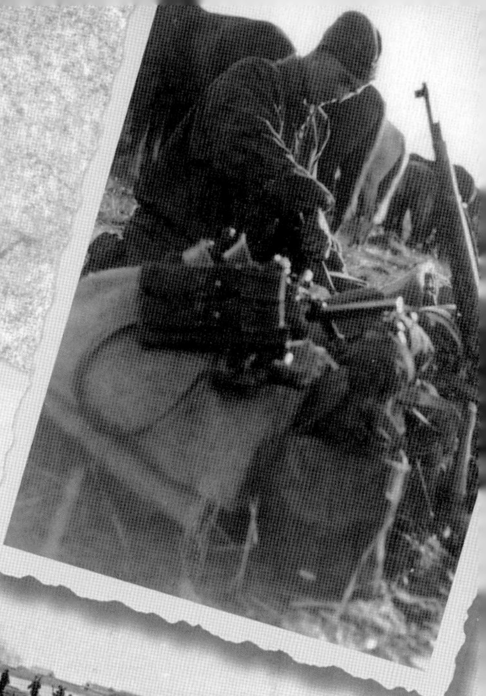

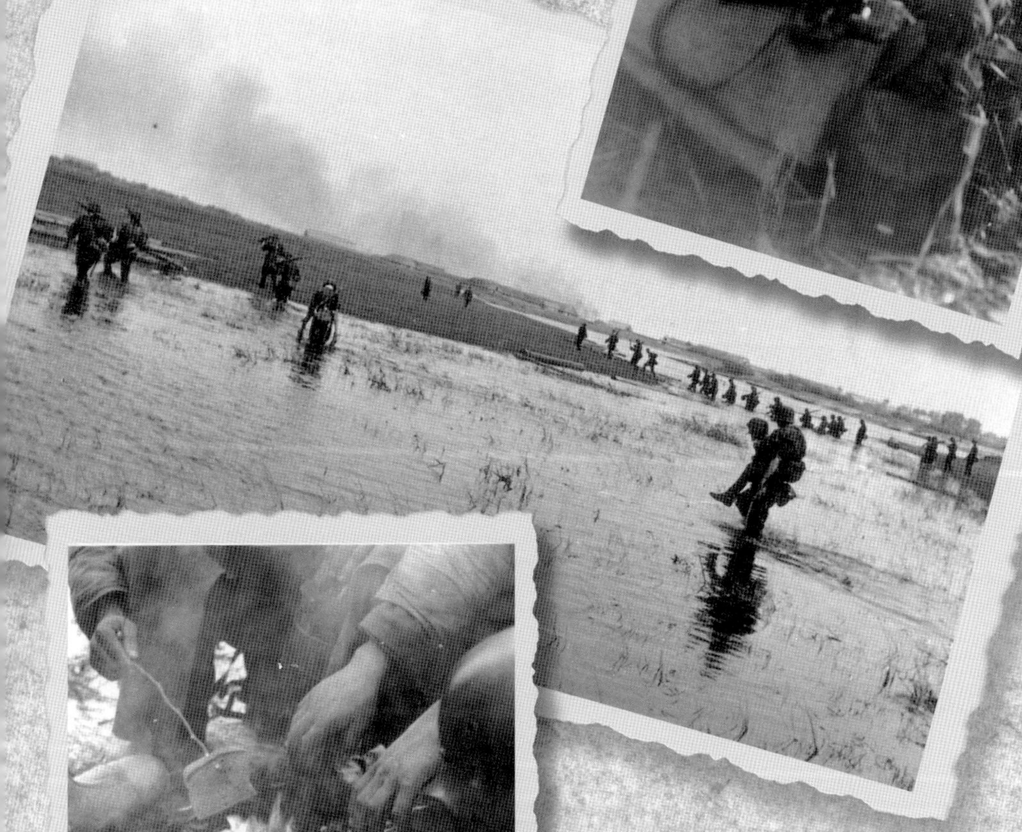

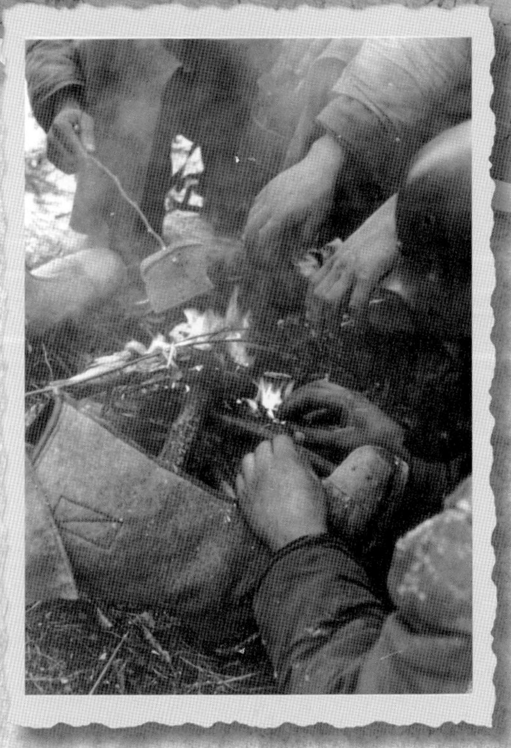

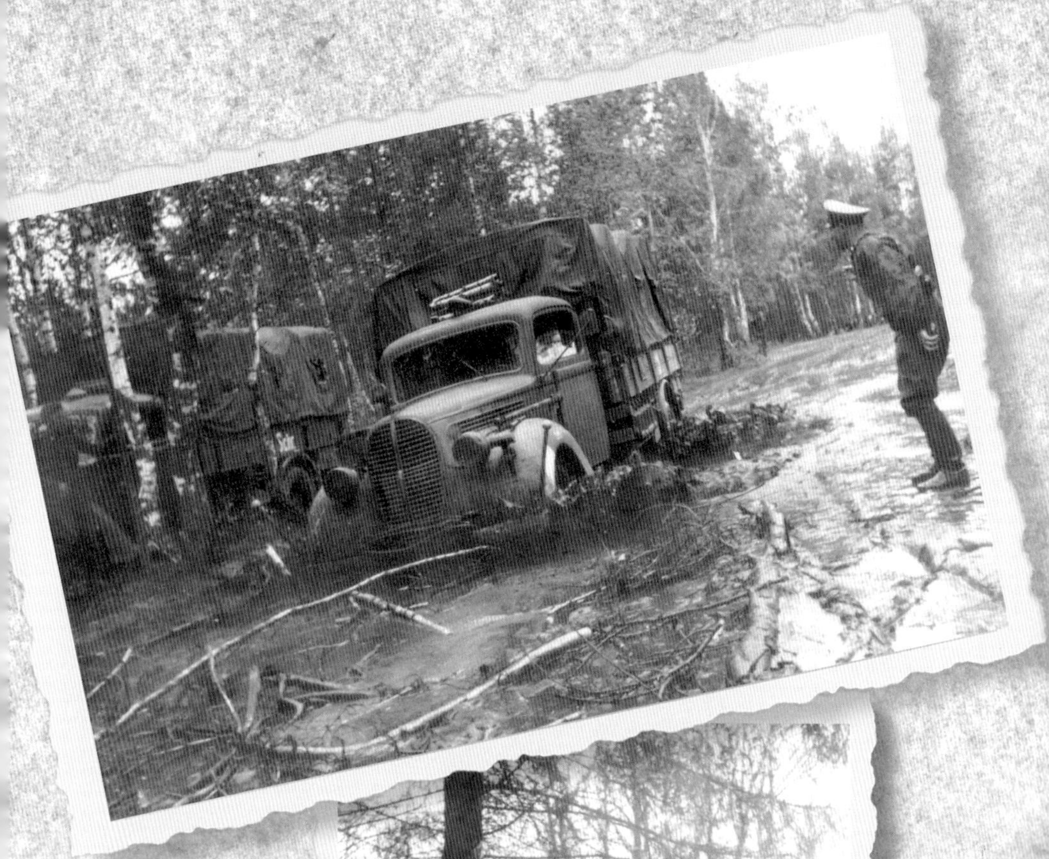

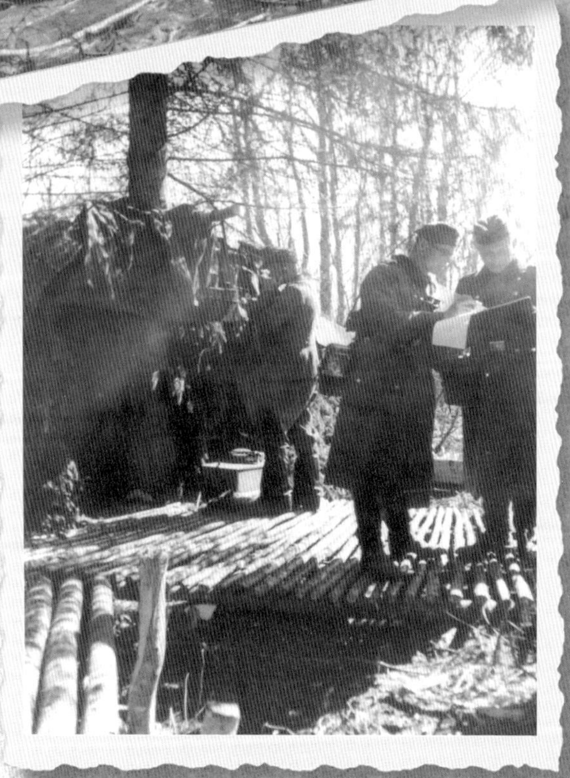

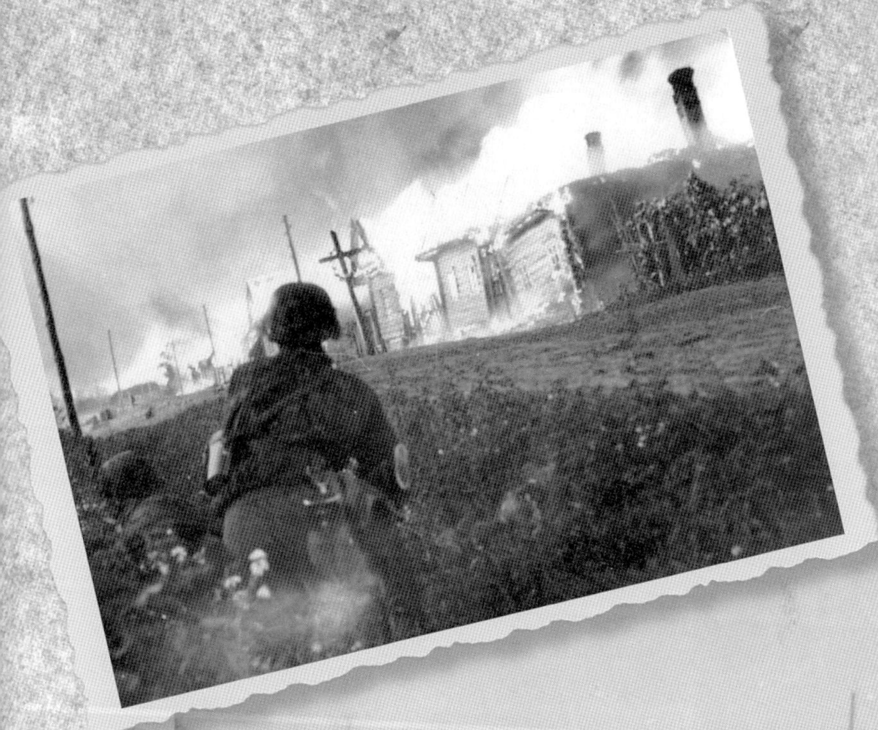

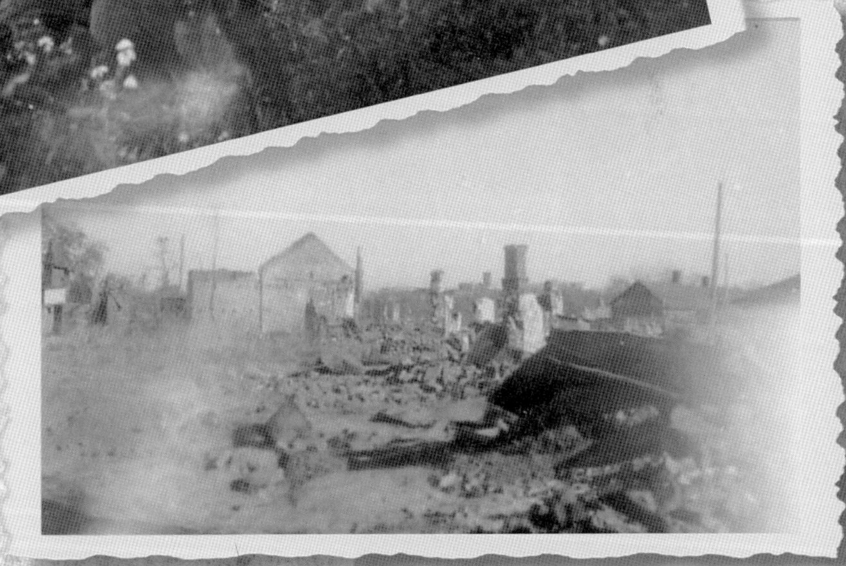

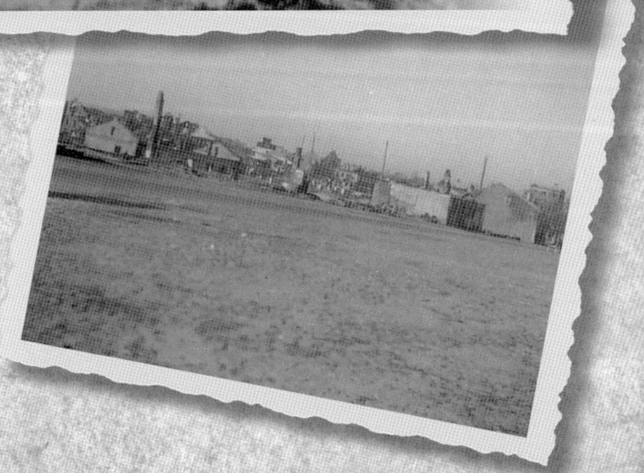

"Anti-partisan warfare" during "Operations Vistula I and II" in the spring of 1943.

Günther Temme – Hermann Fegelein – Gustav Lombard, summer 1943.

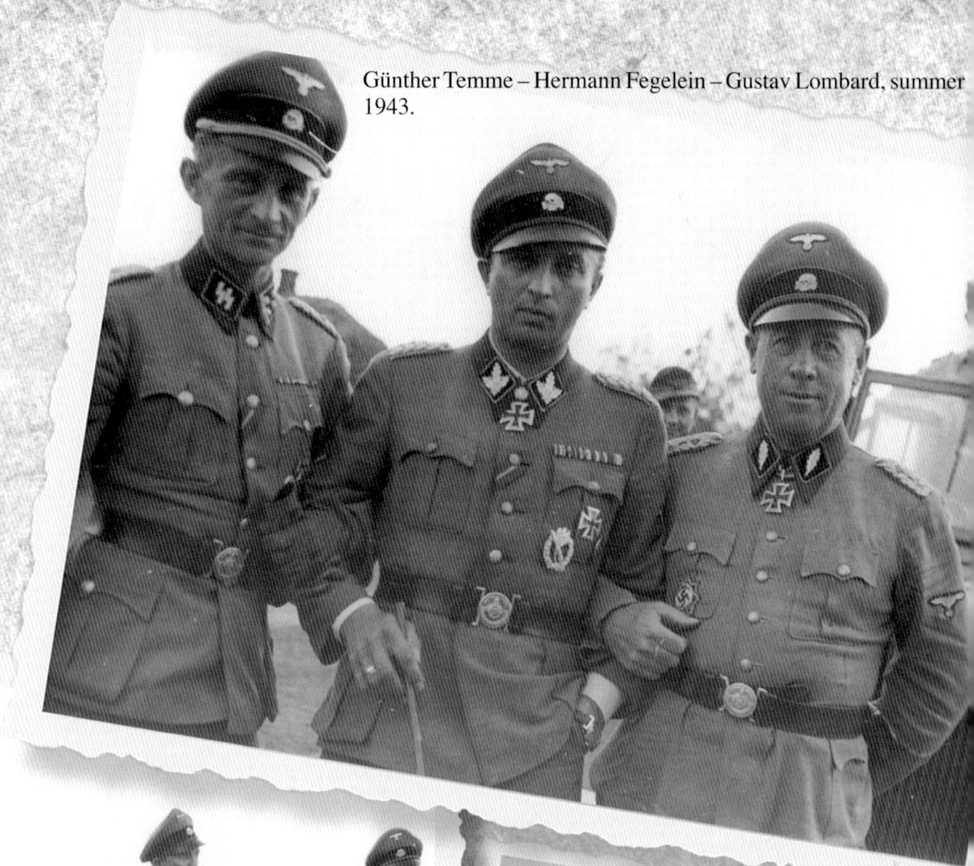

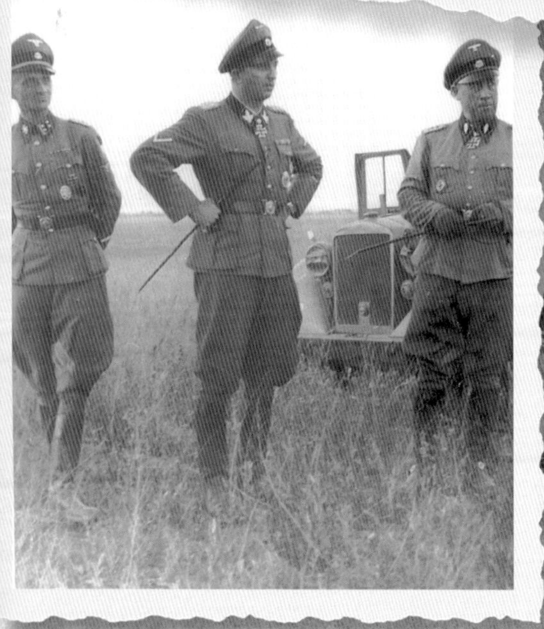

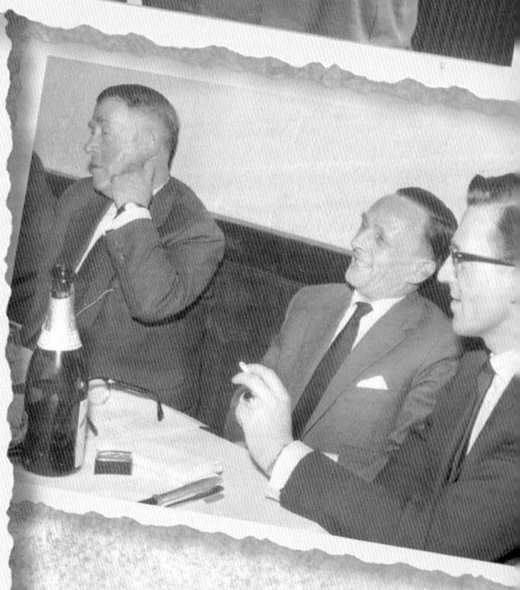

Gustav Lombard and Günther Temme after the war.

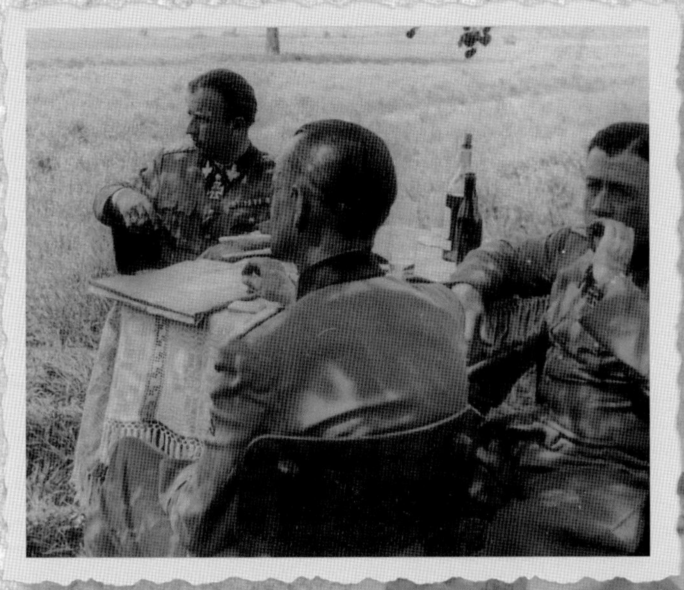

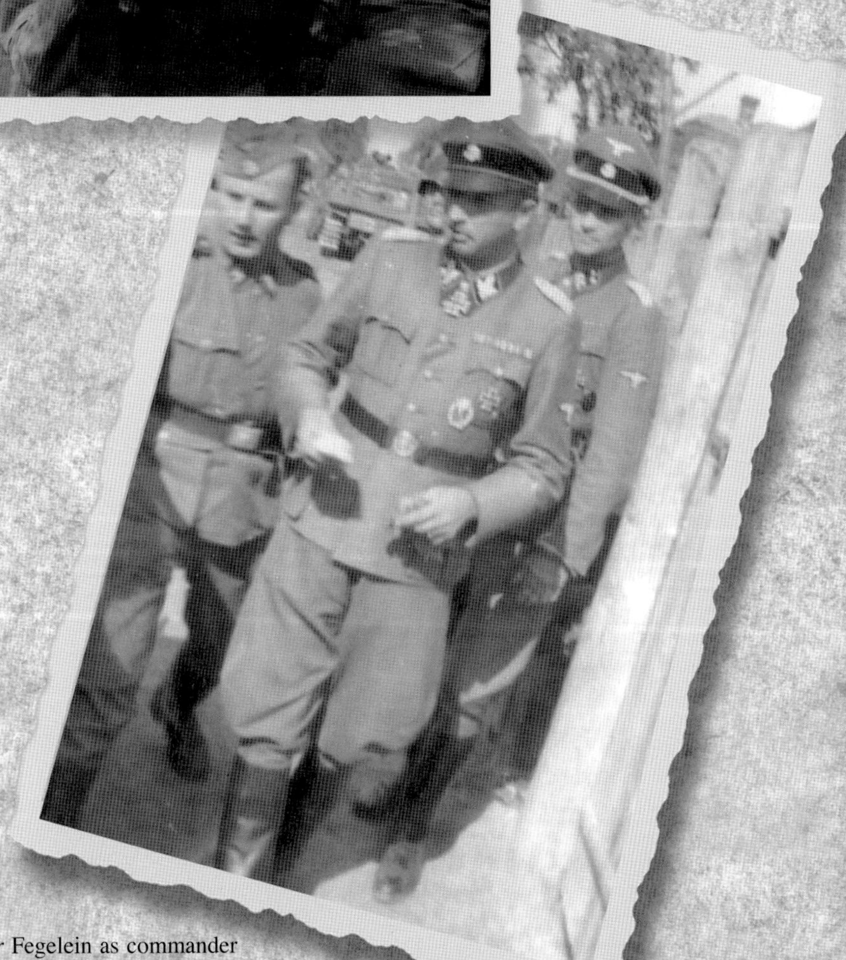

SS-Brigadeführer Fegelein as commander of the 8th SS Cavalry Division (summer 1943).

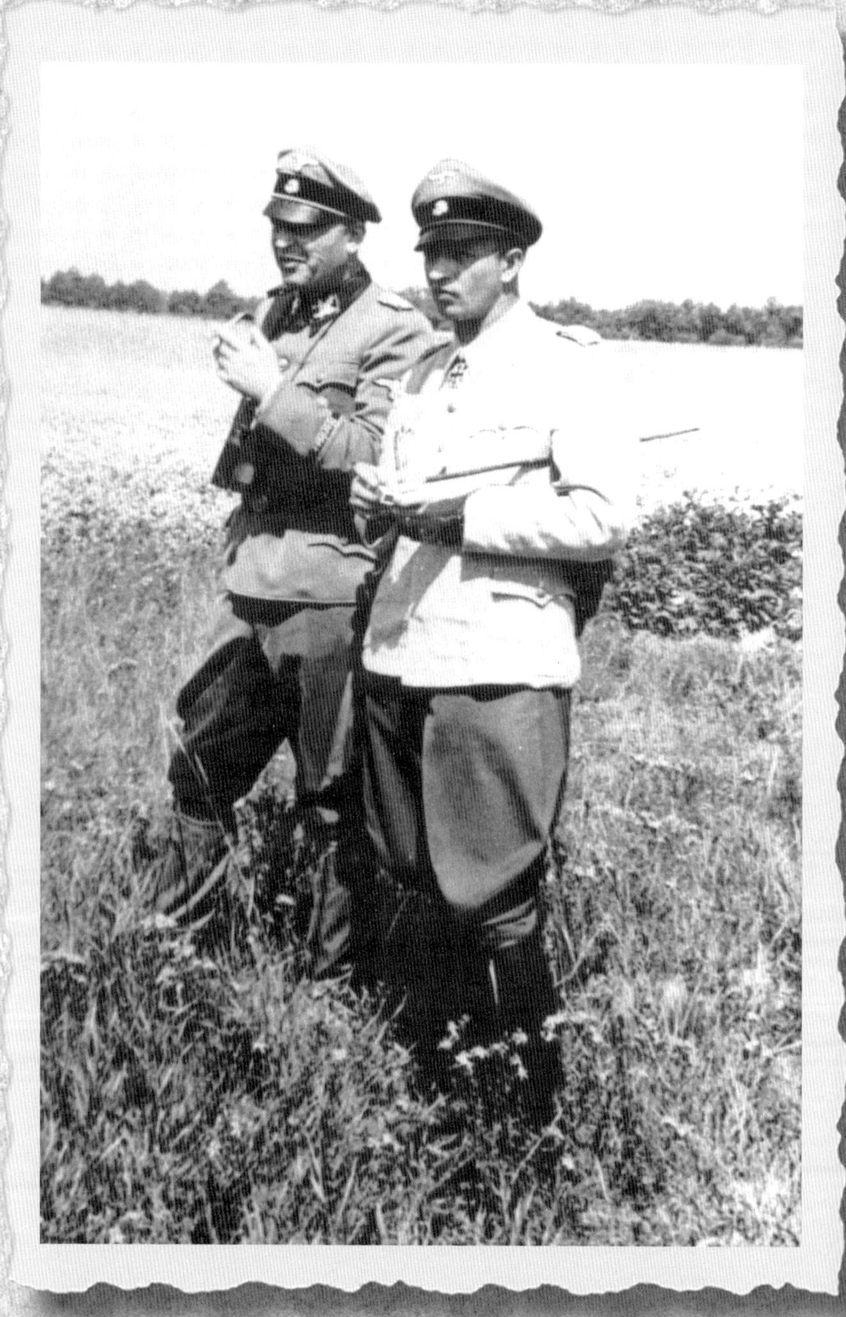

SS-Brigadeführer Fegelein with Senior SS and Police Commander "Ukraine" *SS-Obergruppenführer* Prützmann during "Operation Vistula II" in July 1943.

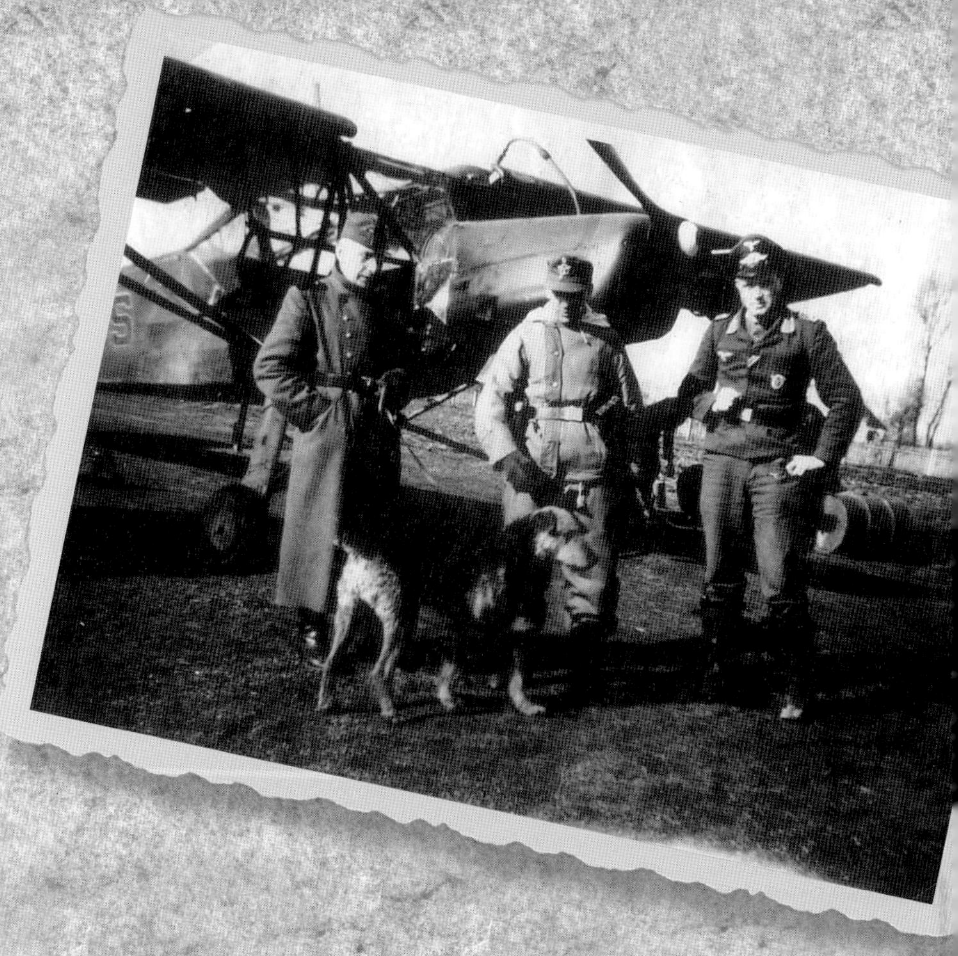

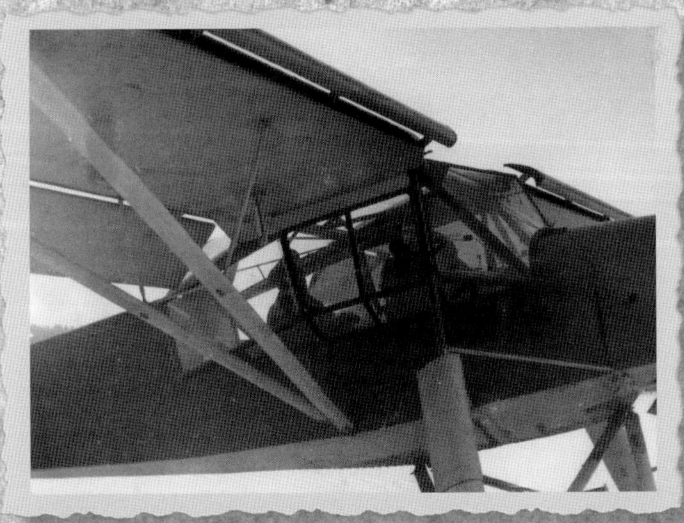

The Fieseler Stork, such as that of the Senior SS and Police Commander, was regularly used on reconnaissance missions during anti-partisan operations.

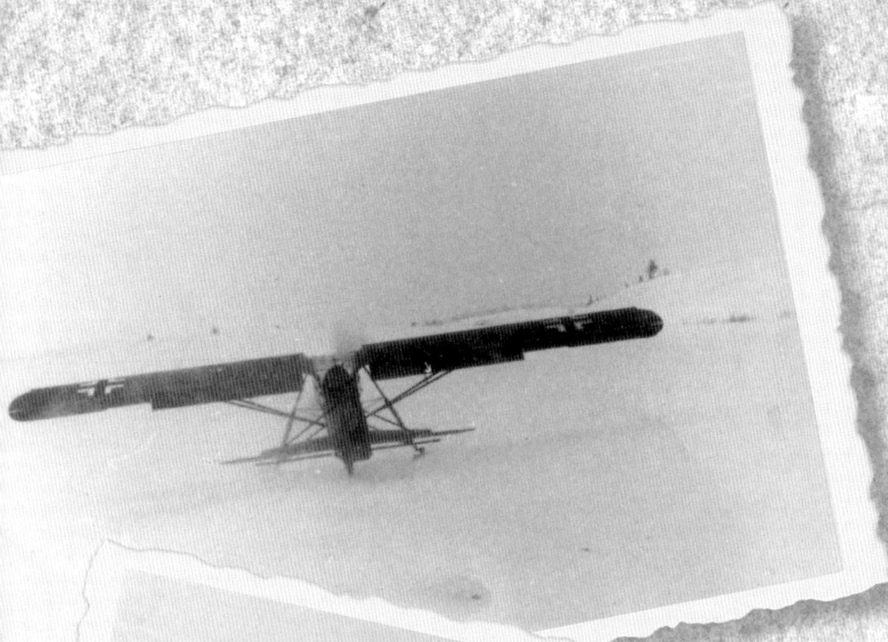

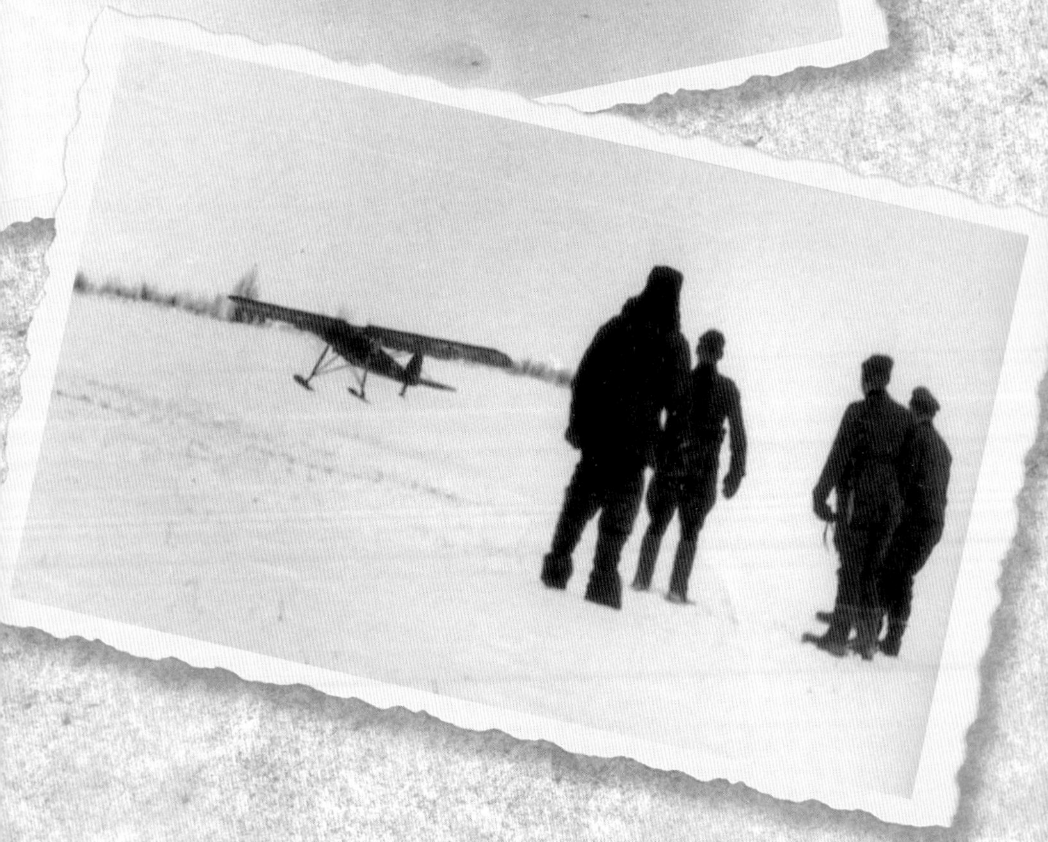

Action at the Front in the Merefa – Mishurin-Rog – Kirovograd Area

Even before the unsuccessful German summer offensive—"Operation Citadel"—was over, the Red Army itself took the offensive and launched a drive towards Kharkov. The SS Cavalry Division subsequently received orders to leave the Mozyr area and move about 500 km to the east to the Merefa area (south of Kharkov). On 21 August 1943 the division reached XXXXII Army Corps (8th Army) with a strength of:

	Officers	NCOs	Enlisted Men	Total
Actual	249	1,364	7,179	8,792
	2.8%	15.5%	81.7%	100%
Authorized	433	2,262	9,926	12,621
	3.4%	17.9%	78.7%	100%

The division was deployed at the boundary with LVII Panzer Corps (1st Panzer Army). In the weeks that followed conditions became chaotic, not because the division was 30% below authorized strength, but because the SS Cavalry Division had not been conceived to take part in large-scale operations against an armored opponent.

XXXXII Army Corps was just making preparations to withdraw to the west bank of the Dniepr. On 26 August 1943, after a fierce artillery bombardment, Soviet armored units attacked and achieved deep penetrations, especially in the division's open flank. The self-propelled guns of the SS Artillery Regiment fought a fierce defensive battle and were able to prevent the worst. The next day the enemy attacked on the same scale as the day before, and three self-propelled guns and two artillery pieces were lost. Elements of the division were encircled during this attack, and in some cases they held out for eight hours before they were relieved by scratch units. Finally a weak, continuous main line of resistance was established.

At the beginning of September 1943 the SS cavalry were attached to LII Army Corps. The commanding general of XXXXII Army Corps, *General der Infanterie* Dostler, bade farewell to the division on 30 August 1943:

"The SS Cavalry Division fought splendidly in the recent fierce defensive battles. To it I express my thanks and appreciation for holding off the powerful enemy attacks, which were preceded by heavy artillery fire. I am certain that the SS Cavalry Division will defeat further such attacks in the future."

From the Tscherk – Bishkin area north of the Donets, the units made a costly fighting withdrawal southwest in the direction of the Dniepr—often operating in small battle groups. They reached the Dniepr on 25 September 1943 and were attached to LVII Panzer Corps in the Mishurin-Rog area. All that could be done was to establish a thin defense line held by men who were at the end of their strength. Two days later the first Soviet infantry units crossed the Dniepr and established a bridgehead south of Mishurin-Rog. The SS Cavalry Division was among the units that took part in the unsuccessful attempt to eliminate the bridgehead. The SS cavalry were initially able to halt Soviet attacks from the bridgehead toward Kommunar to the northwest and Likhovka – Vladimirovka to the southwest. There was especially fierce close-quarters fighting on 29-30 September. On 3 October 1943 the commanding general of LVII Panzer Corps, *General der Panzertruppen* Kirchner, praised SS Cavalry Regiment 1 for its "*outstanding and heroic*" actions in the defense of Kommunar.

At the end of the month the units of the Waffen-SS were numbered consecutively. The new designations were:

8th SS Cavalry Division
SS Cavalry Regiment[9] 15
SS Cavalry Regiment 16
SS Cavalry Regiment 17

The division units also received the number 8.

The positions between Kremenchug and Mishurin-Rog had to be abandoned, and the 8th SS Cavalry Division withdrew into the Kirovograd – Krivoy Rog area. On 27 October 1943 it launched a counterattack near Zapadenka, where the enemy, enjoying massive numerical superiority and tank support, had broken into the German main line of resistance. Hastily-formed battle groups were able to halt and seal off the Soviet attack.

On 5 November 1943 a fight broke out for possession of Vasilyenka. After encountering stubborn resistance, the Soviets sent in bombers to pound the German positions. The Soviet superiority in men and materiel was crushing. Three days later the 8th SS Cavalry Division was attached to XI Panzer Corps. 15 November 1943 was another day of heavy fighting: after heavy artillery preparations the enemy attacked with 200 tanks and powerful infantry forces. By committing their final reserves the Germans were able to hold the line. Five days later the division was again attached to LVII Panzer Corps.

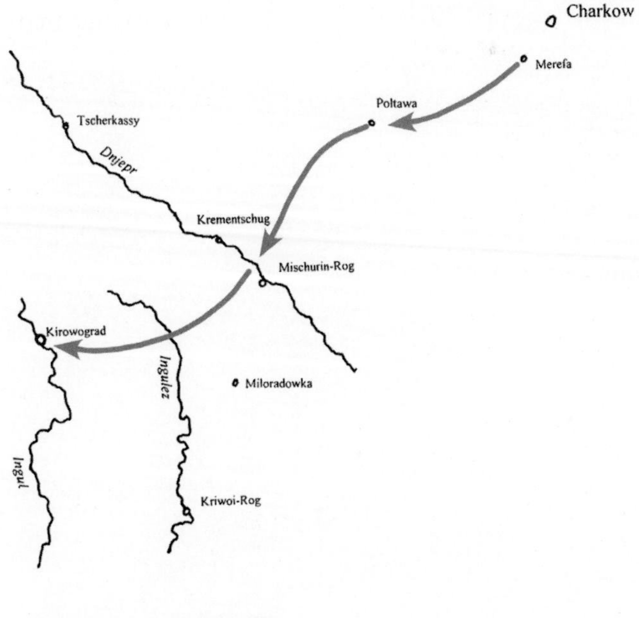

© Michaelis-Verlag Berlin, Oktober 2006

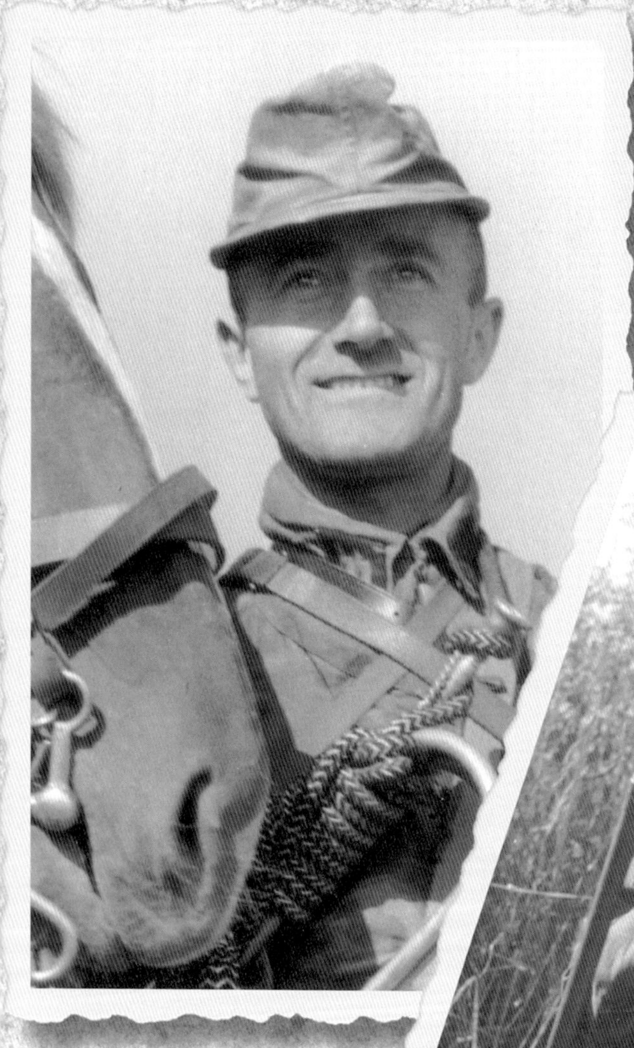

Hornist

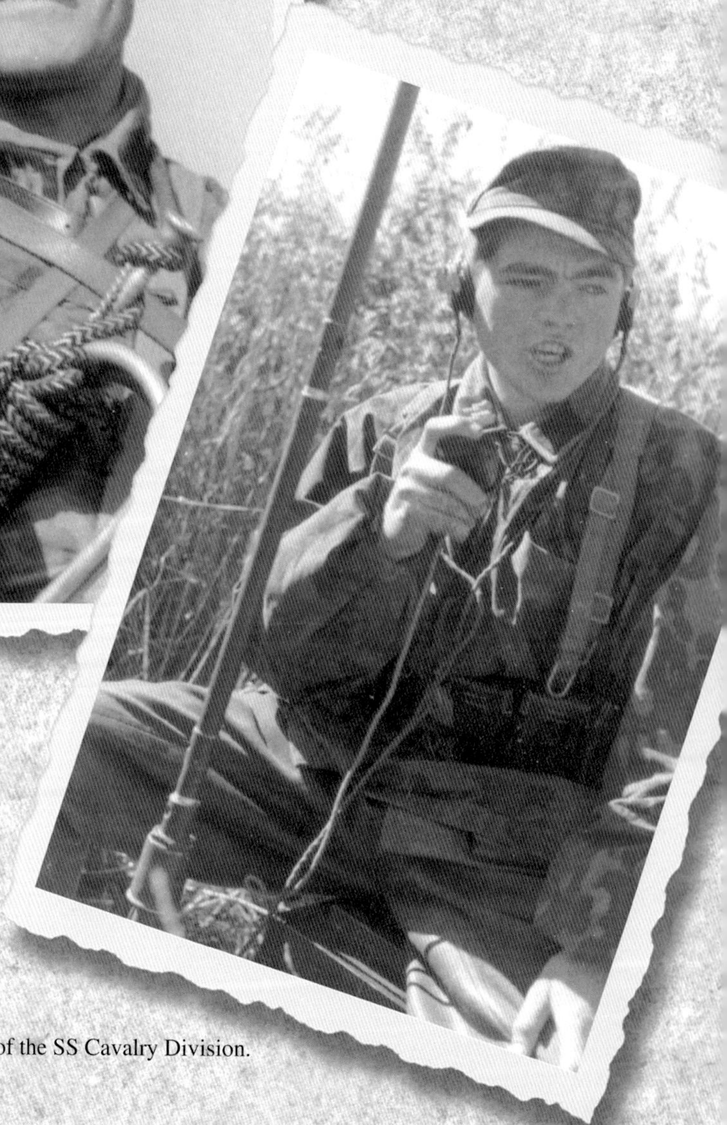

Radio operators of the SS Cavalry Division.

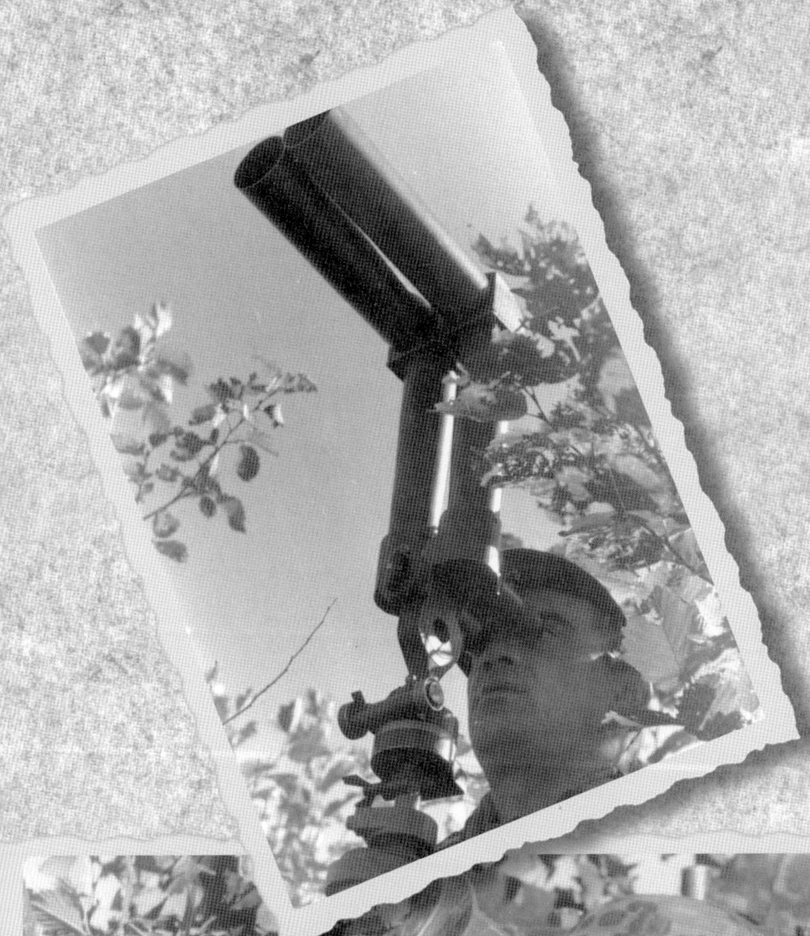

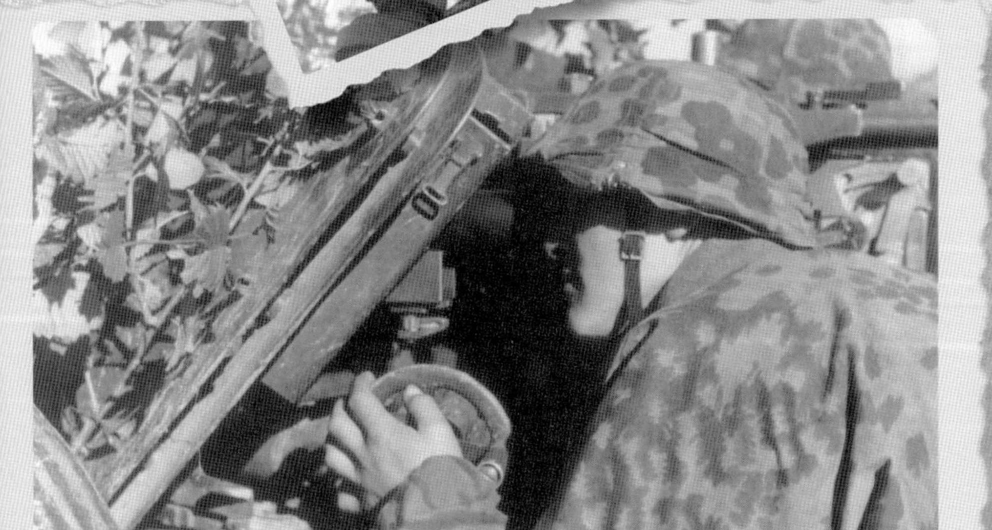

Range-finder and crew of an anti-tank gun.

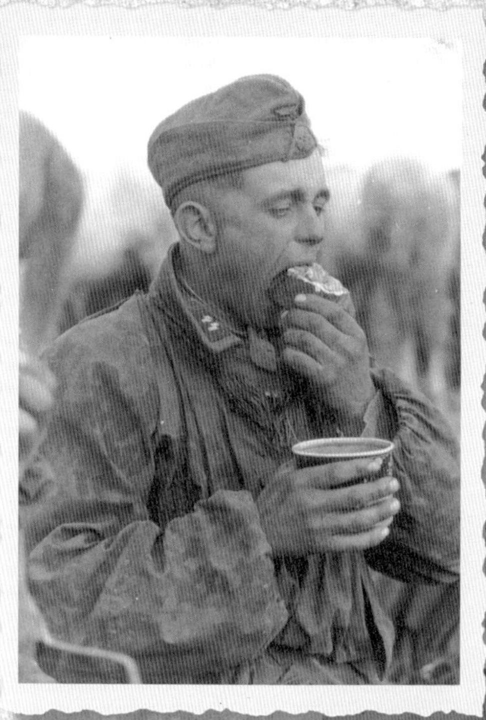
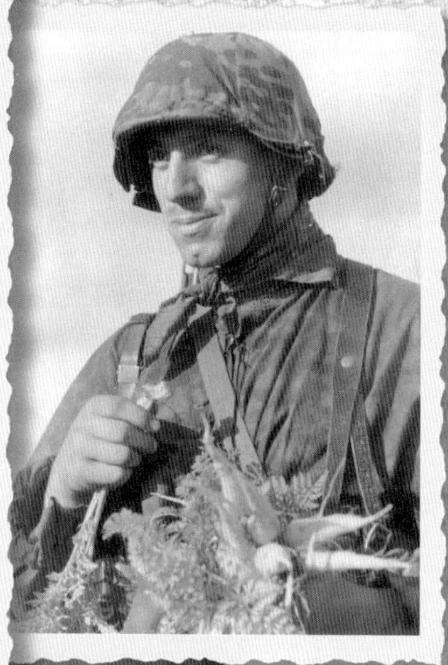
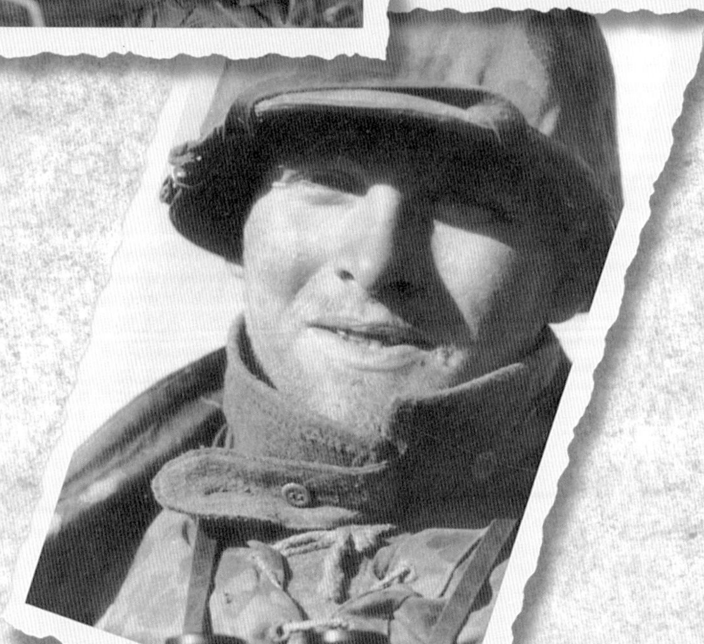

Members of the SS cavalry.

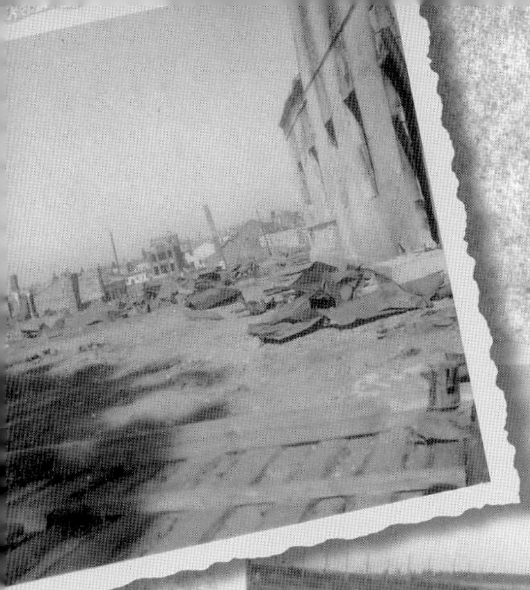

The rear area and "guarding supplies," spring 1943.

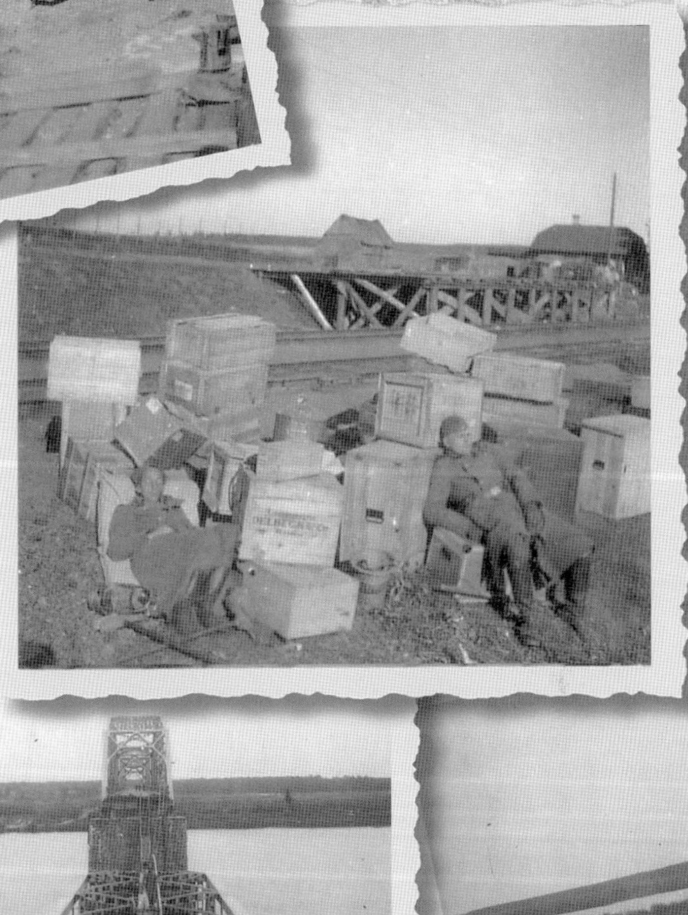

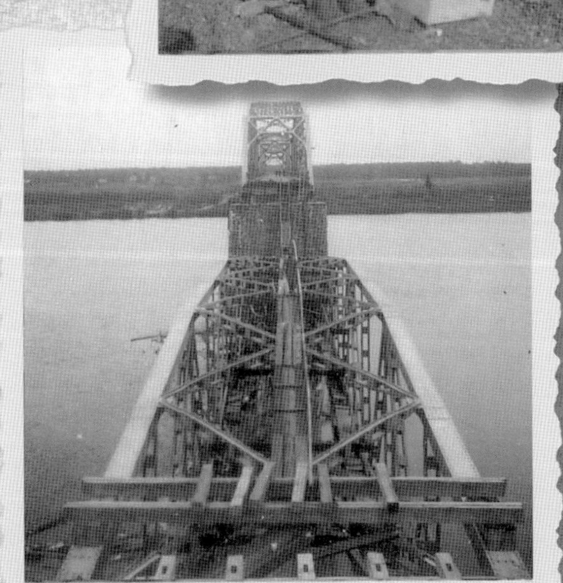

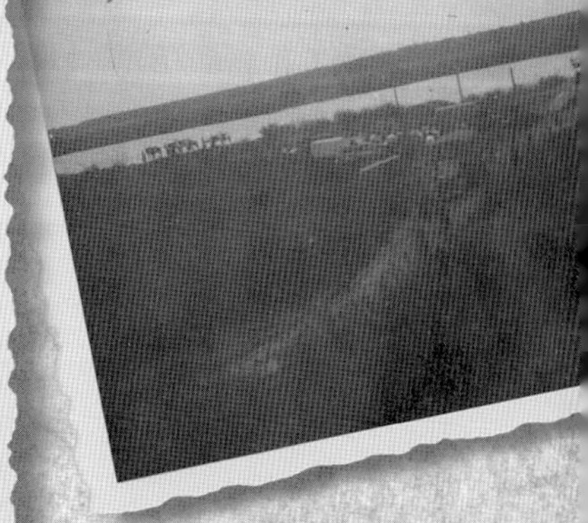

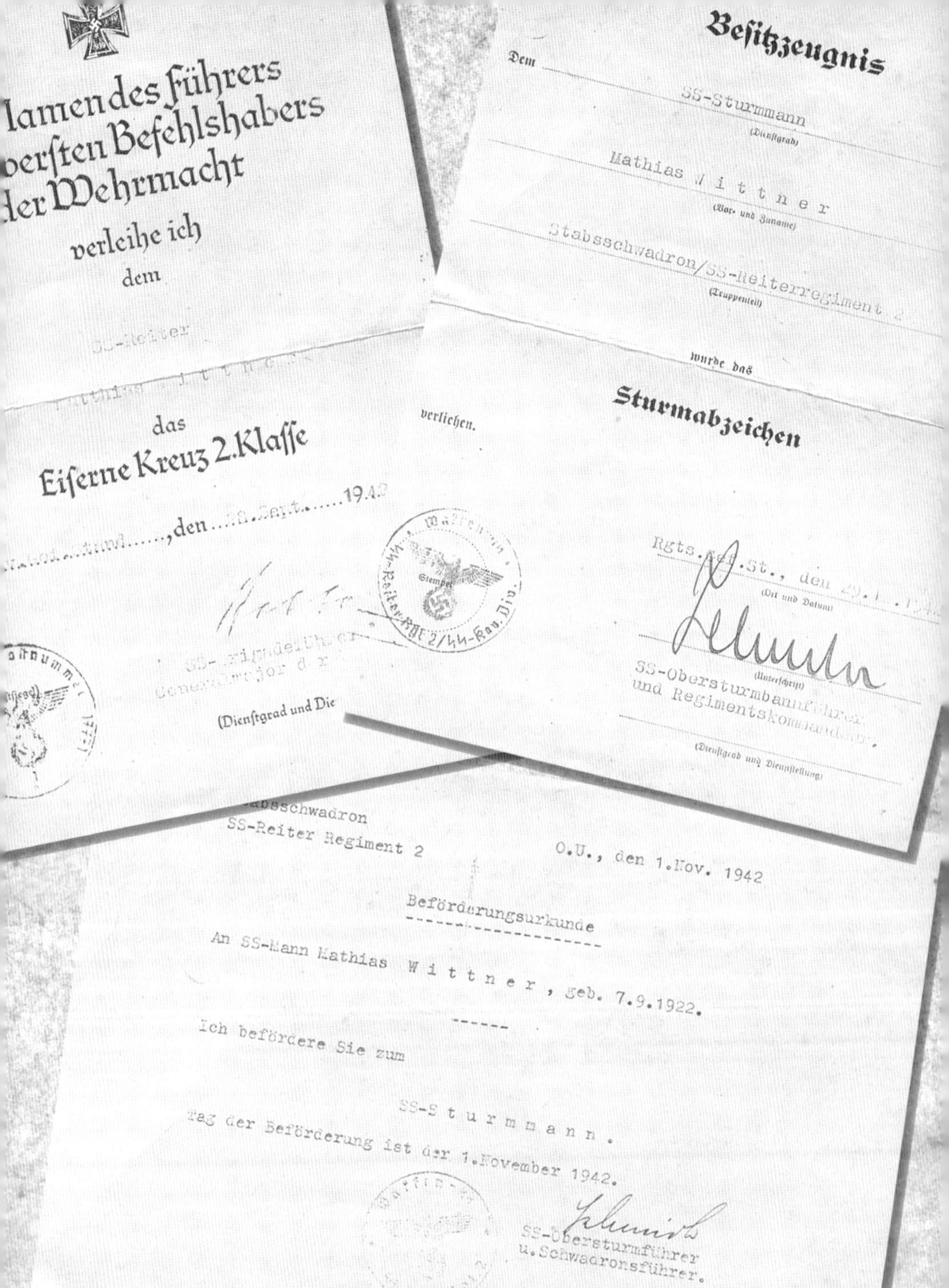

lamen des Führers
berſten Befehlshabers
der Wehrmacht
verleihe ich
dem
SS-Reiter
das
Eiſerne Kreuz 2. Klaſſe
..., den 28. Sept. 19 42
(Dienſtgrad und Die

Beſitzzeugnis
Dem SS-Sturmmann
(Dienſtgrad)
Mathias Wittner
(Vor- und Zuname)
Stabsschwadron/SS-Reiterregiment 2
(Truppenteil)
wurde das
Sturmabzeichen
verliehen.
Rgts.Gef.St., den 29.12.1942
(Ort und Datum)
(Unterſchrift)
SS-Obersturmbannführer
und Regimentskommandeur.
(Dienſtgrad und Dienſtſtellung)

Stabsschwadron
SS-Reiter Regiment 2
O.U., den 1.Nov. 1942
Beförderungsurkunde
An SS-Mann Mathias Wittner, geb. 7.9.1922.
Ich befördere Sie zum
SS-Sturmmann.
Tag der Beförderung ist der 1.November 1942.
SS-Obersturmführer
u.Schwadronsführer.

On 28/9/42 *SS-Brigadeführer* Bittrich awarded *SS-Reiter* Wittner the Iron Cross, Second Class for an act of bravery in the Demechi area.

After fierce fighting against regular enemy troops and powerful partisan forces in the Demechi area, on 29/12/1942 *SS-Obersturmbannführer* Zehender awarded him the Assault Badge (General) for three acknowledged "assault days."

SS-Sturmmann Wittner was awarded the Iron Cross, First Class for an act of bravery in the Merefa area (approx. 20 km SW of Kharkov).

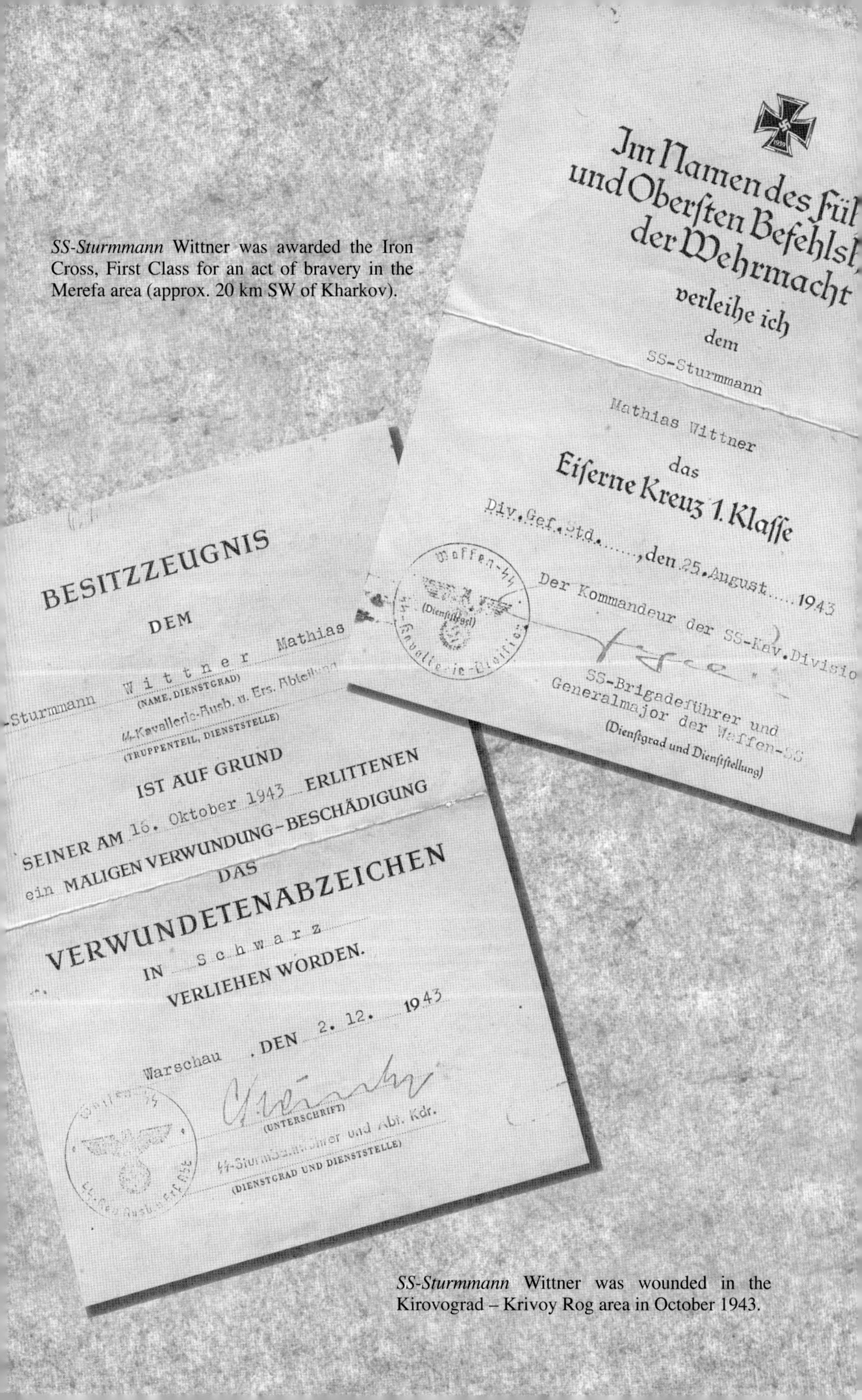

Im Namen des Fü[hrers]
und Obersten Befehlsh[abers]
der Wehrmacht
verleihe ich
dem
SS-Sturmmann
Mathias Wittner
das
Eiserne Kreuz 1. Klasse
Div.Gef.Std. ....., den 25. August 1943
Der Kommandeur der SS-Kav.Divisio[n]
SS-Brigadeführer und
Generalmajor der Waffen-SS
(Dienstgrad und Dienststellung)

BESITZZEUGNIS
DEM
[SS]-Sturmmann Wittner Mathias
(NAME, DIENSTGRAD)
SS-Kavallerie-Ausb. u. Ers. Abteilung
(TRUPPENTEIL, DIENSTSTELLE)
IST AUF GRUND
SEINER AM 16. Oktober 1943 ERLITTENEN
ein MALIGEN VERWUNDUNG-BESCHÄDIGUNG
DAS
VERWUNDETENABZEICHEN
IN Schwarz
VERLIEHEN WORDEN.
Warschau, DEN 2. 12. 1943
(UNTERSCHRIFT)
SS-Sturmbannführer und Abt. Kdr.
(DIENSTGRAD UND DIENSTSTELLE)

SS-Sturmmann Wittner was wounded in the Kirovograd – Krivoy Rog area in October 1943.

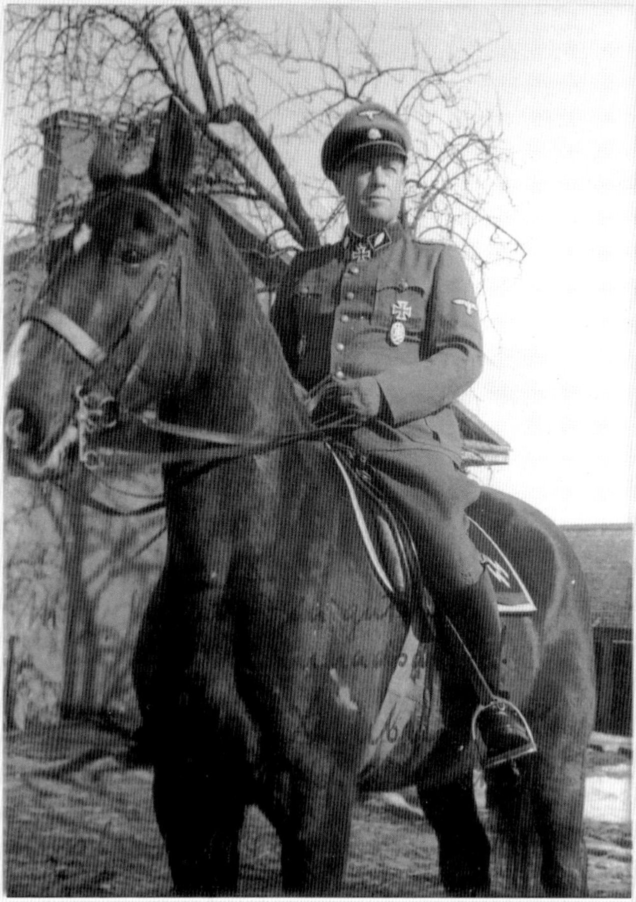

Gustav Lombard — seen here as an *SS-Standartenführer* — led and commanded SS Cavalry Regiment 1 from 19/8/41 to 13/7/44. From 14/7 to 23/8/44 he attended the 12th division commander's course in Hirschberg, and in September 1944 assumed command of the 31st SS Volunteer Grenadier Division.

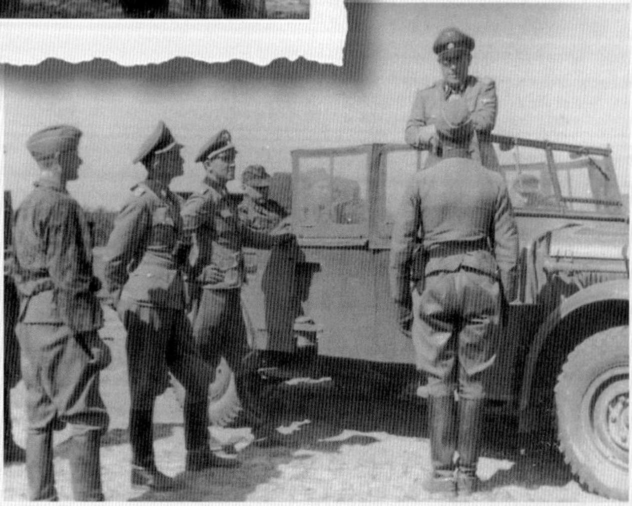

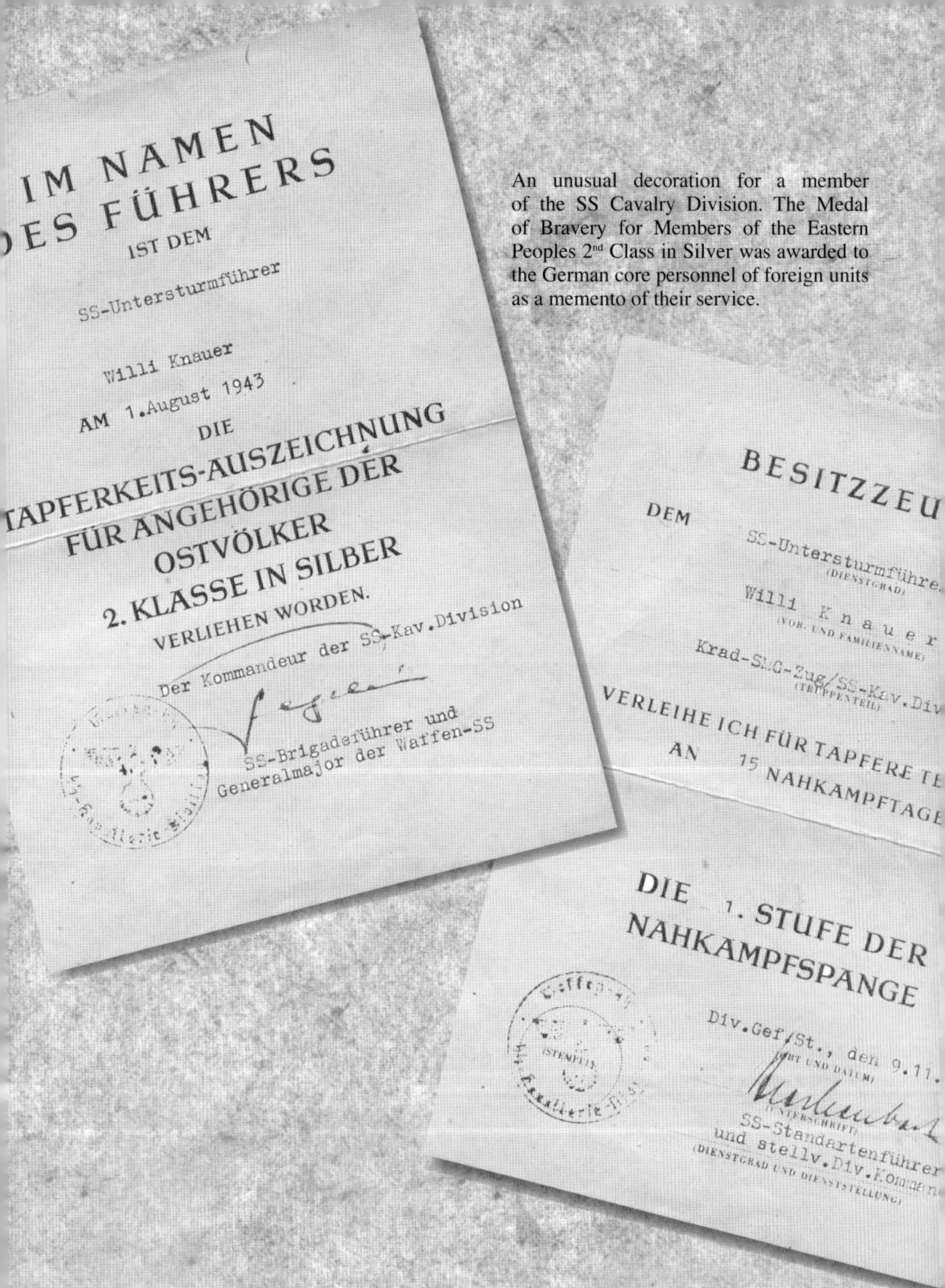

An unusual decoration for a member of the SS Cavalry Division. The Medal of Bravery for Members of the Eastern Peoples 2nd Class in Silver was awarded to the German core personnel of foreign units as a memento of their service.

SS-Standartenführer Streckenbach led the division from September 1943 to April 1944, and on 9 November 1943 he awarded SS-Untersturmführer Knauer the Close Combat Clasp in Bronze.

On 21 November 1943, the Red Army attacked again following a crushing artillery bombardment. In the ice and snow the troops, whose fighting strengths were now down to 15 to 20 men, repulsed the enemy. One week later enemy troops broke into the 8th SS Cavalry Division's left flank near Bashtanka Gorge. Self-propelled guns of SS Artillery Regiment 8 eliminated this penetration too.

The attempt by the 3rd Ukrainian Front to bring about the collapse of the 1st Panzer Army's front initially failed: Krivoy Rog and Zaporozhye were held. On 6 December the 8th SS Cavalry Division even counterattacked and retook the village of Tovarka.

Rest and Reorganization in Croatia

With the unit effectively shattered after the fighting in the Ukraine, on 8 December 1943 Himmler agreed with the head of the Wehrmacht Operations Staff that the 8th SS Cavalry Division should be rested and reorganized as soon as possible. On 21 December, therefore, the first units (SS Reconnaissance Battalion 8 and SS Cavalry Regiment 16) were pulled out of the front and sent to Essig (Croatia) to be reformed. The remaining units stayed with XXXXVII Army Corps as Battle Group Lombard. They would follow to Croatia in January 1944.

On 31 December 1944 the strength of the divided division, less SS Cavalry Regiment 17, was:

	Officers	NCOs	Enlisted Men	Total
Actual	168	1,082	3,932	5,182
	3.2%	20.9%	75.9%	100%
Authorized	433	2,262	9,926	12,621
	3.4%	17.9%	78.7%	100%

In addition, at SS Training Camp "Heidelager" SS Cavalry Regiment 17 (former SS Cavalry Regiment 3) reported:

	Officers	NCOs	Enlisted Men	Total
Actual	38	209	1,573	1,820
	2.1%	11.5%	86.4%	100%

In addition, in November 1943 a fourth cavalry regiment—SS Cavalry Regiment 18—was established for a second SS cavalry division. By 31 December 1943 it had already reached a strength of:

	Officers	NCOs	Enlisted Men	Total
Actual	10	159	1,412	1,581
	0.6%	10.1%	89.3%	100%

A third battalion was also formed for SS Artillery Regiment 18. At the end of 1943 its reported strength was:

	Officers	NCOs	Enlisted Men	Total
Actual	13	64	555	632
	2%	10.1%	87.9%	100%

The former *SS-Unterscharführer* Ludwig Mückl recalled:

"*At the turn of the year 43/44 rumors suddenly began to circulate that we were going to be pulled out of the front and sent back to the Reich for reorganization. There were always such rumors, but this time it was true. We loaded our vehicles onto a train at Vinnitsa station in the Ukraine in the middle of a raging snowstorm. The train had no passenger cars, so we were forced to live and sleep in our vehicles. Luckily we had fur coats and fur-lined boots. The journey took many days and no one knew where we were going, but gradually we realized that we were not headed for the Reich, but rather in a southeasterly direction towards Hungary. We passed through Debrecen and Szeged on our way to Essig, Croatia. The farther south we went, the more spring-like the weather became.*

In the Batchka there were many ethnic German villages, some on the Hungarian side, some on the Croatian. One day the order came to conscript all ethnic German men of an age suitable for military service and take them with us. That was a drama, and often the wives became "hyenas" because they didn't want to let their husbands go.

On one occasion a member of the signals battalion deserted. He was picked up in Belgrade with certain women. This was the second time he had taken off and now he was for it. The military court sentenced him to death for desertion. The entire battalion had to form up in an open square. He was tied to a post and blindfolded. The order was given to fire and he slumped to the ground. I closed my eyes.

We saw little action and spent most of our time training the 17- and 18-year-old replacements from the Reich."

While SS Cavalry Regiment 17 was committed near Kovel, the 8th SS Cavalry Division was at least brought up to strength in personnel through the addition of Reich German and ethnic German replacements. On 12 March 1944 Hitler awarded the cavalry unit the title "Florian Geyer."[10] The division, now officially titled 8th SS Cavalry Division "Florian Geyer," was organized as follows:

SS Cavalry Regiment 15 with 6 troops
SS Cavalry Regiment 16 with 6 troops
SS Cavalry Regiment 18 with 6 troops
SS Artillery Regiment 8 (motorized) with
- 2 battalions each with 3 batteries of 105-mm guns
- 1 battalion with 2 batteries of SdKfz. 124 "Wespe"
- 1 battery of SdKfz. 165 "Hummel"

SS Armored Reconnaissance Battalion 8 with
- 1 company with armored troop carriers
- 3 companies with VW Schwimmwagen
- 1 heavy company

SS Pioneer Battalion 8
SS Anti-Tank Battalion 8
SS Assault Gun Battalion 8
SS Signals Battalion (motorized) 8
SS Flak Battalion 8
SS Veterinary Company 8
SS Medical Battalion 8
SS Economic Battalion 8

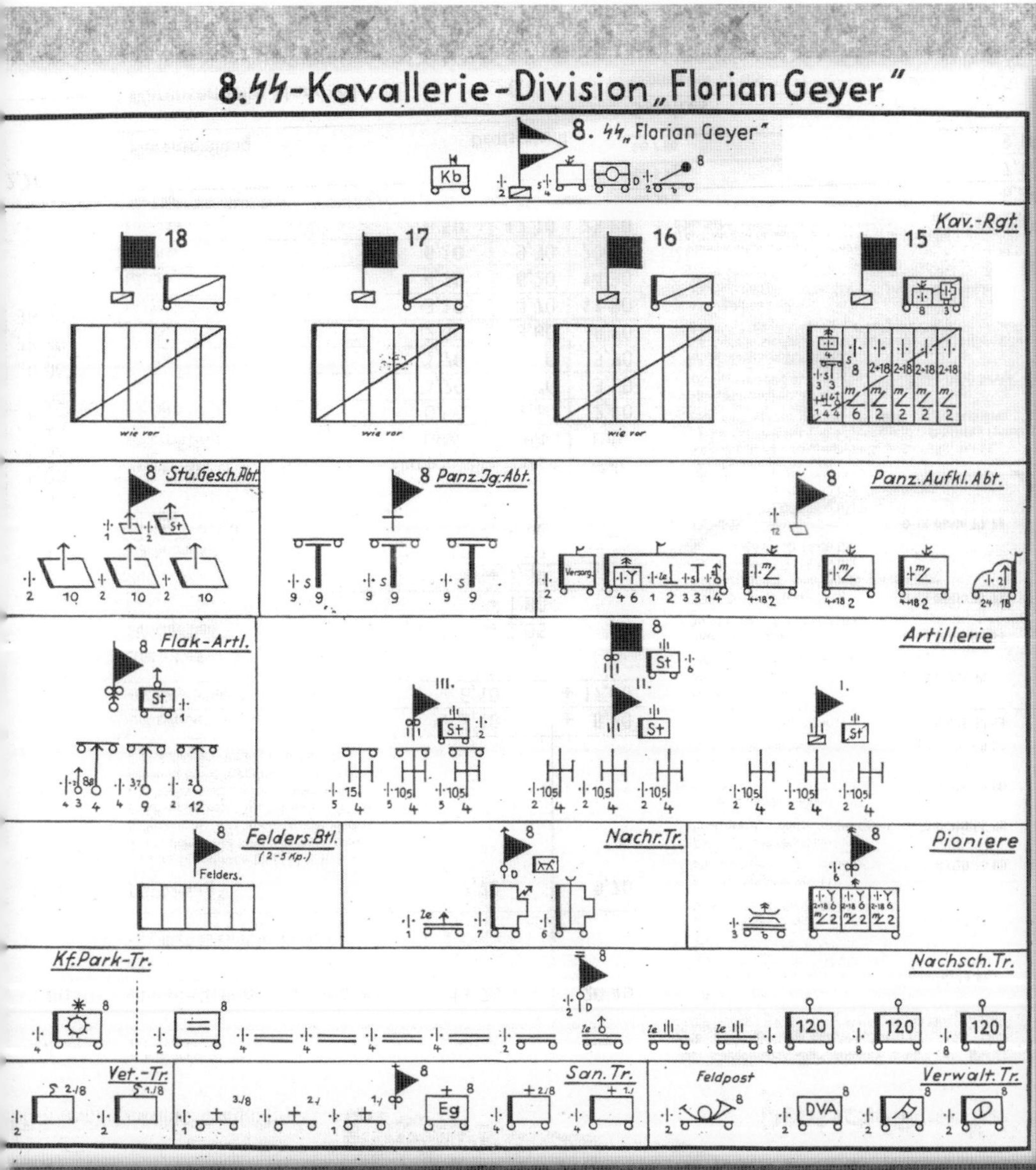
8. SS-Kavallerie-Division „Florian Geyer"
8. SS „Florian Geyer"
Kb
Kav.-Rgt.
18
17
16
15
wie vor
wie vor
wie vor
Stu.Gesch.Abt.
St
Panz.Jg.Abt.
Panz.Aufkl.Abt.
Versorg.
Flak-Artl.
St
Artillerie
St
III.
II.
I.
Felders.Btl.
(2-5 Kp.)
Felders.
Nachr.Tr.
Pioniere
Kf.Park-Tr.
Nachsch.Tr.
120
120
120
Vet.-Tr.
San.Tr.
Eg
Feldpost
Verwalt.Tr.
DVA

In order to create an effective combat formation, much emphasis was placed on motorization and the provision of heavy weapons. The order to expand the SS Assault Gun Battery into a battalion could not be achieved, however, due to a shortage of equipment. An SS Assault Gun Battalion 8 was not formed, and the battery became part of SS Anti-Tank Battalion 8. In fact, the division lacked heavy supporting weapons for the coming battle with the powerful Soviet forces. Georg Ermandraut recalled:

"At the beginning of 1943 at SS Training Camp "Debica," an assault gun battery was formed for SS Artillery Regiment 8. In April 1943 we went to the front as part of Battle Group Streckenbach (C.O. of SS Anti-Tank Battalion 8). "Operation Vistula I" followed in May 1943, and in June 1943 "Vistula II" and "Seydlitz." During these operations our responsibilities included guarding the grain harvest. In August 1943 we were shipped back to the front, and with two of three serviceable assault guns took part in a counterattack. SS-Obersturmführer Göhler was awarded the Knight's Cross after this action. On 16 October 1943, 150 Soviet tanks attempted to break through near Krivoy Rog. The last of our assault guns and self-propelled guns sacrificed themselves in halting this attack. After the division was pulled out of the front, in December 1943 we assembled in Uman and from there were sent to Essig for reformation."

Action at Kovel

While the division was being brought up to strength through the addition of approximately 3,000 replacements, SS Cavalry Regiment 17, which had been newly-established at SS Training Camp "Heidelager" and occasionally used against Polish partisans, received orders to move to Kovel. There the Red Army had broken through the main line of resistance, opening a breach 150 kilometers wide between the 2nd Army and the 4th Panzer Army. The terrain in the area was swampy for the most part; consequently, there was a danger that the enemy might advance rapidly through Kovel, a transportation center, and drive into the *Generalgouvernement*.

SS Cavalry Regiment 17 entrained on 16 January 1944. It was attached to Battle Group von dem Bach, which consisted of:

Pioneer Battalions 50 and 662
1 assault gun battalion
1 artillery battalion
SS Police Regiment 17

The battle group bolstered the forces defending Kovel, which consisted of:

Territorial Battalions 102, 476, 637 and "von Stocki"
Security Regiment 177
Division Supply Office 318
Telephone Repair Company 651
Signals Staff 697
Police Signals Company 41
Transport Column 990

Elements of SS Cavalry Regiment 17 occupied positions near Kolki, on the Styr River (70 km E of Kovel), beyond which lay the swampy region bordered by the Kovel – Okonsst – Sarny – Rokitno – Kies railway line in the north and the Kovel – Lutsk – Rovno – Zhitomir – Kiev line in the south.

The first engagements with regular Soviet troops took place on 29 and 31 January 1944. Partial penetrations into the German main line of resistance were eliminated. The commander of SS Cavalry Regiment 17, *SS-Obersturmbannführer* Zehender, was wounded the next day and replaced by *SS-Sturmbannführer* Janssen. On 9 February 1944 the regiment attacked and retook the village of Rossysze on the Styr. On 22 February the regiment, together with elements of the 7th Panzer Division, attacked across the Styr, enabling XXXXVII Panzer Corps to gather important information on the enemy's strength. One interesting discovery was that the enemy front included large numbers of partisans in addition to regular troops.

At the beginning of March 1944 SS Cavalry Regiment 17 was moved into the area northeast of the Kovel – Povursk railway line. Because of the size of the area to be defended, the regiment's front consisted of a series of strongpoints. Of the unit's original 31 officers, just six were still with the troops—the rest had been

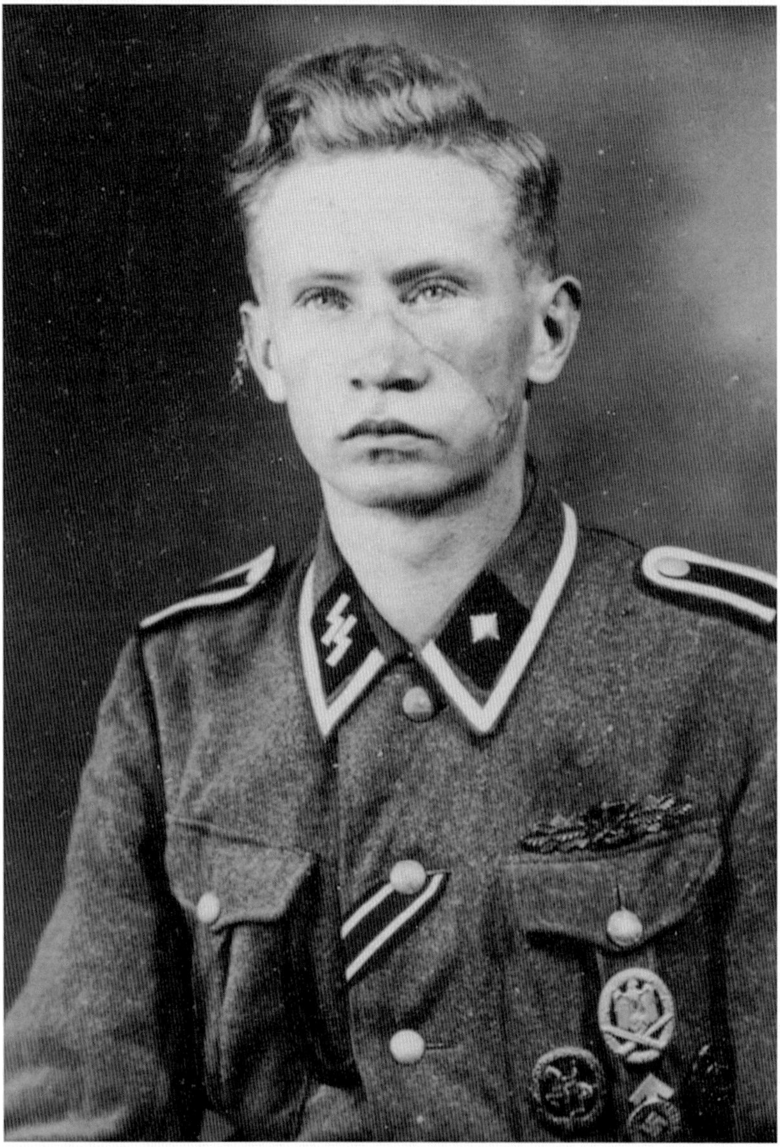

Erich Thöle was inducted into the 1st Company of the SS Cavalry Replacement Battalion in Warsaw on 1 October 1941, and in the spring of 1942 he joined SS Cavalry Regiment 1. After passing through the Radolfzell SS Non-Commissioned Officer's School, he joined SS Cavalry Regiment 17 at SS Training Camp Schieradz. There, in January 1944, the unit was alerted for action at Kovel. Wounded by shell fragments on 15 March 1944, Thöle ultimately joined the 28th SS Volunteer Grenadier Division "Wallonien" by way of the cavalry school in Göttingen.

killed or wounded in the previous six weeks. Fierce fighting broke out on 14 March 1944. Leading the defense had overtaxed *SS-Obergruppenführer* von dem Bach, and on 14 March he was replaced by *SS-Gruppenführer* Gille. Kovel was declared a "fortified place," and on 17 March it was encircled by Soviet forces.

Preparations to relieve Kovel began on 21 March 1944. Elements of the 131st Infantry Division, III Battalion of SS Panzer Grenadier Regiment "Germania," the 8th Company of the 5th SS Panzer Division "Wiking," and a battery from Assault Gun Brigade 190 were sent towards Maciejow. On 30 March the troops set out to relieve Kovel. The relief force, together with elements of the 5th Jäger Division and the 4th and 5th Panzer Divisions, was able to break through the Soviet positions west and southwest of the city, and the almost 2,000 wounded there were evacuated. The commanding general of LVI Panzer Corps, *General der Infanterie* Hoßbach, assumed command in order to widen the narrow corridor and properly defend it. Fighting went on until the end of April in an attempt to drive the last enemy troops from the city and establish a solid main line of resistance. SS Cavalry Regiment 17 was subsequently pulled out of action and moved to the Kisber area in Hungary. There it formed the core of a new mounted unit, the 22nd SS Volunteer Cavalry Division. The former *SS-Standartenjunker* George Beckmann recalled:

"After we were resettled from Riga to Posen/Wartheland, in 1942 I was conscripted by the Reich Labor Service (Labor District XIII) in Magdeburg. In February 1943 I volunteered for the Waffen-SS, on the condition that I be assigned to the cavalry. There were several reasons for this. One was the notion of an elite, which was propagated by "comradeship and reliability"; the other was a conversation with my father, who had been a cavalryman in the Czar's army. He said to me, "Join the cavalry; it's bearable there." Then, in the late summer of 1943 I was called up by the 3rd Regiment of the SS Cavalry Regiment in Schiratz, near Litzmannstadt. We remained at the training camp until the new year, but most of our training was on foot and only rarely did we sit on a horse. In January 1944 I had to enter hospital and thus missed the regiment's departure for Kovel. Together with about 30 to 40 other men, I then formed the regimental after detachment, which caught up with the regiment, bringing equipment and rations. The regiment was on foot and employed as "corset stays," divided into companies formed from railway men, pioneers, etc. As most of the officers had been killed, my company was led by an SS-Unterscharführer. My troop leader, Willi Geyer, commanded a battle sector (battalion strength). In Kovel I was promoted to SS-Sturmmann and was awarded the Assault Badge and the Close Combat Bar in Bronze. After an action southwest of Kovel in which I served as squad leader I was also awarded the Iron Cross, Second Class. Our company was sent across to the west bank of

the Turija and took up position around a collective farm. That same night we were attacked by a large Soviet force and had to withdraw. The west bank was very steep, while the east bank was flat. I covered the withdrawal of the individual squads and platoons, as otherwise they would have been easy targets. My squad and I were the last to leave the west bank. The night before Easter Sunday—shortly before units of the 5th SS Panzer Division "Wiking" opened the pocket—I was wounded by a bullet that passed cleanly through my forearm."

The Occupation of Hungary

Until the occupation of Hungary on 19 March 1944 ("Operation Margarethe"), the unit's duties in Croatia consisted of training replacements and guarding the area against partisans. During the Hungarian operation the 8th SS Cavalry Division "Florian Geyer," under the command of *SS-Oberführer* Streckenbach, moved into the area along the Danube between Mohács and Duna-Földvár:

Division Headquarters	Baja
SS Cavalry Regiment 16	Szekszard
SS Cavalry Regiment 18	Mohacs
SS Artillery Regiment 8	Paks
SS Pioneer Battalion 8	Dunaföldvar
SS Anti-Tank Battalion 8	Pecs
SS Field Replacement Battalion 8	Pecs
SS Armored Reconnaissance Battalion 8	Dunapentele

SS-Obersturmbannführer Rumohr was placed in command of the division effective 1 April 1944. *SS-Oberführer* Streckenbach took over the 19th SS Volunteer Grenadier Division (Latvian No. 2). The division saw no combat; instead, the unit's time in the ethnic German areas proved extremely pleasant for the men. Ludwig Mückl recalled:

"In March 1944 Hungary, which was our ally, wanted to conclude a separate peace with the Allies and jump from our alliance. Our division mobilized, and by dawn everything was ready to go. At that time the Drau River formed the border between Hungary and Croatia. On 18 March 1944 our company crossed a bridge over the Drau into Hungary. At the end of the bridge there was a guard house. Four men jumped from the vehicle and entered the guard house. Hands up! They

were perhaps startled—all were fast asleep! The telephone lines were immediately cut to prevent any messages from getting through to Budapest. By the afternoon the entire division had rolled across the bridge—and we were already deep inside the country before the Hungarian officials in Budapest even learned what was happening. The weather was beautiful as we drove along the Danube, the trees in blossom everywhere. We advanced to Baja, where we were quartered in a school. The usual garrison duties began, with an emphasis on telephone training. Our training exercises frequently took us into the villages. The women still wore the traditional Swabian costume. The wealthier a woman was, the more skirts she wore—often as many as ten. The swineherd was the first to appear in the morning: at the exit from the village he blew loudly on his horn. The farmers opened the doors to the pens and the sows scooted out of their pens at a gallop and into the meadows. Then the cowherd came and led the cattle out of the village. The animals returned in the evening, the swine first. It was something to see them coming rushing along the village street at a fearful pace. On 18 June 1944 Hungary celebrated the 75th anniversary of its independence and the NCO course, in which I again found myself, provided the honor guard."

Many of the German units that had taken part in the occupation of Hungary were soon withdrawn from the country; however, the SS cavalry remained in the security area until the summer of 1944.

On 30 June 1944 the division—less SS Cavalry Regiment 17, which had been designated to form the core of the 22nd SS Volunteer Cavalry Division—reported a strength of:

	Officers	NCOs	Enlisted Men	Total
Actual	258	1,538	11,099	12,895
	2%	11.9%	86.1%	100%
Authorized	433	2,262	9,926	12,621
	3.4%	17.9%	78.7%	100%

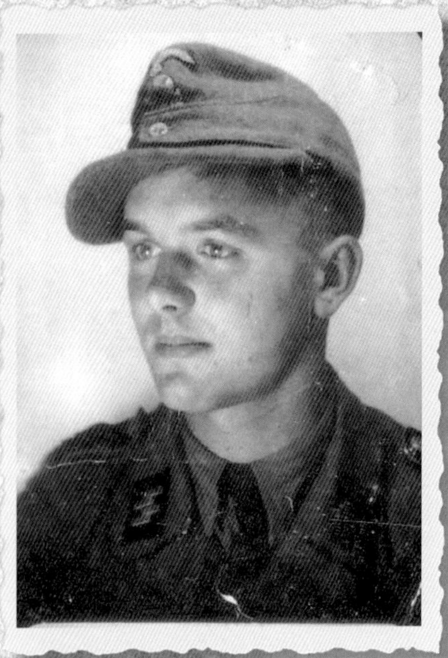

Erwin Keller was called up in March 1944 and joined the SS Cavalry Training and Replacement Battalion in Warsaw. After about three months of training he was transferred to the 8th SS Cavalry Division "Florian Geyer" in Hungary.

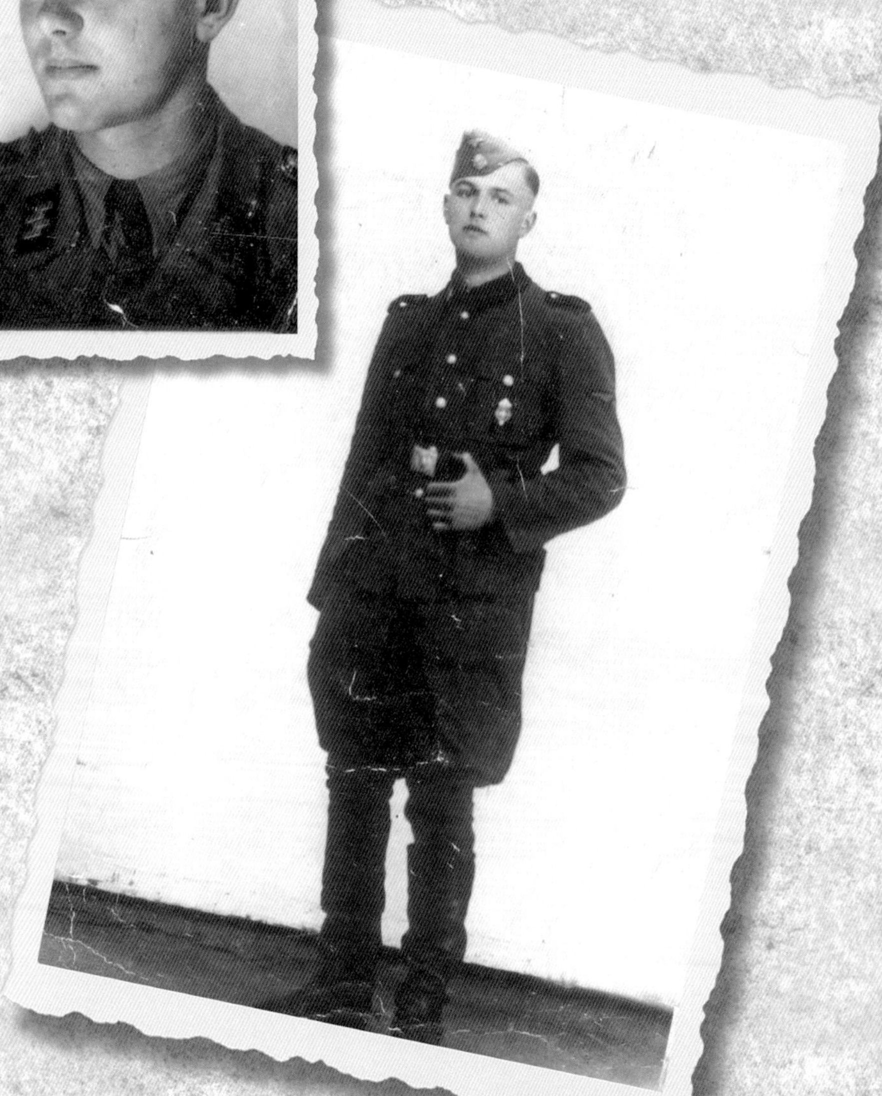

The division had thus achieved its authorized strength for the first time in its existence, and in personnel actually exceeded it. It was, however, still approximately 900 officers and NCOs below strength.

Following the collapse of the front in Rumania, on 20 August 1944 the division headquarters received orders to move to Transylvania. The units had been training for almost nine months. The combination of well-trained recruits and Eastern Front veterans made the division a capable unit. Werner Käser recalled:

"*In March 1944 I was transferred from the SS Anti-Tank Training and Replacement Battalion in Rastenburg, East Prussia, to SS Anti-Tank Battalion 8. We were six young men, eighteen years old, who had undergone very intensive training in a special platoon with approximately 30 officer candidates. Now we were to receive our baptism of fire with the 8th SS Cavalry Division.*

Our marching orders sent us to Essig, from where we were directed on to Sombor for the reformation of SS Anti-Tank Battalion 8. We took part in the occupation of Hungary, and the advance took us through Mohacs, Batszek, and Szekszard to Dunaföldvar, in the south of Budapest, which was surrounded by marshy tributaries of the Danube. My most unpleasant memories of the place are the mosquito plague and the tremendous nightly frog concerts. Soon afterwards the battalion was moved south to Dombovar, where we were housed in private quarters.

I was initially quartered with the egg-seller Tocacs—a Croatian—so that I could use his telephone line until the division had established its own phone communications. This telephone duty freed me from less-enjoyable company and guard duty, and it also brought my stomach an unaccustomed bounty of eggs, so much so that after a few days I had to say no thank you to the well-meaning lady of the house.

Our village, Bikal, was one of those inhabited by German farmers and had a castle. Our relations with the always-hospitable ethnic Germans had been unbelievably warm ever since we entered Hungary, but the reception we were given in Bikal and the surrounding area was unsurpassed. I learned the simple art of animal husbandry there. In the morning the farmers put out the geese, pigs, and sheep at brief intervals, and in the evening they brought them back in, with each animal finding its own way back to its pen. Each animal was marked with a small spot of paint to allow the farmer to keep track.

Our 75-mm Pak 40 anti-tank guns were kept in the castle's sheds. We had to perform guard duty day and night. We guarded the guns and two-man teams patrolled the streets. The population of Bikal consisted almost exclusively of ethnic Germans, who took pains to cultivate their German culture. The older women wore traditional garb, as did most of the younger women. This consisted of a scarf, blouse, bodice, and colorful pleated skirts which, extending almost to the ground, were worn one over another.

Leather footwear was only worn on Sundays or holidays, or when field work made it necessary; otherwise they wore homemade batschkas with woven linen soles, which the wearer removed and carried beneath the arm during longer walks to reduce wear. Almost all of the residents were farmers with respectable holdings of land and cattle.

The farmers of the village donated so much food that the company was able to send a large package containing honey, fats, smoked meat, and other then-precious commodities to the families of every ethnic German.

The residents or the leaders of the ethnic group often invited us to social evenings with dancing. The young beauties of the village were accompanied by their mothers, who took up position on benches along the walls of the hall and kept a watchful eye on their experience-thirsty daughters.

In addition to training our ethnic German comrades, we also helped the farmers with the harvest. I fondly remember the apple or poppy seed strudels we had for lunch. But the pleasant part of the "mercenary" life came to an end at the end of August 1944. Rumors of action circulated and we test-fired our anti-tank guns to select the loaders and gunners."

Action in Transylvania

During the night of 23-24 August 1944, the *Wehrmacht* Operations Staff directed the commanding general in Hungary, *General der Infanterie* von Greiffenberg, to prepare the 8th SS Cavalry Division "Florian Geyer" to move out. This was one of the measures taken by the German side in response to the events in Rumania.

On 23 August 1944 the Rumanian head of state, Marshall Antonescu, was arrested after a conversation with Rumanian King Michael, and a ceasefire with America, Great Britain, and Russia was announced. Hitler's plans to overturn the putsch were foiled by a lack of forces. The Rumanian Army was placed under the command of the Red Army and turned against the German armed forces.

The transfer to Rumania took place at the beginning of September. After a rail journey of about 500 km, the 8th SS Cavalry Division was placed under *SS-Obergruppenführer* Phleps, the Senior SS and Police Commander "Transylvania." As soon as they had detrained in the Neumarkt (Rumanian: Tàrgu Mures) area, the arriving units occupied defensive positions on the northwest side of the Marosch. SS Armored Reconnaissance Battalion 8 (command post: Vaideiul, approx. 40 km west of Neumarkt) was tasked with scouting the bridges over the Marosch and determining which villages were already in enemy hands. As soon as it detrained, SS Cavalry Regiment 15 became involved with Rumanian units and suffered casualties through continuous artillery fire. On 9 September 1944 patrols from SS Armored Reconnaissance Battalion 8 reached Chibed (30 km E of Neumarkt) – Corond (approx. 55 km SE of Neumarkt) – Szekely-Urdvarhely (approx. 50 km SE of Neumarkt) and established contact with LXXII Army Corps (6th Army). In the south they met troops of the Hungarian 20th Reserve Division near Nades.

The defense sector held by the 8th SS Cavalry Division "Florian Geyer" lay between Neumarkt and Ludus to the south and was about 50 km wide. SS Cavalry Regiment 15 was positioned next to SS Cavalry Regiment 18 southeast of Neumarkt. There followed SS Armored Reconnaissance Battalion 8 and SS Anti-Tank Battalion 8. SS Cavalry Regiment 16 was on the division's left flank, where it was in contact with the Hungarian 2nd Armored Division near Ludes. From their positions on the hills south of the Marosch the defenders had an excellent view of the barren, mainly treeless slopes far across the winding valley. This enabled them to easily identify and respond to enemy attacks. In the days that followed there were fierce battles with attacking Soviet troops in heavy rain. The 6th Army also assigned three Hetzer tank-destroyers to the division to deal with possible Russian tank assaults.

On 20 September 1944 the division's reported strength was:

	Officers	NCOs	Enlisted Men	Total
Actual	258	1,597	12,185	14,040
	2%	11.4%	86.8%	100%
Authorized	433	2,262	9,926	12,621
	3.4%	17.9%	78.7%	100%

That day the division was attached to XXIX Army Corps (8th Army). Bolstered by ethnic German recruits from Hungary, the division's actual strength now exceeded authorized strength.

On 1 October 1944 the SS Armored Reconnaissance Battalion assumed responsibility for guarding the XXIX Army Corps' flank to the north in the area of Urmenisu (approx. 40 km N of Ludus). The terrain there was heavily wooded, and thus of a different character than the Marosch hills. A former member recalled:

"In February 1943 a special meeting of the Hitler Youth was called in a school in Nürtingen. When we had gathered in the schoolyard we were sorted by height, hair color, and general appearance. Those who were specially chosen there were given papers that excused them when our age class was called up. On 1 May 1943 we began a one-month course at a pre-military training camp. Two months later I was conscripted into the 1st Company of the 1st SS Infantry Gun Training and Replacement Battalion in Breslau-Lissa. After our training was completed we marched to Czechoslovakia for live firing. I developed a foot inflammation and was sent to the hospital. While I was there my company was transferred to Belgium. When I reported for duty, I was informed that I was not being allowed to follow my company, as new recruits would be arriving in a few days. I had to help out with the issuing of uniforms, weapons, and rations. After completion of this second training period we went to the station to entrain. There I and five others were pulled off the train and informed that we were to leave that evening for the SS NCO school in Posen-Treskau. Later we were transferred to the SS NCO school in Lauenburg.

On 1 July 1944 I was transferred from there to SS Cavalry Regiment 15. We had previously been stationed in various villages in Hungary, lastly in Maria Kemet. As the infantry gun platoon was weakly manned we were assigned recruits—mainly ethnic Germans from Hungary and Rumania. From there we moved by train to Transylvania, near Neumarkt. From the trains we went straight into action. The first village we occupied was inhabited by ethnic Germans. We were welcomed as liberators.

I was a forward observer with the infantry guns and my company commander was SS-Hauptsturmführer Albert Klett. I was wounded by shell fragments on 22 September 1944. My comrades from the firing position got me out of the observation post and risked their lives taking me to the rear. At the main aid station my left leg was amputated below the knee because of gas gangrene. A hospital train took me to a place south of Budapest, where my right leg also had to be removed below the knee. As the Russians had broken through, immediately after the operation I and five other wounded were loaded onto a small truck and taken to Austria. Finally, on 14 October 1944 a hospital train delivered us to the hospital in Vöklasbruck, which was in a monastery. My parents applied to have me moved to a hospital in Reutlingen on 5 December 1944. As the hospital was overcrowded, on 14 February 1945 I was released to go home. I had further surgery on my legs in Reutlingen after the end of the war."

On 6 October 1944 the Red Army, together with Rumanian units, launched a major offensive. Beginning on 9 October, the 8th SS Cavalry Division "Florian Geyer" covered the XXIX Army Corps' retreat from Marosch toward the northwest. Numerous *Wehrmacht* stragglers were incorporated into the division and remained with the SS units until the end in Budapest.[11] The two motorized units (SS Armored Reconnaissance Battalion 8 and SS Pioneer Battalion 8) formed the rear guard. Three days later the *Wehrmacht* communiqué declared:

"*The 8th SS Cavalry Division, led by Knight's Cross wearer SS-Standartenführer Joachim Rumohr and comprised mainly of Germans from the southeast region, fought magnificently in the fighting in Transylvania.*"

Werner Käser recalled his experiences in Rumania:

"Entrainment in Hungary took place in Dombovar. As 1st Company Headquarters Squad dispatch rider I was assigned to SS-Obersturmführer Meier. SS-Rottenführer Kuba, and I set off for the station, the last to leave Bikal. Once again, many of the residents had donated food for us and our company, and there was almost no room for me in the sidecar.

The train headed for Rumania. The 1st Company detrained in the so-called "Szeke Point" and was deployed in the Marosvarsahely area. There we were supposed to intercept as many retreating German troops as possible. But although we advanced south across the Maros, we found almost no stragglers. We were forced to halt the advance and withdraw to the north side of the Maros to find better positions against the Soviet troops and the Rumanians who had gone over to their side.

One of my duties as company headquarters squad dispatch rider was to deliver mail and food to the anti-tank gun positions. I received my baptism of fire during one of my first trips to the forward positions. We were driving our motorcycle down a road toward the front as darkness was falling. Suddenly we found ourselves between a Russian patrol and our dug-in cavalrymen. Kuba drove the motorcycle-sidecar combination into the deep ditch, and we and the food were tossed about. The Rumanians emptied their submachine-guns, as usual without aiming. Having completed their patrol mission the enemy pulled back.

Each day we had to repel several enemy attacks, some with and some without tank support. As most of our anti-tank guns were in forward-slope positions in large cornfields—quite often without supporting infantry—we stayed back when the enemy attacked without tanks. We had the impression that the enemy only wanted to determine the location of our anti-tank guns.

I wanted to take over an anti-tank gun up front, but my company commander refused. I was eager to knock out a couple of Soviet tanks and so prove myself in action. But Meier called me a stupid ass and told me to give some thought to staying where I was instead of going up front. But being a dispatch rider was already dangerous enough, delivering food and mail to the anti-tank gun crews each day. The enemy snipers frequently used me for target practice, and so I varied the timing of my trips to the front.

It was not until a gun commander was killed by a mortar hit on his foxhole that Meyer relented and gave me command of the anti-tank gun. It was part of the Stelly Platoon. At dusk I and several other members of the platoon went up in a 3-ton prime mover to recover the fallen. The heat was unbearable almost all day long. Water was scarce and soon became stale. And so our only resort was the grapes from a vineyard and watermelons from a field about 500 meters away. In the early morning, after a cool night, they were very refreshing, and one or two men would go and pick the fruit. It soon turned out that this was not as risky as we thought, for the enemy was thirsty too. For almost an hour each morning there was a sort of ceasefire as we collected fruit—we at the near end of the piece of land and the Russians and Rumanians at the far end. Of course, each day we got a little closer. This untroubled idyll in the "Garden of Eden" was soon lost, however, when young cavalry replacements functioning as infantry arrived to cover our flank.

They had no appreciation for our heavenly peaceful island. Due to their inexperience, they didn't understand how to take advantage of a situation that benefited both sides. Despite our warnings, they were convinced they had to take target practice using the Russians and Rumanians harvesting at the other end of the field. That was the end of our land of milk and honey.

The enemy attacks increased daily, and they had air and artillery support. We procured barn doors from the nearest village, placed them over our foxholes, and covered them with earth to shield us against the mortar fire. We hoped that this would at least provide some protection from fragments. On the 2nd or 3rd day after I joined the anti-tank guns the enemy attacked with tank support. As usual we received advance warning during the night, as we could hear the sound of vehicles moving about. The enemy probably made as much noise as possible so as to make a psychological impression.

It began at daybreak—the enemy committed everything. Aircraft, artillery, and mortars all took part in the pre-attack bombardment, then the grinding, rattling noise of tanks. They came with infantry, some riding, some walking beside the tanks.

We held our fire until the enemy was 600 meters away. This first tank attack made an indelible impression on me. As gun commander and gunner, it was a mixture of excited tension and nervous anxiety. I was worried that the other members of the gun crew might notice the trembling of my right foot, for the last thing I wanted was to let the others see my anxiety, or even worse pass it on to them. But as soon as the first round stopped one of the two Russian tanks approaching in our sector the anxiety fell away from me. The second tank turned to the right, but although it moved very quickly, the lead was correct and our second round was on target. Our anti-tank guns were spaced at intervals of about 800 meters and the other guns were successful too—except for one that was lost in this attack, The gunner there probably set his sight incorrectly and they hit nothing, even though they were firing from point-blank range. Result: the tank drove over the trail of the gun. The crew suffered few casualties, but they received a severe shock and surely regretted not placing the anti-tank mines—which were on hand for just that reason—in front of the gun.

The two tanks knocked out by our anti-tank gun were reported for confirmation, but the next day they had disappeared. As so often happened, the enemy had towed them away under cover of darkness. I was determined that that should not happen next time. That was two days later. We loaded a high-explosive round into the gun and aimed at the tank. When I heard voices and the sound of a tow vehicle during the night I pressed the button. The round must have been on target—first we heard screams, then the engine noises moved away. The next day the knocked-out tank was still there and our kill was confirmed.

After a few days we were able to go back to the command post in turns to wash and write letters. The command post was about 1,000 meters in the rear in an isolated farmhouse. They also had the elixir of life—water—there, and we were able to wash our clothing too."

The End in Hungary

The German withdrawal on 10 and 11 October 1944 took the 8th SS Cavalry Division in a northwesterly direction to Nontida, where the 2nd Ukrainian Front had achieved deep penetrations against the Hungarian 25th Infantry and 9th Reserve Divisions east of Klausenburg. Between 12 and 16 October the retreat continued toward the northwest to Marghita (approx. 120 km NW of Klausenburg), with the two motorized units providing the rearguard.

On 21 October 1944 the high command of Army Group South ordered Army Group Wöhler, also commanding XXIX Army Corps, to withdraw beyond the Theiß. The next day the 8th SS Cavalry Division "Florian Geyer" withdrew into the area south of Nagy Karoly (NE of Debrecen).

On 23 October 1944 the SS cavalry were manning a 20-kilometer sector of front south of Nyiregyhaza. Together with the 1st Panzer Division, SS Cavalry Regiments 15 and 18 repulsed attacks by Soviet infantry in fierce fighting west of Hajdunanas and Hajdudorog. Three days later a counterattack with the 3rd Mountain

Division and the 23rd Panzer Division resulted in the capture of Nyiregyhaza. The enemy subsequently withdrew towards the south. On 27 October SS Armored Reconnaissance Battalion 8, bolstered by quad anti-aircraft guns, was temporarily attached to the 4th Mountain Division and took part in an attack along the Nyiregyhaza – Ujfeherto rail line.

Two days later the 8th SS Cavalry Division "Florian Geyer" left the area south of Nyiregyhaza, and on 1 November crossed the Theiß, about 30 kilometers away. The SS cavalry regiments moved into the Miskolc area, and SS Cavalry Regiment 15 and SS Artillery Regiment 8 were sent towards the southwest in the direction of Budapest. SS Armored Reconnaissance Battalion 8 crossed the Theiß at Tiszalöc (east of Tiszakeszi) and marched to Tiszakeszi, where it occupied a bridgehead position.

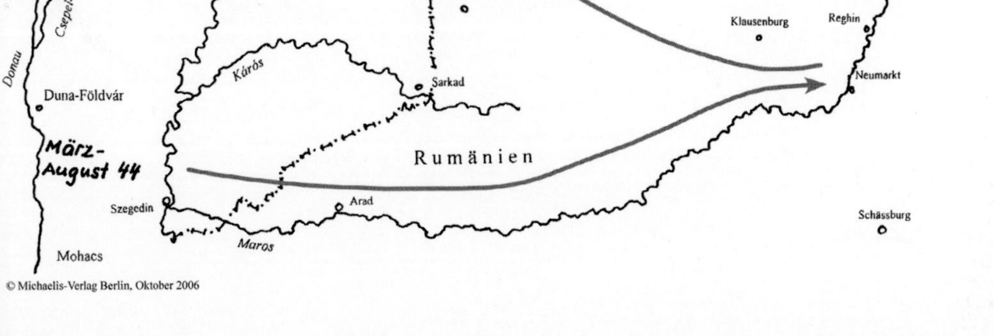

© Michaelis-Verlag Berlin, Oktober 2006

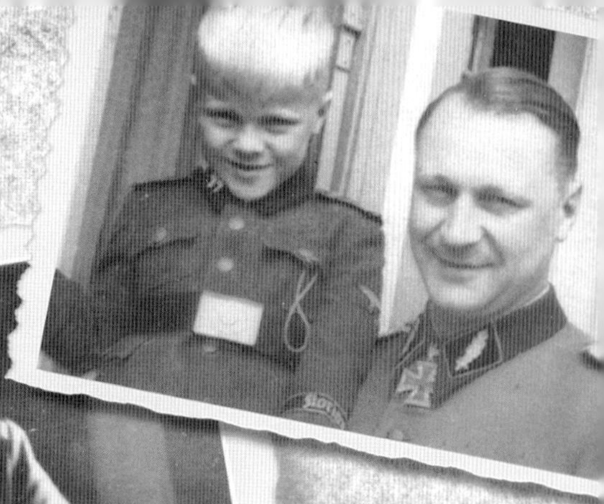

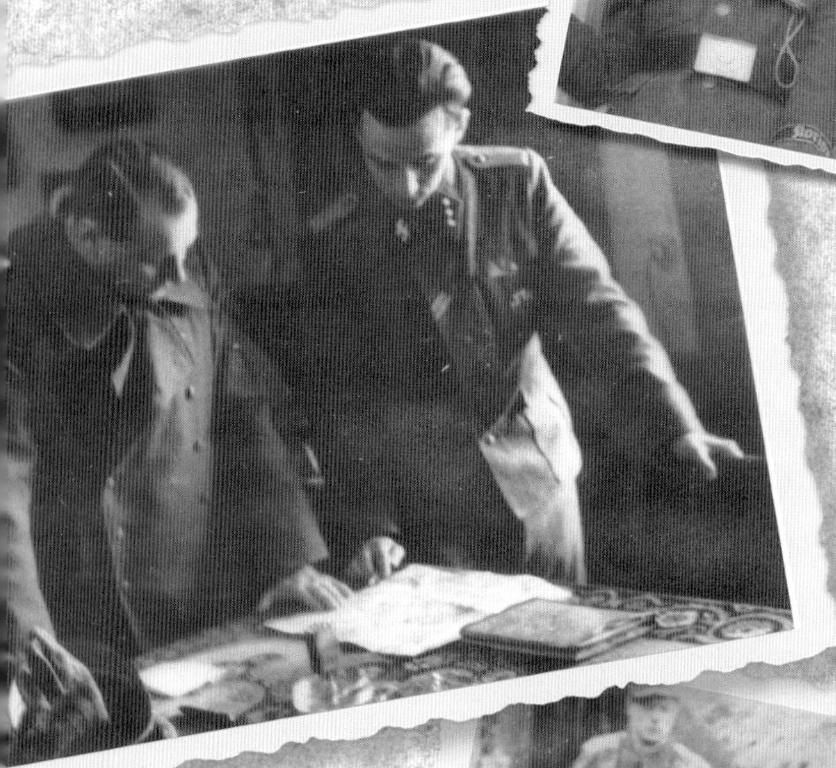

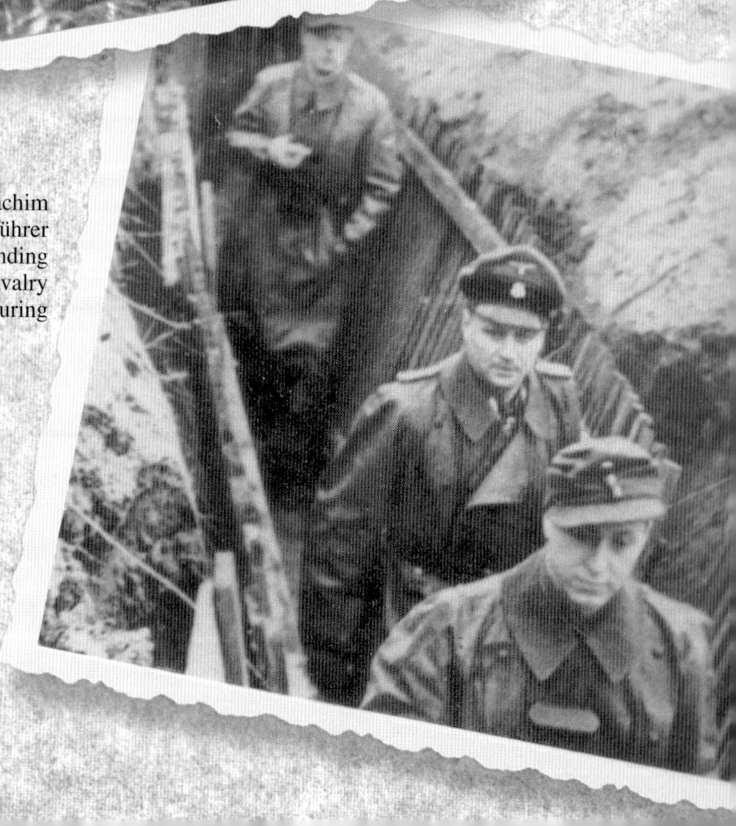

These photos depict Joachim Rumohr as an SS-Standartenführer with his son, and as commanding officer of the 8th SS Cavalry Division "Florian Geyer" during the fighting in Budapest.

Attached to Corps Group Breith (III Panzer Corps), at the beginning of November 1944 the division, together with the Panzer Grenadier Division "Feldherrnhalle," moved into the Pestszentlörinc area (approx. 6 km SE of Budapest) and occupied the line Vecses – Üllö – Peczel. The latter villages were part of the "Karola Position" which, following the line Vecses – Gyömrö – Maglod – Peczel, was supposed to form an outer defense line around the Hungarian capital. Construction of the line had only begun in November, and it was not a proper defense line, as it lacked bunkers and fortified positions.

While the units became increasingly intermixed on account of the frequent creation and disbandment of battle groups, at the end of November 1944 Headquarters, IX SS Waffen Mountain Corps arrived in Budapest from the Balkans, and on 13 December assumed command of III Panzer Corps. Just four days later the first Soviet battalions crossed the Danube and established a bridgehead about 30 kilometers south of the capital.

After several quiet days, on Christmas Day 1944 Soviet troops encircled Budapest. At that time the units of the two cavalry divisions were still on the east bank of the Danube (Pest), holding bridgeheads with *Wehrmacht* units. On 25 December 1944 the 8th SS Cavalry Division received orders to pull out of the eastern bridgehead. Together with units of the Panzer Grenadier Division "Feldherrnhalle," it was to prevent the Soviets from entering the strategically more important western part of the city (Buda).

When Soviet tanks advanced from Bia (approx. 16 km W of Budapest) toward Budakeszi, 14 kilometers away, SS Armored Reconnaissance Battalion 8 was committed to screen Budaörs (approx. 8 km W of Budapest) and defend Budakeszi.

Northwest of Csepel, attacking enemy units crossed the Budapest – Budaörs rail line, and Soviet troops crossed from Budafok to Csepel Island. The German and Hungarian defenders were forced to abandon Vecses, Maglod, Pestszentlörinc, and Rakoscsaba, Fierce house-to-house fighting took place near Budakeszi in temperatures of minus 10 degrees. On 29 December 1944 Soviet Marshalls Malinovsky and Tolbukhin called upon the defenders to surrender. When this was rejected they issued an ultimatum.

As 1944 gave way to 1945, the IX SS Waffen Mountain Corps (strength approx. 33,000 men) consisted of the remnants of:

Hungarian 10th, 12th, and 23rd Infantry Divisions
Hungarian 1st Armored Division
8th and 22nd SS Volunteer Cavalry Divisions
271st Volks-Grenadier Division
Panzer Grenadier Division "Feldherrnhalle"

In the early days of 1945 many members of SS Signals Battalion 8 and SS Artillery Regiment 8 became infantrymen. Most of their equipment was unserviceable anyway. After the *Luftwaffe* proved incapable of supplying the defenders by air a supply ship was sent along the Danube. Water levels were low, however, and the ship ran aground. Nevertheless, smaller boats were able to recover most of the ship's cargo.

As soon as Budapest was surrounded the German command began planning the relief of the Hungarian capital. Given the relative strengths of the opposing forces this was a hopeless undertaking, whose only goal was to buy time to conclude a separate peace with the western powers. On 31 December 1944 IV SS Panzer Corps launched an attack towards Budapest, where there were already about 6,000 wounded whose dressings could no longer be changed and who were subsisting on one slice of bread per man per day.

By 13 January 1945 SS Panzer Grenadier Regiment 10 "Westland" of the 5th SS Panzer Division "Wiking" had reached Pilisszentkereszt, but then Hitler ordered them to halt. The attempt to relieve Budapest, which was almost within reach, had to be abandoned.

The next day IX SS Waffen Mountain Corps reported that it had expended all of its artillery shells, small arms ammunition was running low, and it was out of fuel. Those tanks and guns that were still functional could no longer be used and had to be blown up by their crews.

On 16 January 1945 the eastern bridgehead had been reduced to the area Franz Joseph Bridge – Calvin Square – Elizabeth Ring – Baro Street to the Danube. Margaret Island formed its north tip. The next day the eastern bridgehead was evacuated, and the last intact bridges were blown on 18 January 1945. SS Armored Reconnaissance Battalion 8 occupied positions on the west bank of the Danube at the Margaret Bridge, where they found that the Hungarians had constructed barricades using sacks of flour!

The next day IV SS Panzer Corps launched another relief attempt—this time from the southwest. After initial success, this attack had to he halted on 27 January 1945.

Hungarian units went over to the Soviets and were immediately turned against the Germans. On 29 January 1945 IX SS Waffen Mountain Corps reported that the number of wounded now exceeded that of effectives. The combat zone had by then shrunk to Gellert Hill and the castle. Wounded, soldiers, and civilians took shelter in the numerous underground passageways. The December 1944 casualty figures were issued at the beginning of February 1945. Those of the 8th SS Cavalry Division "Florian Geyer" were:

Killed: 4 officers and 217 other ranks
Wounded: 7 officers and 1,079 other ranks
Missing: 32 other ranks

Thus, approximately 1,300 soldiers had been put out of action during the relatively light fighting in the Karola Position and the first serious battles in the Budapest area after the encirclement of the city. At the beginning of February there was further fierce fighting in the city's streets and houses. By then the number of wounded had risen to about 11,000. Their daily rations consisted of about 15 grams of legumes and a half slice of bread, and there were only sufficient supplies of these for another two days.

On 8 February 1945 the last guns of SS Flak Battalion 8 shot down their 75th confirmed enemy aircraft. In the final days the still intact but useless guns were parked on the grounds of the university near the castle, while the gun crews fought as infantry.

On 9 February 1945 Hitler turned down a request by the IX SS Waffen Mountain Corps to break out, on the grounds that the attempt was doomed to fail and that Fortress Budapest was tying down significant enemy forces. The next day the enemy took Gellert Hill, after which the only resistance came from the castle and the citadel.

On Sunday, 11 February 1945, *SS-Obergruppenführer* Pfeffer-Wildenbruch radioed the OKW that the small pocket was about to be split by Soviet troops, and that continuing to hold out would end in unconditional surrender or destruction. He subsequently decided to break out, for which four groups were formed:

1st battle group: remnants of 8th Company, 8th SS Cavalry Division
2nd battle group: remnants of the 13th Panzer Division
3rd battle group: remnants of the 22nd SS Volunteer Cavalry Division
4th battle group: mixed units (approx. 500 men)

The remnants of the 8th SS Cavalry Division and the 13th Panzer Division would break out to the west and northwest (Szomor – Mariahalom, and Pilis Mountains – Pilisszentlelek), covered by the remaining forces of the 22nd SS Volunteer Cavalry Division. The fourth group was to attempt to escape through the underground sewage system. Despite the strictest secrecy, the Soviets learned the exact hour of the breakout. At 20:00 hours Soviet artillery began pounding the castle. The streets were soon littered with dead and wounded.

On 15 February 1945 the *Wehrmacht* communiqué reported:

"*Following the complete encirclement of Budapest, the defenders have held the city for almost 50 days against fierce enemy attacks by vastly superior Soviet forces. Its ammunition and food gone, as per orders, the courageous German and Hungarian garrison has broken through the siege ring. The first elements have already reached our front west of Budapest.*"

The first and subsequent elements were a total of 785 men from about eight divisions! On 14 February 1945 they reached the German positions in the area of Zsambek (approx. 25 km W of Budapest). Most of the soldiers were killed or captured by the Soviets during the breakout. The approximately 100 survivors of the 8th SS Cavalry Division were ultimately integrated into the 37th SS Volunteer Cavalry Division then being formed, along with those from the 22nd SS Volunteer Cavalry Division. Helmut Schreiber recalled those days in Budapest:

"*I was born in 1924, and on 15 April 1942 I was inducted in the Uhlan Barracks in Warsaw. From there I was sent to the SS Cavalry Replacement Battalion in Chelm, near Lublin, for basic training, after which I went to the so-called Heidelager training camp at Debica, where the 8th SS Cavalry Division was being formed. I was assigned to the artillery and was with it when our division went into action.*

On Christmas Eve 1944 we were ordered to change positions, to the inner city of Budapest. Early in the morning the opening was closed and the Russians sealed the pocket. As we were about out of ammunition for our guns (Type 18 light field howitzers, 105-mm) we immediately became infantrymen. I was initially assigned to the battalion command post as a forward observer. Our poor horses had already died of hunger or had been killed by shellfire or bombs. At least they benefited the hungry civilians. The horses were butchered in no time.

From Gellert Hill I was able to observe the blowing of the bridge over the Danube. At the beginning of January 1945 the remaining battery personnel (train) were placed under my command as a small battle group. Aiding me were an officer cadet and an NCO from the 2nd Battery who was separated from his unit. There was almost no communication with the other group. Each group was more or less on its own, whether searching for something edible or ammunition.

I still remember well an incident in one of the houses we occupied, near the post office on Vienna Street. While searching the house we found a man in bed in an apartment. He was allegedly ill. Behind his bed was the door to a pantry full of sausage, bread, and other foods. What to do? First we satisfied our own hunger, then we took a wash basket full to the hungry residents in the cellar. After I was wounded two of the women there also gave me first aid.

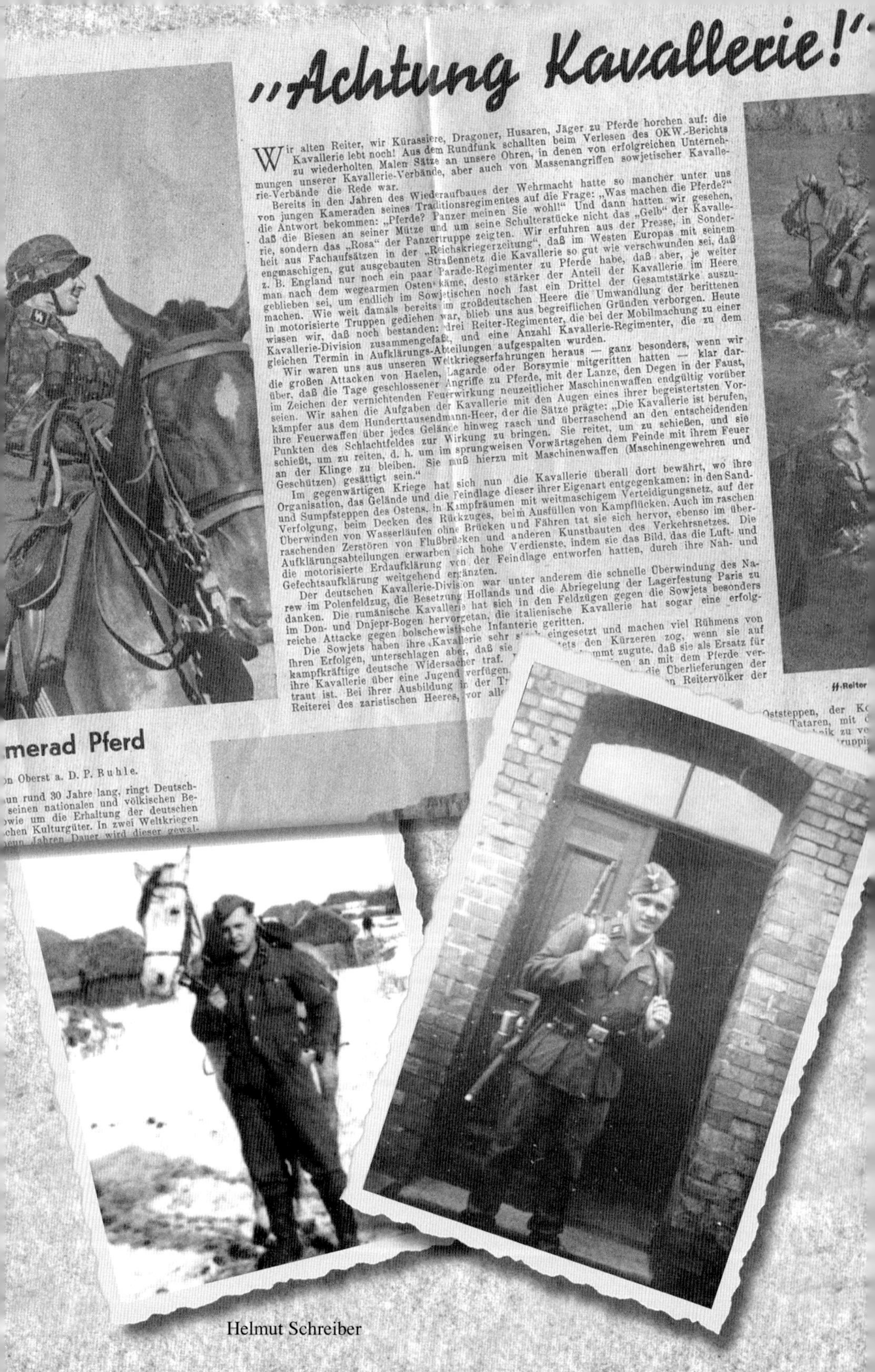

„Achtung Kavallerie!“

Wir alten Reiter, wir Kürassiere, Dragoner, Husaren, Jäger zu Pferde horchen auf: die Kavallerie lebt noch! Aus dem Rundfunk schallten beim Verlesen des OKW.-Berichts zu wiederholten Malen Sätze an unsere Ohren, in denen von erfolgreichen Unternehmungen unserer Kavallerie-Verbände, aber auch von Massenangriffen sowjetischer Kavallerie-Verbände die Rede war.

Bereits in den Jahren des Wiederaufbaues der Wehrmacht hatte so mancher unter uns von jungen Kameraden seines Traditionsregimentes auf die Frage: „Was machen die Pferde?“ die Antwort bekommen: „Pferde? Panzer meinen Sie wohl!“ Und dann hatten wir gesehen, daß die Biesen an seiner Mütze und um seine Schulterstücke nicht das „Gelb“ der Kavallerie, sondern das „Rosa“ der Panzertruppe zeigten. Wir erfuhren aus der Presse, in Sonderheit aus Fachaufsätzen in der „Reichskriegerzeitung“, daß im Westen Europas mit seinem engmaschigen, gut ausgebauten Straßennetz die Kavallerie so gut wie verschwunden sei, daß z. B. England nur noch ein paar Parade-Regimenter zu Pferde habe, daß aber, je weiter man nach dem wegearmen Osten käme, desto stärker der Anteil der Kavallerie im Heere geblieben sei, um endlich im Sowjetischen noch fast ein Drittel der Gesamtstärke auszumachen. Wie weit damals bereits im großdeutschen Heere die Umwandlung der berittenen in motorisierte Truppen gediehen war, blieb uns aus begreiflichen Gründen verborgen. Heute wissen wir, daß noch bestanden: drei Reiter-Regimenter, die bei der Mobilmachung zu einer Kavallerie-Division zusammengefaßt, und eine Anzahl Kavallerie-Regimenter, die zu dem gleichen Termin in Aufklärungs-Abteilungen aufgespalten wurden.

Wir waren uns aus unseren Weltkriegserfahrungen heraus — ganz besonders, wenn wir die großen Attacken von Haelen, Lagarde oder Borsymie mitgeritten hatten — klar darüber, daß die Tage geschlossener Angriffe zu Pferde, mit der Lanze, den Degen in der Faust, im Zeichen der vernichtenden Feuerwirkung neuzeitlicher Maschinenwaffen endgültig vorüber seien. Wir sahen die Aufgaben der Kavallerie mit den Augen eines ihrer begeistertsten Vorkämpfer aus dem Hunderttausendmann-Heer, der die Sätze prägte: „Die Kavallerie ist berufen, ihre Feuerwaffen über jedes Gelände hinweg rasch und überraschend an den entscheidenden Punkten des Schlachtfeldes zur Wirkung zu bringen. Sie reitet, um zu schießen, und sie schießt, um zu reiten, d. h. um im sprungweisen Vorwärtsgehen dem Feinde mit ihrem Feuer an der Klinge zu bleiben. Sie muß hierzu mit Maschinenwaffen (Maschinengewehren und Geschützen) gesättigt sein.“

Im gegenwärtigen Kriege hat sich nun die Kavallerie überall dort bewährt, wo ihre Organisation, das Gelände und die Feindlage dieser ihrer Eigenart entgegenkamen: in den Sand- und Sumpfsteppen des Ostens, in Kampfräumen mit weitmaschigem Verteidigungsnetz, auf der Verfolgung, beim Decken des Rückzuges, beim Ausfüllen von Kampflücken. Auch im raschen Überwinden von Wasserläufen ohne Brücken und Fähren tat sie sich hervor, ebenso im überraschenden Zerstören von Flußbrücken und anderen Kunstbauten des Verkehrsnetzes. Die Aufklärungsabteilungen erwarben sich hohe Verdienste, indem sie das Bild, das die Luft- und die motorisierte Erdaufklärung von der Feindlage entworfen hatten, durch ihre Nah- und Gefechtsaufklärung weitgehend ergänzten.

Der deutschen Kavallerie-Division war unter anderem die schnelle Überwindung des Narew im Polenfeldzug, die Besetzung Hollands und die Abriegelung der Lagerfestung Paris zu danken. Die rumänische Kavallerie hat sich in den Feldzügen gegen die Sowjets besonders im Don- und Dnjepr-Bogen hervorgetan, die italienische Kavallerie hat sogar eine erfolgreiche Attacke gegen bolschewistische Infanterie geritten.

Die Sowjets haben ihre Kavallerie sehr st[…] eingesetzt und machen viel Rühmens von ihren Erfolgen, unterschlagen aber, daß sie […]tets den Kürzeren zog, wenn sie auf kampfkräftige deutsche Widersacher traf. […]mmt zugute, daß sie als Ersatz für ihre Kavallerie über eine Jugend verfügen, […]en an mit dem Pferde vertraut ist. Bei ihrer Ausbildung in der Tr[…] die Überlieferungen der Reiterei des zaristischen Heeres, vor all[…]n Reitervölker der Oststeppen, der Ko[…] Tataren, mit […]nik zu ve[…]ruppi[…]

ℌ-Reiter

[Ka]merad Pferd

[Vo]n Oberst a. D. P. Buhle.

[N]un rund 30 Jahre lang, ringt Deutsch[land um] seinen nationalen und völkischen Be[stand so]wie um die Erhaltung der deutschen [...]chen Kulturgüter. In zwei Weltkriegen [...] neun Jahren Dauer wird dieser gewal[...]

Helmut Schreiber

One night we were almost out of ammunition, but luckily the crew of a damaged armored troop carrier gave us some, so that we were at least able to continue defending ourselves. On 30 January 1945, during the house fighting, I was wounded. First I was hit in the head, but luckily the bullet failed to pierce my steel helmet, and ten minutes later I was hit by a bullet which lodged in my right collar bone. A comrade took me to the aid station, which was in the underground passageways beneath the castle. An emergency dressing was applied to the wound. The cellar vaults were filled with badly wounded men, lying on the floor without beds, covered with paper. Rations consisted of a slice of bread and a cup of tea. Two days later my comrades came to get me out of there. Their reasoning: if we're going to go to the dogs, then we want to go together!

On 10 February 1945 the order came for all the walking wounded to assemble in the castle's underground vaults, where the Swedish Red Cross was supposed to take charge of them. Nothing came of it. During the night of 11-12 February 1945 word went round that those who could still fight were going to try to break out. Many of the walking wounded went along, but before long many returned in disappointment. The breakout had more or less failed. On 12 February the Russians fetched us out of the cellars. What happened then was hell. Those who could not walk were shot. During the march to Budafok we saw evidence of the horror of the final days. The bullet-riddled bodies of German soldiers lay everywhere in small defense positions. We were taken via Rumania and the Black Sea to Odessa. This was the start of a nine-year trek through half of Russia to the Urals."

The total casualties suffered by the 8th SS Cavalry Division "Florian Geyer" since 22 July 1941:

Killed: 110 officers and 3,063 other ranks
Wounded: 222 officers and 9,381 other ranks
Missing: 19 officers and 1,098 other ranks

The unit's casualties were thus almost equal to its entire personnel complement. Raised and equipped for use in the rear area, the SS Cavalry Brigade, later SS Cavalry Division, was repeatedly sent to the front as the last reserve, where initially it was able to help stabilize the situation. In 1943, by which time the Red Army's materiel superiority had become too great, the division was shattered in action southwest of Kharkov. In keeping with this situation, at the beginning of 1944 an attempt was made to turn the division into a unit capable of front line combat by adding motorized heavy supporting units, such as a motorized artillery battalion. The materiel superiority of the Red Army and the weakness of the German and Hungarian units prevented a successful deployment in Transylvania. Finally, after the loss of all their heavy weapons and equipment, the units were employed as infantry in Budapest, where they were destroyed in February 1945. For their actions in the rear area against partisans and civilians the survivors received the most severe punishments, and most did not return from the USSR until 1955-56.

The 22nd SS Volunteer Cavalry Division

(*Die 22. SS-Freiwilligen-Kavallerie-Division*)

The SS-FHA began making plans for a second SS cavalry division—to be created using ethnic Germans from Hungary—in autumn 1943. In November 1943 orders were issued for the formation of a fourth SS cavalry regiment, which at first was to be part of the 8th SS Cavalry Division. On 31 December 1943 SS Cavalry Regiment 18's reported strength was:

	Officers	NCOs	Enlisted Men	Total
Actual	10	159	1,412	1,581
	0.6%	10.1%	89.3%	100%

By that time more than 22,000 ethnic Germans had already been inducted into the Waffen-SS. Now another agreement between the two nations was going to allow a significant increase in this figure. On 23 March 1944, during the change of government in Budapest, the treaty was quickly ratified. The drafting of ethnic Germans between the ages of 17 and 60 years of age began in April 1944.

Realizing this potential, on 29 April 1944 the SS-FHA issued orders for the formation of an SS volunteer cavalry division,[12] which was already planned, to go ahead in Hungary. The designation "volunteer" was used because the unit's personnel were required to meet army suitability requirements, not those of the SS.

The Commander of the SS in Hungary, *SS-Obergruppenführer* Keppler, was made responsible for the activation of the division, which was to take place between Kisber (approx. 70 km W of Budapest) and Györ (approx. 95 km NW of Budapest) and be completed by 30 October 1944.

Instead of the planned SS Cavalry Regiment 18, SS Cavalry Regiment 17, which had just taken part in the fighting at Kovel, would form the core of the division. The new formation was to be organized as follows within half a year:

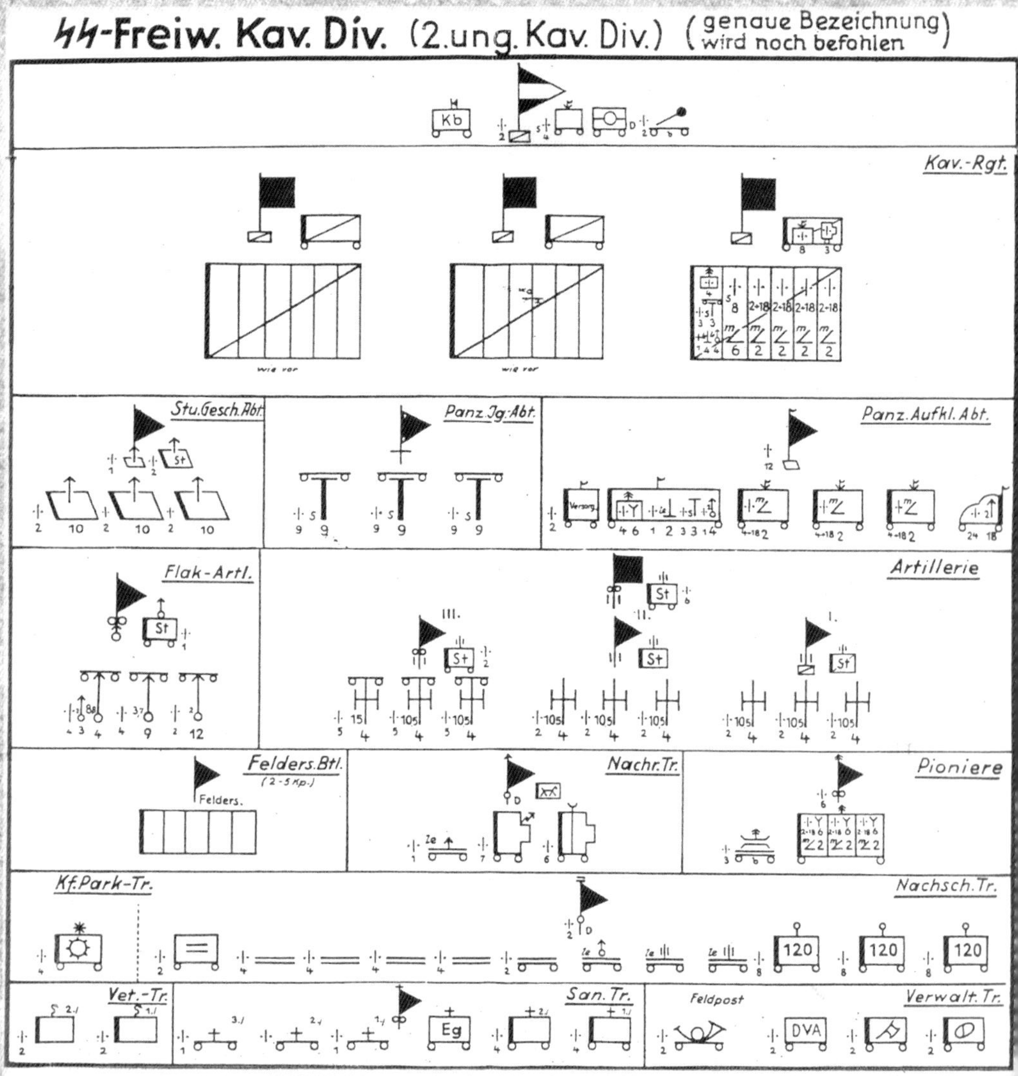

Interestingly, the title at the top of this table of organization for the 22nd SS Volunteer Cavalry Division from SS Operational Headquarters dated May 1944 includes the suffix "*(2nd Hungarian Cavalry Division)*."

Here, as was often the case, a potential title was chosen by a high-level office. Presumably the "1st Hungarian Cavalry Division" was the unit formed mainly from Hungarian ethnic Germans in 1942, which later became the 8th SS Cavalry Division "Florian Geyer."

Division Headquarters
SS Volunteer Cavalry Regiment 52[13]
SS Volunteer Cavalry Regiment 53
SS Volunteer Cavalry Regiment 17[14]
SS Volunteer Artillery Regiment 22
SS Armored Reconnaissance Battalion 22
SS Pioneer Battalion 22
SS Anti-Tank Battalion 22
SS Signals Battalion 22
SS Flak Battalion 22
SS Field Replacement Battalion 22
SS Medical Battalion 22
SS Economic Battalion 22

Eight weeks later division commander *SS-Brigadeführer* Zehender reported a strength of:

	Officers	NCOs	Enlisted Men	Total
Actual	96	570	4,248	4,914
	2%	11.6%	86.4%	100%
Authorized	433	2,262	9,926	12,621
	3.4%	17.9%	78.7%	100%

In July 1944 the unit was renamed the 22nd SS Volunteer Cavalry Division, and by 20 September 1944 its strength reached:

	Officers	NCOs	Enlisted Men	Total
Actual	112	616	11,715	12,453
	1%	5%	94%	100%
Authorized	433	2,262	9,926	12,621
	3.4%	17.9%	78.7%	100%

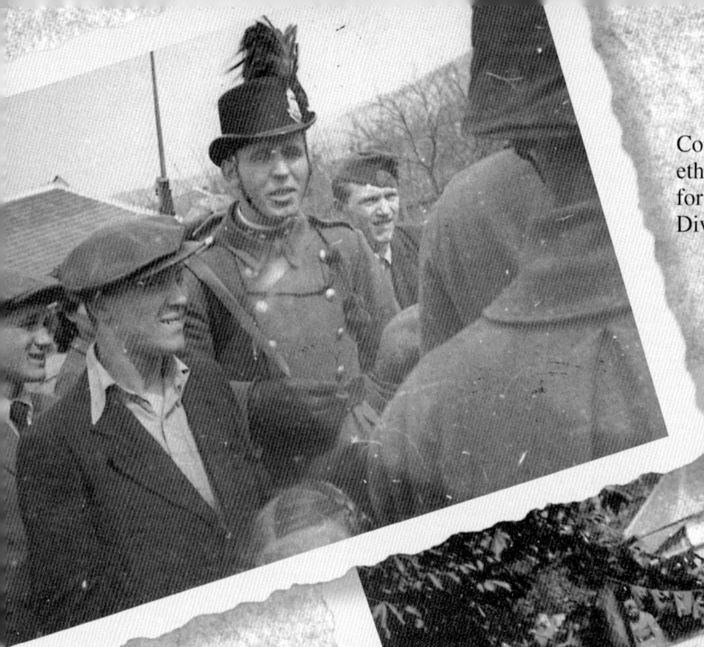

Conscription and training of young ethnic Germans from Hungary for the 22nd SS Volunteer Cavalry Division.

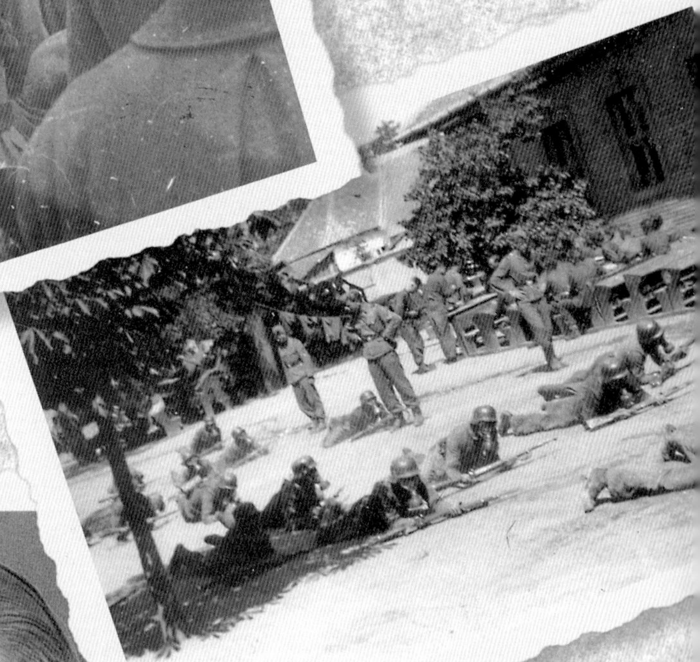

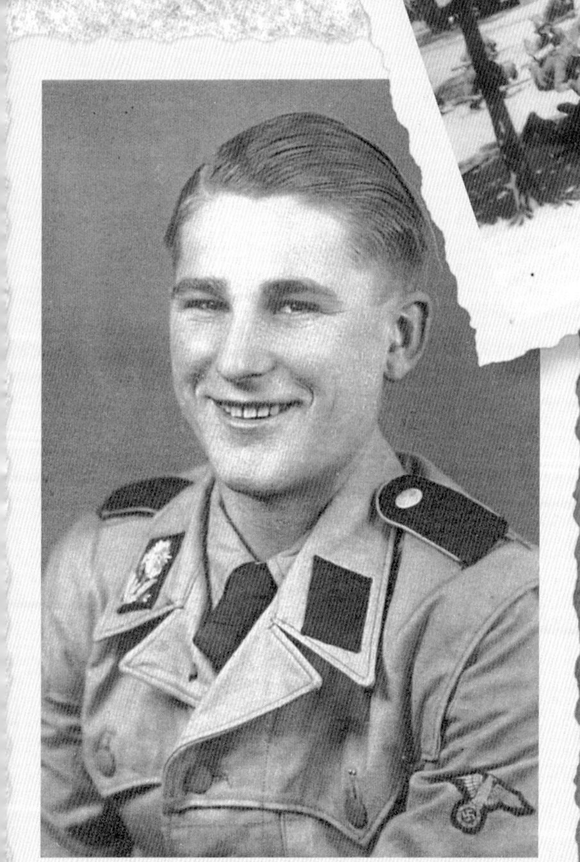

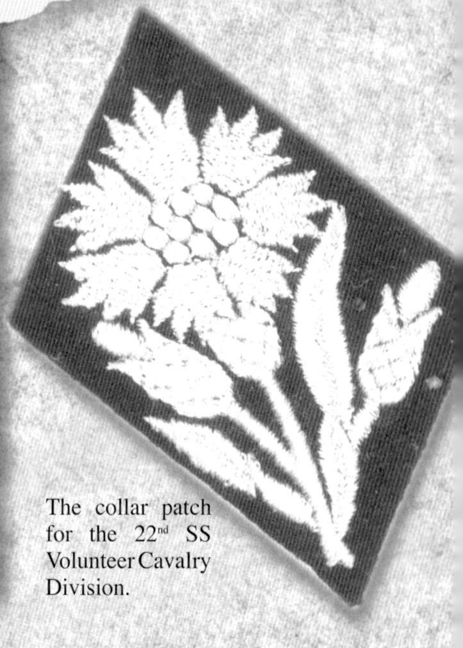

The collar patch for the 22nd SS Volunteer Cavalry Division.

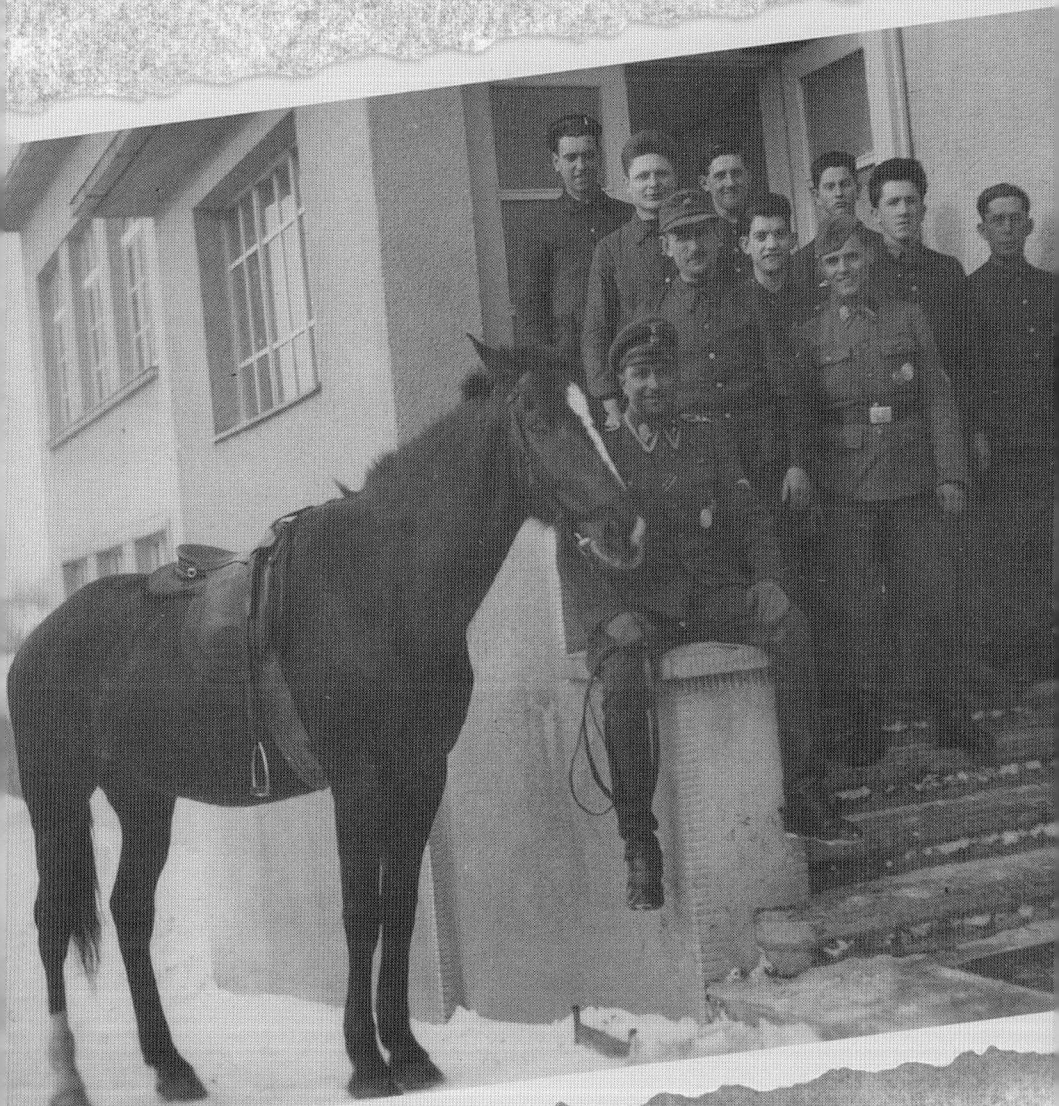

An *SS-Hauptscharführer* and an *SS-Sturmmann* of SS Volunteer Cavalry Regiment 17 of the 22nd SS Volunteer Cavalry Division together with ethnic German recruits from Hungary (November 1944).

While nominally it had achieved its authorized strength, the division was not yet operational. It was still short about 2,000 officers and NCOs, and had yet to be trained on and equipped with heavy weapons. And so, despite urgent requests by the Commander-in-Chief of Army Group South, *Generaloberst* Frießner, the division was only capable of forming a battalion-strength battle group for action at the hard-pressed front.

Battle Group Ameiser

Under the commander of SS Volunteer Cavalry Regiment 52, *SS-Sturmbannführer* Wiedemann, approximately 1,000 members of his regiment with supporting units saw action at the front. After Wiedemann was killed *SS-Hauptsturmführer* Ameiser took over the battle group, which was subsequently named after him. The battle group was made up of:

elements of SS Volunteer Cavalry Regiment 52
1 infantry gun troop
1 platoon of Vierlingsflak
1 motor transport column

Sent to LVII Panzer Corps in the Hungarian-Rumanian border area near Sarkad, the SS battle group was deployed with the Hungarian 4th Infantry Division. After the Hungarian units offered almost no resistance to the Soviet assault, on 2 October the SS cavalry were surrounded. After four days *SS-Hauptsturmführer* Ameiser ordered a breakout to the German lines. Some of the men completed the perilous journey, crossing the Körös and Theiss Rivers and rejoining LVII Panzer Corps at the end of October 1944. From there they were sent on to the 22nd SS Volunteer Cavalry Division's formation area west of Budapest to rest and reequip. The cavalry had succeeded in various ways in inflicting serious losses on the enemy in men and materiel, and Ameiser was promoted to *SS-Sturmbannführer* and awarded the Knight's Cross of the Iron Cross.

Action during "Operation Panzerfaust"

While SS Battle Group "Ameiser" was deployed about 200 km from the Hungarian capital, other elements of the 22nd SS Volunteer Cavalry Division were placed on alert in mid-October 1944. As the Hungarian Reich Administrator and Regent Admiral Horthy was preparing to take his country out of the war, Hitler decided to remove him for good—especially after the events in the spring of 1944. "Operation Panzerfaust" was carried out on 16 October 1944 under the command of *SS-Sturmbannführer* Skorzeny. The 22nd SS Volunteer Cavalry Division was tasked with sealing off the government quarter—the Budapest Castle—and occupying the railroad stations and other strategically important installations. The takeover of the government by the right-wing Arrow Cross Party under Szálasi took place without causing much of a stir. On 22 October the elements of the 22nd

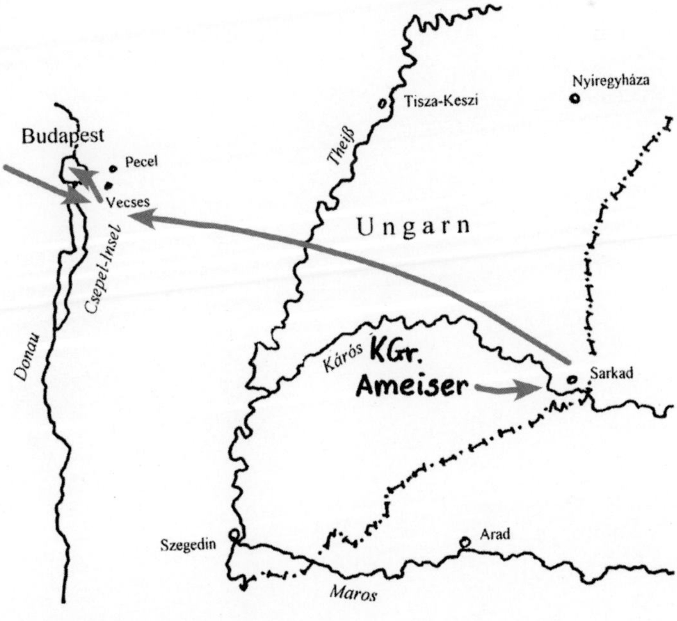

© Michaelis-Verlag Berlin, Oktober 2006

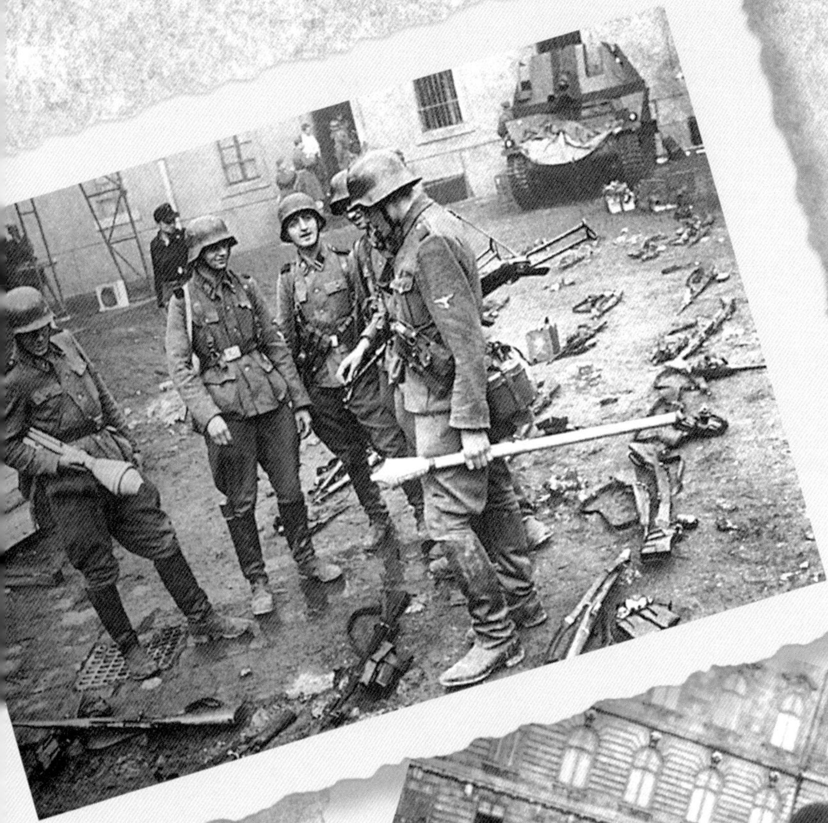

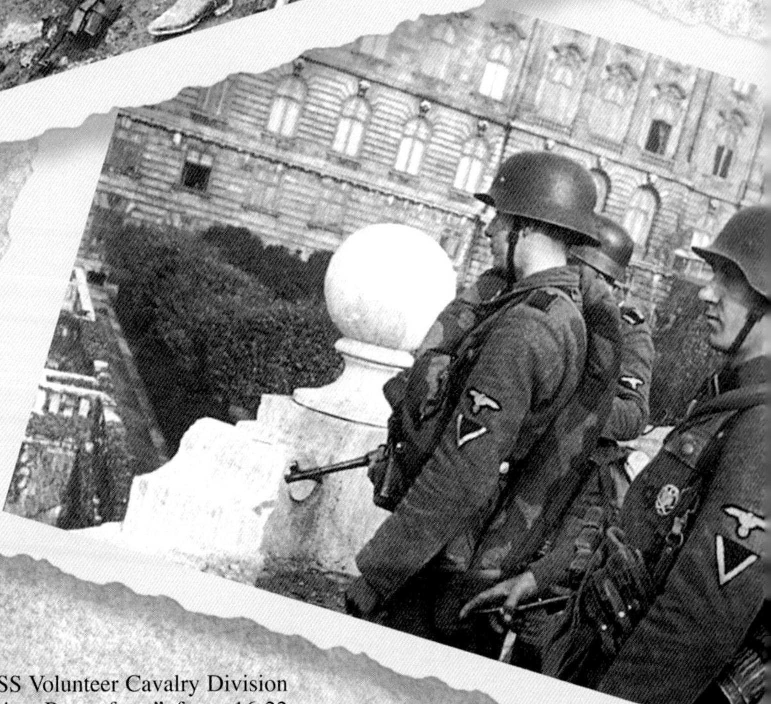

Elements of the 22nd SS Volunteer Cavalry Division took part in "Operation Panzerfaust" from 16-22 Oct. 1944, during which they occupied the Budapest castle.

SS Volunteer Cavalry Division that had taken part in the operation marched back to their quarters west of the capital. Werner Käser recalled:

"At the end of September 1944 we six officer candidates received orders to proceed to Beneschau – Woykau Castle in Bohemia-Moravia. In open freight cars we headed in the direction of Budapest. Employees of the Hungarian railroad rerouted us through Debrecen into the northeast of Hungary, probably due to the threat of sabotage. The train suddenly stopped in Tokay. With my last Pengös [Hungarian coins] I bought two bottles of wine, a real delicacy. Before we reached Budapest one bottle had been emptied and the other stolen!

We arrived in Budapest at the beginning of October 1944, and despite our marching orders we were picked up by the "hero thieves" (station guards) and whisked to the Hotel Imperial on the east side of the Danube, where a staff of senior officers was quartered. They immediately formed scratch units, which were deployed around the Hungarian Prime Minister because of the uncertainty of the situation. No one knew how the Hungarian Army would react to the fall of Admiral Horthy.

I was assigned to a unit led by Skorzeny. He led every available vehicle through the narrow streets up to the seat of the Hungarian government, castle hill, to arrest Horthy and the members of his disloyal government. The operation was quick and successful, and the few security personnel on the hill offered no serious resistance.

The Arrow Cross Party, which was well-disposed toward Germany, was formed in Budapest, and the threat of a conflict with Hungarian Army units was averted. Just one day later we were able to carry on to Bohemia-Moravia to begin the course. The military situation was then critical, however, and the course was cancelled after a few weeks. Most of the course participants went to Chulm, while I was transferred to Rastenburg. A new odyssey followed at the beginning of 1945."

The End in Budapest

Just one week later the unit was again placed on alert and attached to III Panzer Corps. Without the units of the battered SS Battle Group "Ameiser," *SS-Brigadeführer* Zehender led about 4,000 members of the division to the front southeast of Budapest.[15] Functioning strictly as infantry, the units occupied the line Alsonemedi (approx. 24 km S of Budapest) – Soroksar (approx. 10 km S of Budapest) – Budapest in the area of the Karola Position between Csepel Island and Vecses. By 2 November the SS cavalrymen, most of them young with no combat experience, were locked in a fierce defensive struggle.

After Headquarters, IX SS Waffen Mountain Corps had relieved Headquarters, III Panzer Corps for the Battle of Budapest, from 13 December 1944 the 22nd SS Volunteer Cavalry Division was under the command of *SS-Obergruppenführer* von Pfeffer-Wildenbruch.

After the Red Army completed the encirclement of the Hungarian capital at Christmas 1944, the strategic focus shifted to Buda, on the west bank of the Danube. The 8th SS Cavalry Division and large parts of the 22nd SS Volunteer Cavalry Division were moved to Buda from the so-called eastern bridgehead in Pest. Pest was abandoned on 17 January 1945 after the last bridges were blown and all subsequent fighting took place in Buda.

The situation there became apocalyptic. With no food or medical care and under constant enemy artillery fire a growing apathy spread. On 11 February 1945 the commanding general of IX SS Waffen Mountain Corps ordered a breakout from Budapest. Less then 100 members of the 22nd SS Volunteer Cavalry Division reached the German lines. The operational component of the SS unit had thus been destroyed in 10 weeks of combat operations.

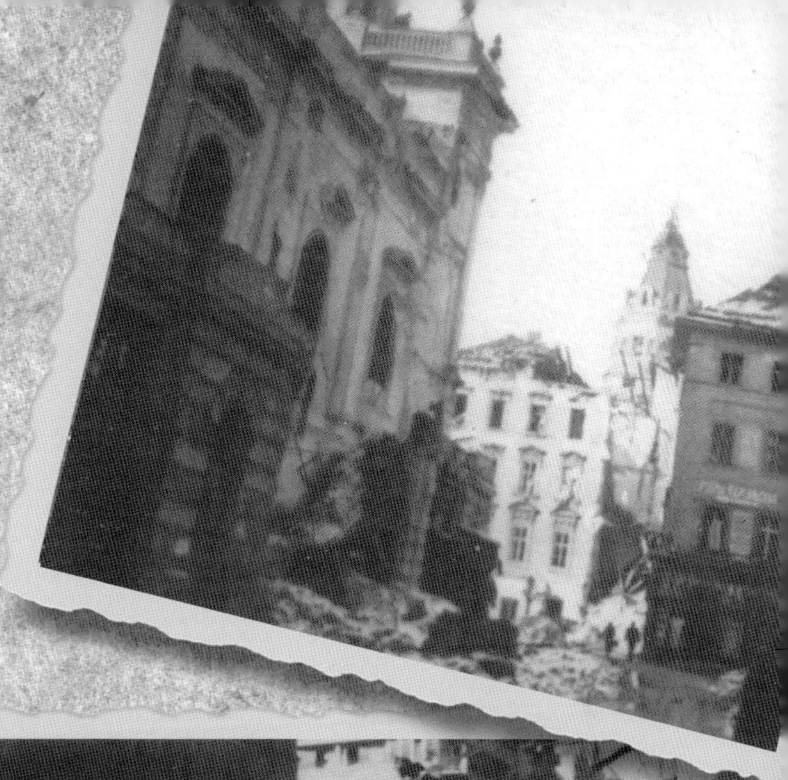

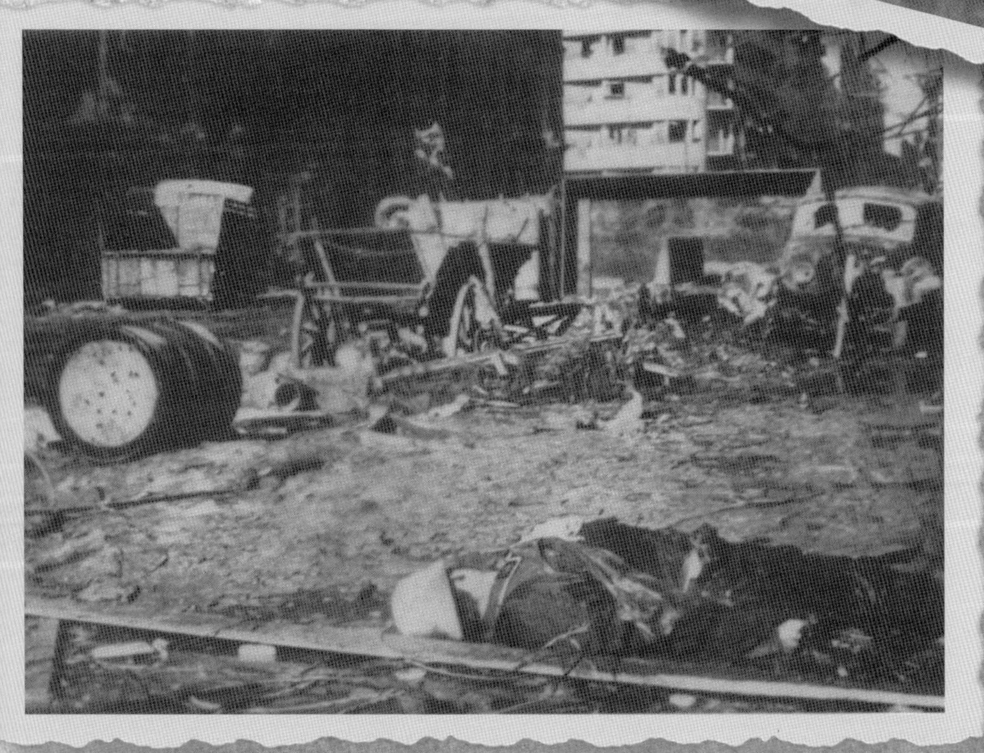

Budapest 1945.

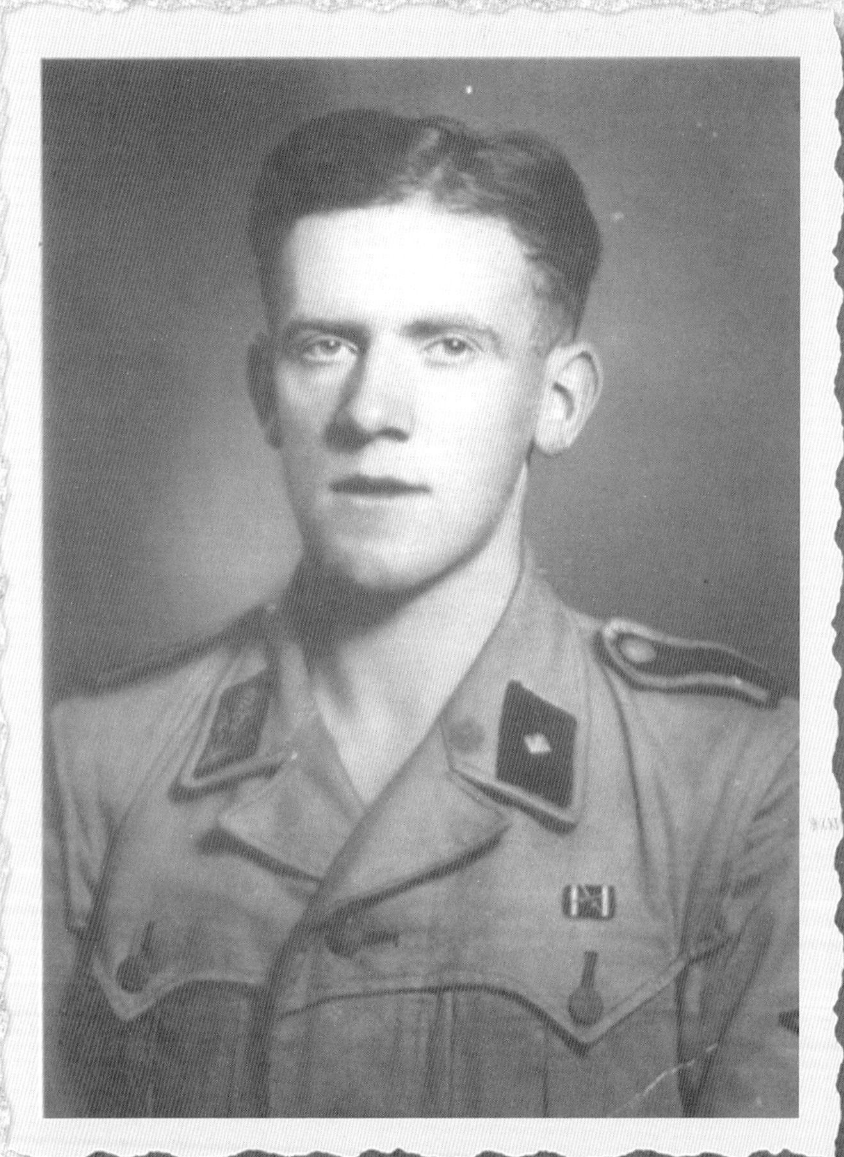

Werner Saß.

Johann Schwendemann recalled:

"I first joined the 22nd SS Volunteer Cavalry Division in October 1944 and was slightly wounded on 4 November. After a stay in hospital in Baden, near Vienna, at the beginning of December I was assigned to the 6th Company, then 14 days later to the 4th Company of SS Volunteer Cavalry Regiment 53. On 8 January 1945 I was wounded again in Soroksár and remained at the aid station until the breakout."

Walter Saß gave a very vivid description of his time in the division:

"From the summer to autumn of 1944 my company, the radio company of the 22nd SS Volunteer Cavalry Division, was stationed in Hungary for organization of the unit and training of the new recruits (mainly ethnic Germans from Hungary). We were quartered in Bia – Torbacy. The radio training took place under primitive conditions: there were shortages of training equipment, and consequently much emphasis was placed on infantry training. There was a reason for this, as we later learned. At the beginning of October 1944 a part of our company was sent into action to prevent Hungary from changing sides, as we were told. I was assigned as a squad leader in the streets bordering Budapest's castle hill and later in the inner castle grounds. Six days later we returned to Bia, luckily with no casualties. Late in the evening on 31 October 1944 we received orders to move out to a position east of Budapest. Our first contact with the enemy occurred on 2 November. We were employed as infantry, and during the morning hours of 8 November the Russians launched their anticipated offensive against our positions. We were initially forced to give up our village. We assembled at the exit from the village, and then in the late morning hours launched a concentrated counterattack. The Russians had to get out. In the fierce house-to-house fighting we lost contact with the unit on our right. I was ordered to reestablish contact. During the attempt to do so I was wounded in the knee. The platoon leader and two men took me to the aid station, which had been set up in a garden. My right knee was shattered, and I was taken in an ambulance to Budapest. There they told me that my leg could not be saved and would have to be amputated. Totally despairing and depressed, I arrived in Prague by hospital train."

After only a part of the division was ordered into the "Karola Position" as infantry, in February 1945 what was left was combined with the remnants of the 8th SS Cavalry Division and Hungarian volunteers to form the 37th SS Volunteer Cavalry Division.

The 37th SS Volunteer Cavalry Division

(*Die 37. SS-Freiwilligen-Kavallerie-Division*)

On 8 February 1945 the SS-FHA ordered the creation of the 33rd SS Cavalry Division. The division number was changed, however, with the simultaneous renaming of the following units:

SS Waffen Grenadier Brigade "Charlemagne" became:
the 33rd SS Waffen Grenadier Division "Charlemagne" (French No. 1)
SS Volunteer Grenadier Brigade "Landstorm Nederland" became:
the 34th SS Volunteer Grenadier Division "Landstorm Nederland" (Dutch No. 2)
Polizei Brigade "Wirth" became:
the 35th SS Police Grenadier Division
SS Assault Brigade "Dirlewanger" became:
the 36th SS Waffen Grenadier Division

As a result, by 19 February 1945 the *Reichsführer-SS*' field command office was already making reference to a:

37th SS Volunteer Cavalry Division

This was supposed to be created:

"*from remnant elements of the 8th SS Cavalry Division destroyed in Budapest and the 22nd SS Volunteer Cavalry Division plus […] Hungarian ethnic Germans and Hungarian volunteers.*"

Making up the core of the division were the approximately 6,000 ethnic Germans inducted in August-September 1944 who had not been sent to the front, and SS Cavalry Regiment 17, which was in the process of being reformed. They were transferred into the area Senec – north of Bratislava, where SS Field Recruit Depot 8 was located. Replacements came from a variety of sources, including the SS Cavalry Training and Replacement Regiment in Beneschau. Chosen to command the division was *SS-Obersturmbannführer* Gesele, who since 8 January 1945 had been envisaged as a training group commander at the SS Cavalry School in Göttingen.

The 37th SS Volunteer Cavalry Division, with only a brigade headquarters, was supposed to be established at Training Camp "Lesser Carpathians" in the Gajary – Malacky – Stupava area east of the Morava River, with the following organization:

Brigade Headquarters
SS Volunteer Cavalry Regiment 92 (I – II Battalion)
SS Volunteer Cavalry Regiment 93 (I – II Battalion)
SS Tank-Destroyer Company
1 "Ofenrohr" anti-tank rocket platoon
1 81.4-mm mortar platoon
1 50-mm anti-tank gun platoon
SS Artillery Battalion 37[16]
SS Pioneer Battalion 37[17]
SS Division Signals Company (partially motorized) 37[18]
SS Division Administration Company 37

Although this organization was supposed to be seen as binding, there were several deviations in the actual organization of the division. Basically they adhered to the framework of an Infantry Division 45 in abbreviated form, with a strength of approximately 6,600 men. And so the following units were also created:

SS Anti-Tank Battalion 37
1st Company (75-mm anti-tank guns, towed)
2nd Company (Jagdpanzer 38 (t) "Hetzer" dank destroyers)
SS Reconnaissance Battalion 37
3 (bicycle) troops
1 heavy troop

While two battle groups went into action in various front line sectors, in mid-March the unit activation staffs of the various units moved to the Znaim area. From there, on 4 April 1945 they were sent to the units of the 8th Army then in the process of activation. Together with attached army units, the division elements were supposed to close the gap extending to the 6th Army in the area between Marchegg and the mouth of the Danube. The next day the 96th Infantry Division with the attached Battle Group "Ameiser" crossed the Morava and took over the defense sector north of the river. SS Battle Group "Keitel,"[20] on the other hand, did not return under the command of the 37th SS Volunteer Cavalry Division.

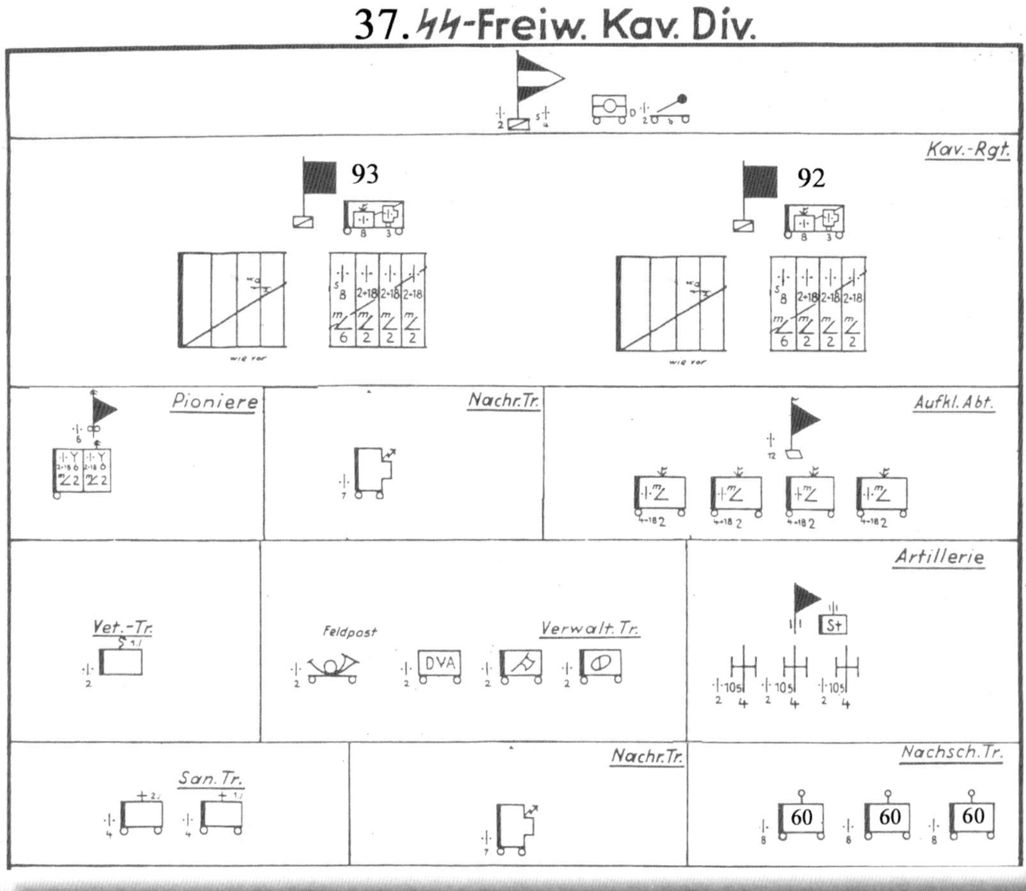
37. SS-Freiw. Kav. Div.
Kav.-Rgt.
93
92
wie vor
Pioniere
Nachr.Tr.
Aufkl. Abt.
Artillerie
Vet.-Tr.
Feldpost
Verwalt. Tr.
DVA
St
San. Tr.
Nachr.Tr.
Nachsch.Tr.
60
60
60

At this time the reinforced Grenadier Regiment 284 of the 96th Infantry Division, Panzer Grenadier Replacement and Training Battalion 82 of the 232nd Panzer Division, and Volkssturm battalions (including from Krems) were attached to the division. The fragmentation, command relationships, and composition of the units—elements of the 96th Infantry Division in exchange with units of the 37th SS Volunteer Cavalry Division—clearly illustrate the situation that existed then. Shattered units, like those of the 96th Infantry Division, were nevertheless viewed as strong enough to act as corset stays of the defense.

The 37th SS Volunteer Cavalry Division, whose first units had been alerted for action several weeks after they were formed, fought as infantry with no supporting heavy weapons. From the outset, therefore, the likelihood of a defensive success was almost non-existent, even though the old-growth forests along the Morava made it impossible for the enemy to commit tanks.

The improvised units fielded by the Germans were unable to prevent the Red Army from crossing the Morava; instead, the German unit fragments were forced to continuously withdraw. On 12 April 1945 the XXXXIII Army Corps (8th Army) was organized as follows:

Battle Group/25th Panzer Division
Battle Group/101st Light Infantry Division
Battle Group/96th Infantry Division with attached
SS Battle Group "Ameiser"
Grenadier Brigade 92 (motorized)
Battle Group/37th SS Volunteer Cavalry Division with:
Grenadier Regiment 284 (96th Infantry Division)
Panzer Grenadier Replacement and Training Battalion 82
Volkssturm

The units under Headquarters, 37th SS Volunteer Cavalry Division fought in the Rußbach – Aspern area near Vienna. The next day Grenadier Regiment 284 returned to the 96th Infantry Division. On 15 April 1945 *SS-Standartenführer* Gesele temporarily took over a sector northeast of Vienna. Three days later the division headquarters was pulled out of the front and moved to the Pisek – Tabor area for further activation of the division. Like SS Battle Group "Keitel," SS Battle Group "Ameiser" remained in action. The division command had thus functioned solely as a staff unit commanding various attached units (including a Hitler Youth tank-destroyer brigade and Honved troops). The former *SS-Unterscharführer* Franz Wunsch recalled the end of the war:

"In the last days of April 1945 elements of the 37th SS Volunteer Cavalry Division were in the villages of the Bohemian Forest, south of Prague, for activation. The division headquarters was in a small town with the name Beching. My unit, the SS Reconnaissance Battalion (anti-tank platoon), had found shelter in the village of Wostrowitz. It may have been the 2nd or 3rd of May when, during the early morning briefing, we received marching orders for St. Pölten, in Lower Austria. Our chief, SS-Obersturmführer Suß, instructed the men to stock up on gasoline, as fuel was only available in limited quantities. Sitting in a meadow were some brand new Kübelwagens wearing unusual camouflage. On closer examination we found that their identity plates still bore the WM code (Wehrmacht Marine, or Armed Forces Navy). The next surprise was that barely every second motor started. As there was no time for repairs, the unserviceable vehicles were attached to the intact ones with tow cables. Then an anti-tank gun was hitched behind each of them. We were ready to move out in less than two hours. We of the anti-tank platoon had been quartered in the town joinery, and we bade farewell to the friendly Czechs with whom we had been billeted.

About 90% of the young enlisted men were ethnic Germans from Hungary, Transylvania, and Yugoslavia. Only a few had any combat experience, and so they had not yet been welded into a team. The platoon leader was an SS-Oberscharführer from Berlin, a member of the SS Police Division. We four NCOs were from the 8th and 10th SS Divisions, the Luftwaffe, and I from the 32nd SS Division "30th of January." For days the atmosphere had been tense in all of the former Czechoslovakia. Our spirits low, we set off south towards Austria. We overtook a steady stream of units from our division, some on horseback, some walking, all moving in the same direction over the Bohemian roads. The first to fall by the wayside was a Luftwaffe NCO with his men. Then in the afternoon our tow vehicle also ran out of fuel. A dispatch rider reported that one of our division's assembly points was just a few kilometers ahead. So I decided to borrow teams of horses from the farmers to pull our vehicles. A growing number of village residents came out to gaze in astonishment at our colorfully camouflaged vehicles with the anti-tank guns. Young Czechs on bicycles and even motorcycles repeatedly passed us, grinning with malicious glee. The entire country seemed to be in revolt. Everything was decorated with Czech banners and flags waved from many houses. Finally one of the men returned with news that he had found a farmer willing to lend us horses. We all helped push up a long hill, as one of the vehicles was loaded with anti-tank ammunition. Otherwise the trip to our assembly point was uneventful. We gave the Czech some preserves and then discharged him "from our service." After refueling we continued under motor power toward Austria. In Pisek we (about 20 men) stopped near a park and tried to obtain fuel. This resulted in complications with the local German commander. Two of my men had already "organized" fuel from the Wehrmacht fuel dump, which had been turned over to the Czechs. "Don't you know that stealing fuel is punishable by death?" I was asked. An older Hauptmann from a rear-echelon unit, about 1.6 meters tall, stole the show, declaring to the local commander that the Czech farmers had previously made regular deliveries of butter, eggs, chickens, and so on, but that they no longer did so on the grounds that the SS was taking everything. After an argument, during which I drew my pistol, we were able to resume our journey toward St. Pölten. In Budweis we came upon members of our battalion, including the battalion commander, which increased the size of our group to about 150 men. We were able to refuel our vehicles again there. Soon afterwards, on 7 May 1945, we reached Austrian soil near Schremms. There we dropped off some civilians we had picked up along the way. By then signs of disintegration in the German military were visible everywhere. Only a few units maintained discipline in this situation. The roads were clogged and progress was slow. On the other side of Zwettl we learned of the end of the war and the surrender of the German armed forces. My spirits were therefore lower than they had ever been before. We were briefed in a large clearing in a wood. The battalion commander was there with a radio truck and his staff. A mood of defeatism surrounded us. Our comrades tossed their weapons, ammunition, and equipment into a large fire in the clearing. It was a miracle that nothing happened. We listened to the last Wehrmacht communiqué, and with sunken shoulders each of us spent a while lost in his own thoughts…."

Actions by
Division Headquarters and the SS Battle Groups "Ameiser" and "Keitel"
from February 1945.

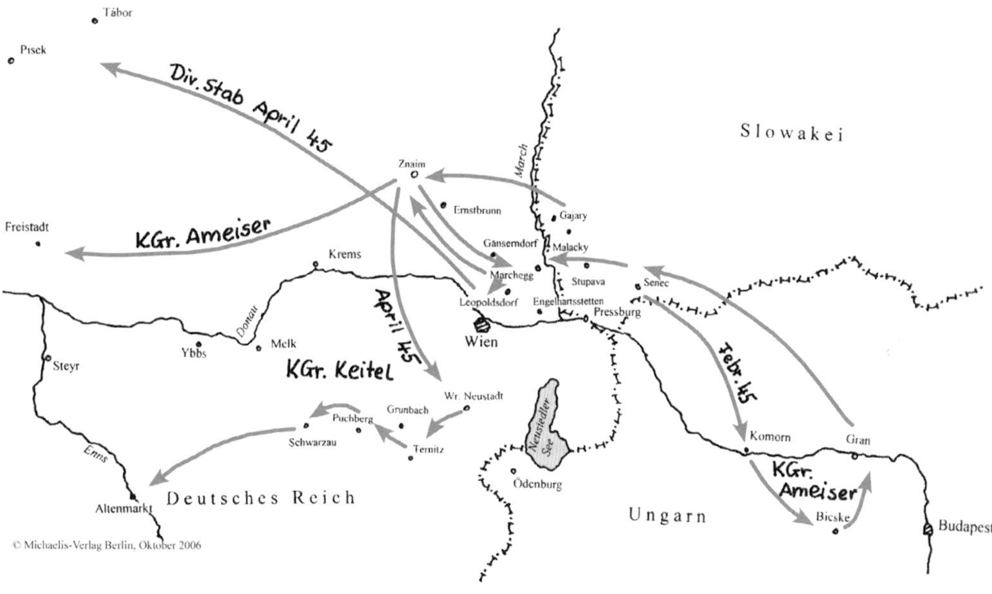

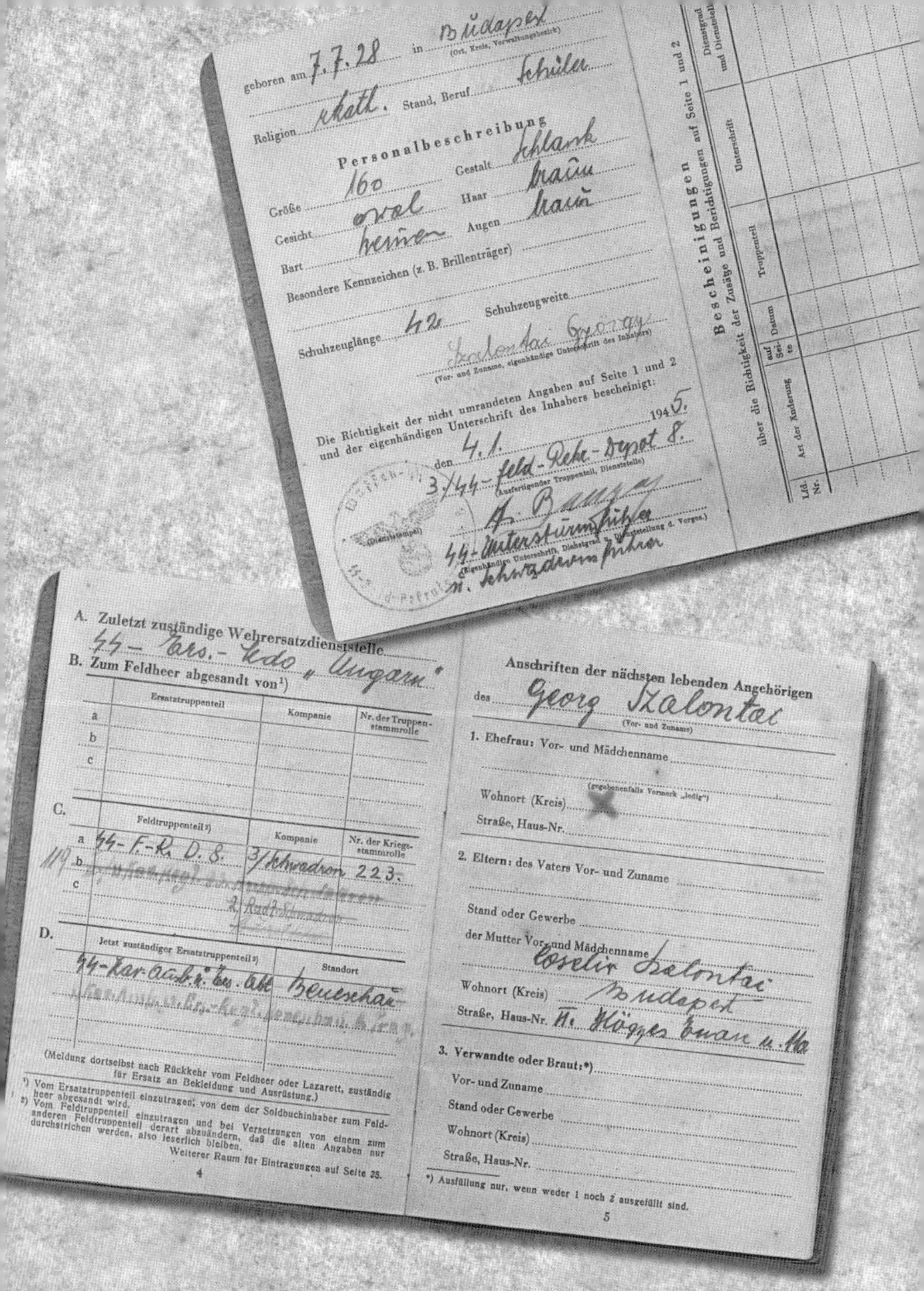

György Szalontai, a Hungarian volunteer just 16 years old, was a member of the Tank Harassment Troop of the II Battalion, SS Volunteer Cavalry Regiment 93. He was killed near St. Corona (Austria) just before the end of the war.

SS Battle Group "Ameiser"

In February 1945 *SS-Sturmbannführer* Ameiser, who had been decorated with the Knight's Cross while commanding a battle group from the 22nd SS Volunteer Cavalry Division in November 1944, was placed in command of SS Volunteer Cavalry Regiment 92. His former battle group headquarters staff and the remains of his battle group served as SS Activation Staff "Ameiser" in the Senec area.

Not longer afterwards, on 25 February Ameiser received orders to form a new battle group which was to be sent to Army Group Balck for the coming "Spring Awakening" offensive. Approximately 1,400 men strong, SS Battle Group "Ameiser" consisted of:

SS Volunteer Cavalry Regiment 92
1 battery of SS Artillery Regiment 37
1 company of SS Pioneer Battalion 37
1 platoon of SS Signals Unit 37
elements of SS Supply Services 37

Attached to the 96th Infantry Division (Hungarian VIII Army Corps), on 5 March 1945 the SS cavalry took up positions in the Bicske area. After the failure of "Operation Spring Awakening," on 16 March 1945 the Red Army launched its own offensive. Three days later the enemy broke through between the units of the 96th Infantry Division and the 1st Hungarian Armored Division. The troops positioned to the north finally established the German Gran bridgehead.

XXXXIII Army Corps was directed to guard the nearby oil refineries east of Komorn and assumed command of the German forces in the bridgehead. Operating as part of the 96th Infantry Division, Battle Group "Ameiser" made possible the evacuation of the heavy weapons to the north bank of the Danube, repulsing six Soviet attacks on 24 March 1945 alone. After the Soviets crossed the Gran to the north orders were issued to abandon the bridgehead.

On 26 March 1945 the enemy launched an offensive from his own Gran bridgehead, and the 96th Infantry Division with SS Battle Group "Ameiser" was forced back across the Neutra into the area north of Bratislava (Preßburg).

On 1 April 1945 XXXXIII Army Corps was organized as follows:

Battle Group/711 Infantry Division
Battle Group/96th Infantry Division with attached
SS Battle Group "Ameiser"
Machine-Gun Battalion 417 (*Hauptmann* Mark)
1 battalion of the 6th Panzer Division
1 Hungarian cavalry battalion
elements of the 711th Infantry Division
Battle Group/211th Volks-Grenadier divisions with
1 battalion of the Panzer Grenadier Division "Feldherrnhalle" 2
Anti-Tank Battalion "Feldherrnhalle" 2
2 battalions of the 711th Infantry Division

On 5 April 1945 the 96th Infantry Division and attached units crossed the Morava River and occupied a security sector from the Danube-Morava triangle to Marschegg, which recently had been held by the units sent from the 37th SS Volunteer Cavalry Division. The 37th SS Volunteer Cavalry Division detachment was subsequently assigned the line between Grub up to and including Marschegg. SS Battle Group "Ameiser" remained with the 96th Infantry Division as division reserve, while Grenadier Regiment 284 was attached to the 37th SS Volunteer Cavalry Division.

From 7 – 9 April 1945 SS Battle Group "Ameiser" was deployed in the Stopfenreuth – Engelhartstetten area with Grenadier Regiment 287. The enemy crossing of the Morava was followed by two days of fighting near Markgrafneusiedl. There the SS cavalry ended their attachment to the 96th Infantry Division and returned to the command of the 37th SS Volunteer Cavalry Division.

During the fighting it was observed that the new units quickly lost their ability to resist. Again and again scratch units were formed from less capable personnel, Viennese policemen for example. Without training and equipment they suffered enormous losses.

Until 18 April 1945 the units fought in the Kreuztal – Hautzendorf area under their own division command. After it was pulled out of the front to continue activation of the division the units again saw action under the 96th Infantry Division. Finally SS Battle Group "Ameiser" was also pulled out of action and marched through Znaim into the Freistadt area. There, next to the 3rd Panzer Division, it initially secured the area. Subsequently attached to the 6th SS Panzer Army, it surrendered to American forces.

SS Battle Group "Keitel"

On 26 March 1945, one month after the formation of SS Battle Group "Ameiser," *SS-Standartenführer* Gesele was ordered to assemble another battle group for action at the front. Attached to the 6th Army, it was to help halt the Red Army's advance out of the Ödenburg/Sopron area.

Formed in the Znaim area, the unit of about 1,600 men was led by the commander of SS Volunteer Cavalry Regiment 93, *SS-Sturmbannführer* Keitel,[21] and organized as follows:

SS Volunteer Cavalry Regiment 93
SS Anti-Tank Battalion 37
1 battery of SS Artillery Battalion 37
1 company of SS Pioneer Battalion 37
1 platoon of SS Signals Unit 37
elements of SS Supply Services 37

On 1 April 1945, SS Battle Group "Keitel" and elements of the 356th Infantry Division were attached to I SS Panzer Corps in the Wiener Neustadt area. The next day west of Ternitz the battle group barred the enemy from the entrance to the Siering Valley and later occupied positions in the Grünbach – Puchberg area. In the mountainous terrain, with few roads usable by heavy vehicles, the German troops succeeded in halting the enemy's advance. SS Battle Group "Keietel," too, held its own in various, often fierce battles.

On 12 April 1945 I SS Panzer Corps was organized as follows:

Battle Group/1st SS Panzer Division
Battle Group/356th Infantry Division
SS Battle Group "Keitel"
Battle Group/12th SS Panzer Division

On 7 May 1945 the remnants of SS Battle Group "Keitel" left their positions and marched through Schwarzau to Altenmarkt. As the River Ems formed the demarcation line between the U.S. forces and the Red Army an attempt was made to surrender to the Americans. No contact could be made with the detachment of the 37th SS Volunteer Cavalry Division, whose headquarters staff was at Beching/Bechnye (south of Prague), and the units went into captivity separately.

The then *SS-Untersturmführer* Simon recalled:

"*On 11 February 1945, as an SS-Standarten-Oberjunker, I was sent from the SS Cavalry School in Göttingen to the newly-activated 37th SS Cavalry Division, and in Deutschwagram occupied quarters for the 8th Troop. At the end of the month the son of Keitel senior arrived to command SS Cavalry Regiment 93. The regimental headquarters was 18 km away in a castle in Obersiebenbrunn. It was there that we were introduced to Keitel. Our personnel arrived gradually, 16 to 18 year old Hungarians, relatively enthusiastic, determined to rid their homeland of the Russians. The core personnel were the remnants of the former 8th SS Cavalry Division and came from Pecs, in Hungary. The language of command was German, translated by an interpreter into Hungarian. The equipment was relatively good, as were the horses from Hungary and the eastern horse hospital. In two months an attempt was made to teach the people the basics of soldiering plus discipline, steadfastness, and especially the handling of weapons. Given the time available this was relatively successful.*

From 26 to 30 March I was detached to Untersiebenbrunn to serve as entraining officer. Our destination was Wiener Neustadt.

Then, with the Russians advancing, we were forced to proceed, in the direction of Pottenstein, north into the Vienna Woods via Heiligenkreuz – Grub to Klausenleopoldsdorf. We dug ourselves in at the Schöpfl fence—to our right were elements of the 12th SS Division and left the 1st Panzer Division. We took many casualties there. The fighting extended over the Schöpfl [the highest hill in the Wienerwald mountains]. The Russians had unfortunately occupied it before us and could not be dislodged. All they had to do was lob hand grenades down at us. An attempt by our battalion commander and several officers also failed.

We were relieved by graduates of the Vienna officer's school. Unfamiliar with Russian fighting tactics, they dozed instead of watching the dense undergrowth and lost 15 men whose throats were cut. The old colonel, who I had briefed the night before and was convinced that he knew the Russians better than I, was close to a crying fit.

We drove into the Pax Valley to the Gasthaus Hutbauer, which still existed then. II Battalion, SS Battle Group "Keitel" set up its command post there. My post was in the Hutbauer chapel. There we were able to wash with 4711 eau de cologne and change clothes—after all there was still snow everywhere!

No one can imagine what went on there. German soldiers came from everywhere, all rushing in the direction of Altenmarkt. Coming the other way were Honved convoys, with women and children, trying to get back to Hungary. Anything that was in the way and would or could not yield was pushed down the left bank. Many motor vehicles were immobilized without fuel.

On 10 May 1945 we reached the bridge and safety. On the other side of the river we surrendered our weapons to the Amis (so-called Rainbow Division)."

Thus ended the three-month history of the 37th SS Volunteer Cavalry Division. As was the case with many other units, the military situation prevented it from achieving its authorized strength in personnel and equipment, and it never became a fully effective division. Nevertheless, two regiment-strength battle groups were formed and sent into action. Consisting for the most part of ethnic Germans inducted in August-September 1944, who had at least six months of training behind them, the battle groups were usable in the infantry role.

The SS Cavalry Training and Replacement Regiment

(*Das SS-Kavallerie-Ausbildungs- und Ersatz-Regiment*)

When the *SS-Totenkopf-Reiterstandarte* (SS Death's Head Cavalry Regiment) was formed in September 1939, a replacement troop was established in Munich. When the regiment was sent to the *Generalgouvernement* the troop followed to Warsaw.

When the SS Cavalry Brigade was activated in the spring of 1941, the replacement troop provided the framework for the SS Cavalry Replacement Battalion, which consisted of three cavalry troops, a heavy troop, and a driver training troop. Beginning on 19 April 1943 the battalion, with a strength of 10 officers and 450 other ranks, took part in the clearing of the Warsaw ghetto under *SS-Brigadeführer* Stroop, the SS and police commander in the District of Warsaw. One member of the SS Cavalry Replacement Battalion was killed and 29 were wounded in this action, which ended on 16 May 1943 and saw 56,000 Jews deported to Lublin and Auschwitz.

Effective 22 October 1943 the unit was renamed:

SS Cavalry Training and Replacement Battalion 8

In 1943 Jan Gwizdalla, then an *SS-Untersturmführer*, was a member of SS Cavalry Training and Replacement Battalion 8. He recalled an incident in the *Generalgouvernement*:

"*In 1943 I was ordered to bring some recruits from Warsaw to Kielce. They still had no concept of military life, to say nothing of handling weapons. The train stopped just south of Radom, as the track was blocked by derailed cars. The tracks were torn up, and because something like that didn't happen by itself the partisans must have had their hands in the game. A small Wehrmacht unit had gone after the wrongdoers and had not come back. Good advice was hard to come by, and no one wanted or was able to make a decision. I debated whether or not it was advisable to undertake something with my pupils. On the train, however, there were two dozen men in SS uniforms. Their language revealed them to be from the Ukraine. They were Galician SS volunteers on their way to SS Training Camp "Debica," and they were less than enthusiastic when I placed them under my command to do what had to be done. We gathered up all the ammunition we could find on the train.*

It was enough to give us a certain amount of firepower, and I set off with the Ukrainians. Moving on foot, we came to a small village where several individuals tried to take to their heels. That was always suspicious, and after the first aimed shots many raised their hands. And then I was amazed to see my brave Mennonites from the Ukraine, who in the beginning wanted nothing to do with the operation, apply the necessary force to get out of them what we wanted to know. With submachine guns held to their heads they led us to where the Wehrmacht soldiers lay. The partisans had first shot and then massacred them, or vice versa. When we found the personal effects of the murdered soldiers in a farmer's cottage the case was clear. We turned out the entire village and assembled everyone in the marketplace. I then gave the entire clan ten minutes to think things over, and when my men positioned themselves to fire the "evildoers" were standing alone—any sign of solidarity had disappeared. The statements were clear enough, and so I pronounced sentence in their own language. 15 German soldiers bestially murdered. The penalty followed quickly. Immediately afterwards I made the residents of the village carry the bodies of our comrades back to the railroad tracks. Returning after two hours, I heard a Wehrmacht pioneer major, who had arrived while we were gone, say: "Why didn't you level the entire nest, why is even one of them still alive?!""

Transferred to SS Training Camp "Bohemia" in July 1944, only about 100 SS cavalry took part in the Warsaw Uprising, which began on 1 August 1944. The then *SS-Unterscharführer* Schwenn recalled:

"In July 1944 the various replacement troops were withdrawn from Warsaw and transferred to Training Camp Bohemia in Czechoslovakia. Each troop still had a skeleton crew in its old garrison, however, when the Warsaw Uprising began precisely at 17:00 on 1 August 1944. SS-Sturmbannführer Plänk, our battalion commander, and the battalion headquarters had stayed behind and were in an embassy building on Victory Avenue, opposite the Copernicus Observatory and Belvedere Park, formerly the seat of the Polish president.

My friend Hans Miebs and I sat at the window in our quarters and talked. It was an amazing scene. Our comrade at the hut by the signpost dashed forward and took cover behind the cannon at the entrance. Then he began blasting away with his submachine-gun. All of this amazed and amused me in equal parts. But this couldn't go on for long. Hans had also taken a look outside and quickly realized what was going on: Take cover, they're shooting at our building! And so they were. Bullets smacked into the wall to the corridor, knocking dirt from the ceiling.

Together with the police and every other kind of arms bearer, we took part in the fighting until the beginning of November 1944. There was shooting and dying everywhere. When we left Warsaw, what remained was a burning city with desperate survivors. For three whole months and several days we had waged a pitiless war in Warsaw. Essentially it had all been for nothing.

We rolled westwards through Upper Silesia into Czechoslovakia, then the "Protectorate of Bohemia and Moravia," towards SS Training Camp "Bohemia." This training camp was the new home of the SS Cavalry Replacement Battalion. The towns of Seltschan, Tschorschowitz, Jannowitz, Drachkau, and Boskowitz were the troops' new homes. We had gotten to know a proper barracks in 1942, and the recruits of March 1944 were able to exist reasonably and comfortably in a Warsaw school, but not so the recruits of autumn 1944 and all of the following men who had the honor to serve in the SS cavalry. Their quarters were abandoned farmers' cottages which their former owners had been forced to leave. Much emphasis was placed on hygiene, but achieving it was never possible because of the primitive conditions."

After the formation of a second cavalry division (the 22nd SS Volunteer Cavalry Division) had begun in early May 1944, on 15 August 1944 the unit was enlarged to become the:

SS Cavalry Training and Replacement Regiment

When the Red Army advanced to the Oder in January 1945, the regiment was placed on alert and a battle group was ordered to Silesia, to the area about 50 km southwest of Breslau. Werner Barmann recalled:

"*In January 1945, at SS Training Camp "Beneschau," south of Prague, the 7th Company of the SS Cavalry Training and Replacement Regiment was placed on alert. Our troop was made up entirely of officer candidates. In the course of this alert we were issued winter uniforms and live ammunition. Our clothes and personal things were packed in so-called "cavalry feed bags," which stayed with the train. We spent one day and one night in our quarters in full uniform without arms and equipment. One thing that stands out in my memory from that time is that some of the handful of "especially popular" non-commissioned officers came to our room quite often and addressed us as "comrade." They were wondering whether they would have to go with us to the shaky front—you could literally see the bad conscience in their eyes. "Battle Group Plänk"—named after our commanding officer—was to be sent to an unidentified sector as a blocking unit. On the second day it was all called off and we returned to our usual routine. But the rumor mill was buzzing. It said that officer candidates could not be sent to the front as a unit. Instead we would be assigned to individual troops, 10 to 15 each. This was due to the possibility of excessively heavy casualties.*

At Watzlawitz we completed the preparation course for officer candidates that we had missed at the SS Cavalry School in Göttingen. Meanwhile Battle Group Plänk was formed using other troops and was deployed in the Waldenburg district."

About four months later, on 5 May 1945, the Prague uprising broke out. Once again orders were issued for the formation of a battle group under the regimental commander, *SS-Obersturmbannführer* Plänk, to help put down the uprising in the Prague area. There the battle group alone lost 112 missing. Hermann Melcher, then 16 years old, was a member of SS Battle Group "Plänk." He recalled:

"Born in 1928 and raised in a Christian home, I nevertheless came into contact with the German Jungvolk and the Hitler Youth at an early age. I enjoyed the activities there and was enthused about the pre-military training. During the selection of the gifted I was chosen to attend the Strassbourg National-Socialist Instructor Training Institute in Bad Rippoldsau. There I also volunteered for service in the Waffen-SS. I received my call-up from the Waffen-SS in the first days of March 1945 while serving in the Reich Labor Service. Training at the SS Cavalry Training and Replacement Regiment in Beneschau was very quick. At Marschowitz and Watzlawitz we were on our feet day and night, and they worked us so hard that one could have thought that it was we who were to pull the much trumpeted final victory out of the fire. Then we saw our first action. I was wounded while assaulting a railroad bridge over the Save River near Tschertschan, which was held by a group of partisans. I was sent to the military hospital in Watzlawitz, where we heard one piece of bad news after another on the radio. The news of Hitler's death in Berlin hit us like a blow from a club. Afterwards Hermann Frank, the Minister of State in the Protectorate, gave a speech and warned the Czechs not to revolt. Soon afterwards our hospital was disbanded. Those who could walk were sent back to their units as "fit for front line duty." The bullet wound in my right calf wasn't healed, but "the wound looks good," and so on 5 May 1945 I set off in the direction of Prague in light rain. With mixed feelings and our hands under out tent square sections, we trotted through the night at the reins of our horses. They had told us that we were going to entrain in Teinitz, but we had long since passed Teinitz.

As we were riding through a wooded area, a soft rustling in the undergrowth brought us to a high state of watchfulness. Suddenly bullets began flying and we had a hard time staying on our horses. From up ahead came a shout for a medic. When our side opened fire on the bushes with submachine-guns the nocturnal confusion was complete. With just one wounded, we subsequently rode onto the grounds of an obviously abandoned factory. Our platoon leader, SS-Untersturmführer Köhler, had all the married men with children step forward: "Take charge of the horses. You are responsible for their safety, well being, and constant readiness. In case of a trap we must be able to immediately mount up and ride away." Functioning as infantry, we advanced in a skirmishing line toward Cunratice—a residential suburb of Prague—and took up position there. I was acting as second gunner and carried two boxes of ammunition, a barrel protector, and a spare barrel. With about five paces separating me from the man ahead we walked along park-like gardens to our assigned positions.

7 May 1945, twelve noon. The sun burned hot from a brilliant blue May sky. We were lying in groups, smoking cigarettes, in the grass beside the road, waiting for what was to come. We were supposed to advance to the right of the main road to Prague and march on through a suburb with the 7th and 4th Troops on our right and left towards Prague. At first we made rapid progress. Our troop leader, SS-Obersturmführer Ertl, walked with our platoon for a while, before he moved over to the center. We made first contact with the enemy about 400 meters from the town. Suddenly it seemed as if there was fire coming from every corner, and we took cover in the furrows of a plowed field to avoid being shot down like rabbits in a hunt. Giving covering fire, we worked our way forward. The shooting stopped as quickly as it had begun. The silence was downright eerie as we advanced toward the first houses in a skirmishing line. It was clear to us that the rebels were dug in behind a barricade, about 200 meters above the road. The partisans began shooting again and Ertl ordered: "Prepare to attack!" Pistol drawn, he emerged from behind the wall of a house and dashed onto the road. At that instant a shot rang our and Ertl collapsed groaning onto the road. SS-Junker Dürrwitz dragged him back behind the wall and paid for it with a through-and-through wound in the back. Chalk-white in the face and foaming at the mouth—SS-Obersturmführer Ertl. Blood-smeared, squatting by the wall, and spitting out teeth—SS-Junker Dürrwitz. SS-Unterscharführer Häussler laid Ertl, who had a belly wound, on a ladder. We fetched a feather mattress from a house and used it to cushion the wooden frame. We then fought our way house by house towards the barracks. When caught, the residents of some houses fell to their knees in supplication, while the smoking shell casings from their treacherous ambush lay at the front door. From close by a loudspeaker blared: "German soldiers, surrender! Your situation is hopeless. We guarantee you a free withdrawal!" The word was passed down: "Work back in stages and give mutual covering fire!" I dashed toward the rear. At the starting point, where Ertl had been wounded, I found our squad— which was missing several men. A runner brought the order that we were to withdraw in the direction of Cunratice, back to our original starting position.

On 8 May 1945 we were in the first houses of Cunratice facing the forest. The Rumanian Ludescu and I were sitting in wicker chairs on a balcony. Two men, armed with a submachine-gun and a 98 carbine, were staring in boredom at the area in the direction of a wood. The previous night, after our return to Cunratice, we had taken up quarters here at the edge. The residents were downright charming, but they noticeably avoided crossing paths with us. The hours that followed were filled with checking weapons and equipment and the issuing of ammunition and cold rations. At 15:00 our troop received a new marching order. We were to spearhead an attack in the direction of Prague. Suddenly SS-Unterscharführer Häussler appeared: "Listen up! The marching order has been withdrawn. We must continue to hold here until the German civilian population is safe. You will spread yourselves out in individual nests and strongpoints." We moved out. The other squads followed at intervals. The men came out of the adjoining houses and advanced toward the wood in a skirmish line. Our squad had taken up quarters in a garden shed enclosed by shrubs. I was designated a field sentry. All of my senses were strained to the utmost. Behind every rustle and snapping of twigs one suspected the worst. Suddenly a voice rang out not far from our position and I saw the crouched figure of a man approaching. I shouted, "Halt! Who goes there? Password!" He stopped abruptly. Again I shouted "Halt, who goes there?," so excited that I had my finger on the trigger. The unidentified man finally answered "Horseback" and then added "troop runner Ludescu!" Ludescu came up and gasped, "The war is over! Pull back immediately. The ceasefire has been in effect for some time. We've lost the war! Unconditionally." Dumbfounded, I stared at the figure in front of me."

The former *SS-Standartenjunker* George Beckmann:

"After I was wounded at Kovel I spent about six weeks in hospital. I was with the SS in Warsaw when they tried to assassinate Hitler. Afterwards I went to Josephstadt to attend the preparation course for SS officer candidates. From there, in August 1944 I joined SS Panzer Grenadier Regiment "Schill," with which I experienced the Slovakian National Uprising. At the big farewell parade in Banska Bistrica I received the Iron Cross, First Class and the Close Combat Clasp in Silver. I returned to the cavalry school in Göttingen, and on 20 April 1945 was promoted to SS-Standartenjunker and sent to Prague-Werschowitz. On 3 May 1945, with the SS Cavalry Training and Replacement Regiment in Beneschau, I took over a platoon of Hitler Youth to take them to the Reich. We left for Pisek on 6 May. A few days later we were held, by the Americans at first, and later handed over to the Soviets. We were initially held in a large police barracks in Tabor. Having no tattoo I claimed to be a Wehrmacht NCO. That probably saved my life."

Cossacks in the Waffen-SS

In preparation for the establishment of the 1st Cossack Division by the *Wehrmacht*, in March 1943 *Generalfeldmarschall* von Kleist, Commander-in-Chief of Army Group South Ukraine, ordered all able bodied Cossacks to assemble in Kherson on the Dniepr. These men were used to form one Don Cossack and two Kuban Cossack regiments. The units were transferred to Training Camp "Mlawa" (west of Warsaw), where the formation of the division began under *Generalmajor* von Pannwitz. The unit was organized as follows:

- I Cossack Cavalry Brigade "Don"
  - Don Cossack Cavalry Regiment 1 (I and II Battalions)
  - Ural Cossack Cavalry Regiment 2 (I and II Battalions)
  - Svodno Cossack Cavalry Regiment 3 (I and II Battalions)
- II Cossack Cavalry Brigade "Caucasus"
  - Kuban Cossack Cavalry Regiment 4 (I and II Battalions)
  - Don Cossack Cavalry Regiment 5 (I and II Battalions)
  - Terek Cossack Cavalry Regiment 6 (I and II Battalions)
- Artillery Regiment 55
  - Don Cossack Artillery Battalion I
  - Kuban Cossack Artillery Battalion II
- Pioneer Battalion 55
- Signals Battalion 55
- Supply Services 55
- Administration Services 55
- Veterinary Services 55
- Medical Services 55

Of significance is the fact that numerous units, such as anti-tank or flak units, were not formed. The German armaments industry was having great difficulty making good the losses suffered at Stalingrad and Tunis, but these units were intended for security duties in the Balkans, where such units were not yet essential.

After about six months of formation, at the end of September-beginning of October 1943 the division was moved to the Syrmia region of Slavonia (Croatia), between Ruma (approx. 12 km NE of Mitrovica) and Belgrade. There the division was to be employed against Tito's partisans as part of the 2nd Panzer Army. In mid-October 1943 the entire division took part in an operation in the area of the 539-meter-high Fruska Gora (south of Neusatz). The division subsequently moved west into the Sid – Vukovar – Vinkovci – Vrpolje area to guard the main transportation net between Agram and Belgrade.

In December 1943 I Cossack Cavalry Brigade "Don" took over the quartering and security area of the 11th SS Volunteer Panzer Grenadier Division "Nordland," which was leaving for the Eastern Front. The area encompassed Sisak – Glina – Kostajnica. At the same time II Cossack Cavalry Brigade "Caucasus" marched through Brod into the north of Bosnia, where its mission was to guard the Brod – Doboj – Maglaj – Sarajevo rail line. At the beginning of January 1944 the three regiments of the II Brigade were ordered back to Croatia, where they moved into the area formerly held by I Cossack Cavalry Brigade "Don." During the pull-back, known partisan groups were engaged in an operation dubbed "Napfkuchen" (deep-dish cake).

From the area south of Sisak, elements of I Cossack Cavalry Brigade moved northwest into the adjacent Karlovac – Metlika area, and elements of II Cossack Cavalry Brigade east into the area between Drau and Save near Daruvar – Pozega – Brod – Bosnian Gardisca. Finally, elements of the two brigades began guarding the Agram – Brod railway line.

While operations were becoming steadily more difficult, the assassination attempt against Hitler on 20 July 1944 changed a great deal. *Reichsführer-SS* Heinrich Himmler took over the Replacement Army, and the SS Operational Headquarters set up the so-called Volunteer Leitstelle "Ost" in Amtsgruppe D. The new office administered the non-Russian volunteer units from the eastern area (Ukrainians, White Russians, Cossacks, Caucasians, etc.), which were to be transferred to the Waffen-SS.

At the end of July 1944 there were numerous conversations with the commander of the 1st Cossack Division. He was informed of the creation of a 2nd Cossack Division. During a meeting with Himmler on 26 August 1944, *Generalleutnant* von Pannwitz was informed that he had been chosen to lead a Cossack Cavalry Corps within the Waffen-SS.

On 29 September 1944 Himmler directed the Senior SS and Police Commanders to report the Cossack units deployed in their areas—most within the *Ordnungspolizei*—for the establishment of the XV (SS) Cossack Cavalry Corps.

The order for the formation of the XV Cossack Cavalry Corps, to be made up of two SS Cossack divisions and a Cossack Rifle (Plastun) Brigade, was issued two months later. As the bulk of the German core personnel had no interest in being taken into the Waffen-SS, the officers and other ranks remained members of the army. It was also feared that there would be unrest among the Cossacks if they were officially designated and uniformed as members of the Waffen-SS. So while the SS-FHA did send SS officers and other ranks to serve as core personnel in the new units being formed, the bulk of the division's personnel continued to wear the Wehrmacht Cossack uniform. The "SS" prefix was not used in association with unit designations in official correspondence for the duration of the war. The only exception was internal correspondence within the SS-FHA. On 1 February 1945 the SS-FHA advised that "*all indigenous members of the Cossack units attached to the Waffen-SS*" were considered transferred to the Waffen-SS. This directive had no effect on rank designations or uniform insignia, however.

The end of 1944 saw the beginning of the reorganization of the 1st Cossack Division into the XV Cossack Cavalry Corps. Numerous other army Cossack units were brought in, and the resulting corps organization looked like this:

1st SS Cossack Division
Commander: Oberst Wagner
Don Cossack Cavalry Regiment 1
Siberian Cossack Cavalry Regiment 2
Kuban Cossack Cavalry Regiment 4
Cossack Artillery Regiment 1
Reconnaissance Battalion 55
Pioneer Battalion 55
Signals Battalion 55

2nd SS Cossack Division
Commander: Oberst Schulz
Kuban Cossack Cavalry Regiment 3
Don Cossack Cavalry Regiment 5
Terek Cossack Cavalry Regiment 6
Cossack Artillery Regiment 2
Reconnaissance Battalion
Pioneer Battalion
Signals Battalion

3rd (SS) Cossack Plastun (Rifle) Brigade
Commander: Oberst Kononow
Cossack Plastun Regiment 7
Cossack Plastun Regiment 8
Reconnaissance Battalion
Pioneer Battalion
Signals Battalion

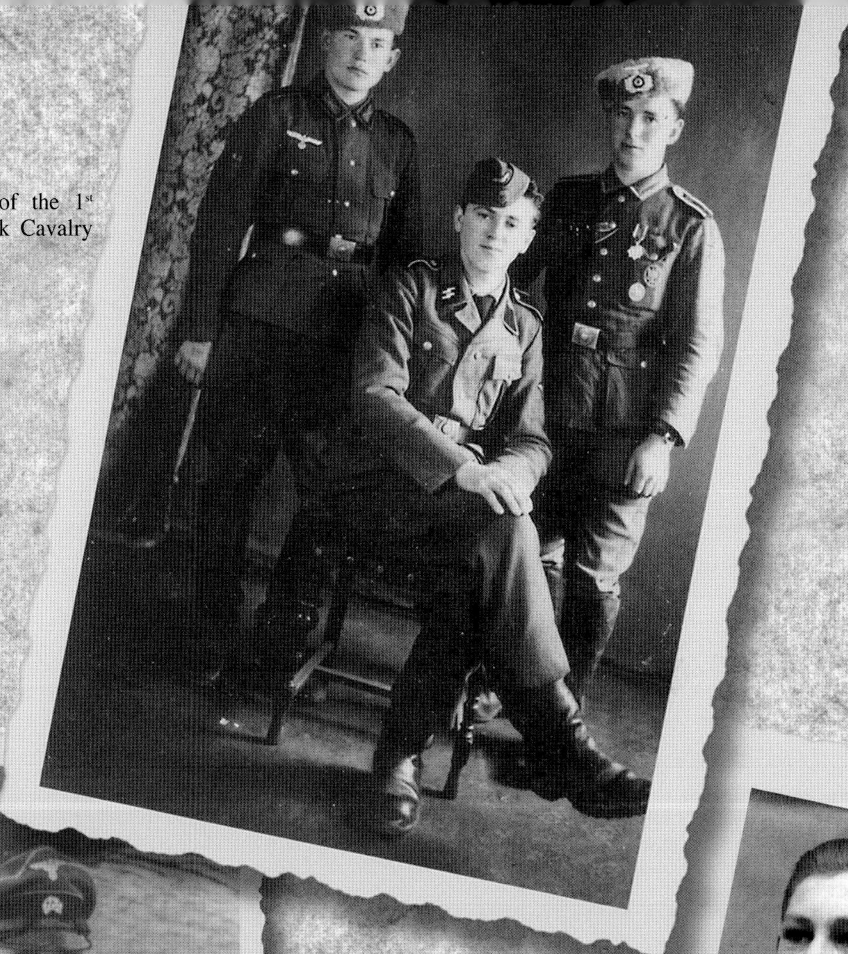

Members of the 1st SS Cossack Cavalry Division.

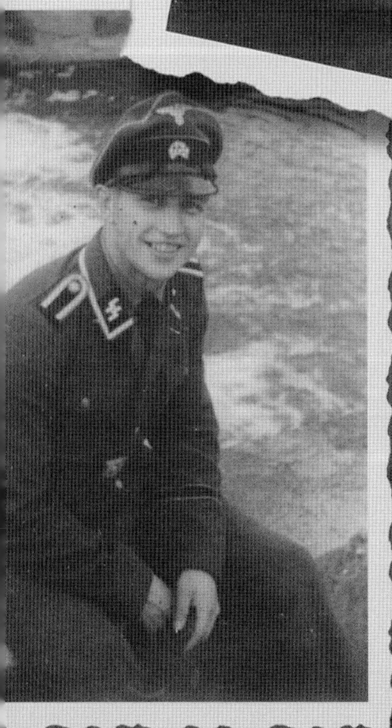

Rudi Kirchner was transferred to the 1st SS Cossack Cavalry Division as signals officer in autumn 1944.

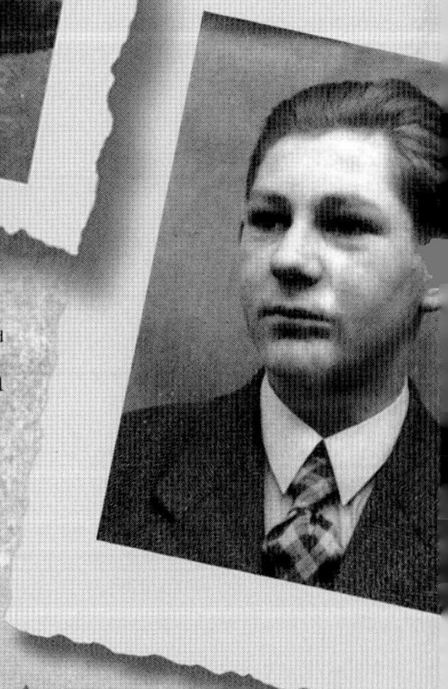

Eduard Kickel joined the 2nd SS Cossack Cavalry Division on 13/2/45.

F.S.Nr.5o64 SS F.H.A.-Amt II/Org.IE/IV(1)
Mit Wirkung vom
13.2.45
zur
2./ϟϟ Kosacken/Kavallerie/Division
versetzt.

In the winter of 1944-45 the newly-formed units were committed in the Sisak – Koprivnica area. On 25-26 December, elements of the 2nd SS Cossack Division saw action against regular Soviet troops for the first time, on the Drau Front near Koprivnica – Virovitca. Elements of the 2nd Cossack Division pushed back elements of the Soviet 133rd Rifle Division near Pitomaca and captured a great deal of materiel.

While the bulk of the units were deployed south of the Drau, elements of the 1st Cossack Division took part in "Operation Spring Awakening" in the Donji – Miholhac area (NW of Essig). They subsequently linked up with elements of the 2nd Cossack Division in the Sokolavac – Koprivnica – Drau area, after which the retreat began at the end of April 1945.

The Cossacks marched northwest towards Windisch-Feistritz and finally reached Lienz by way of Unterdrauburg, Völkermarkt, and Klagenfurt. On 28 May 1945 the British, with the use of force, handed the members of the XV Cossack Cavalry Corps over to the Red Army near Judenburg. For most this meant death. Of about 800 German core personnel barely 200 returned to Germany in the years up to 1955.

Appendices

Ethnic Germans in the SS Cavalry

Several thousand ethnic Germans—mainly from Hungary and Rumania—served in the three Waffen-SS cavalry divisions. What follows is a brief description of the agreements between Germany and those states that allowed these foreign nationals to serve in the Waffen-SS.

Rumania

Approximately 540,000 foreign Germans lived in Rumania, where they formed a German *Volksgruppe*, or national minority, under Andreas Schmitt. Unlike in Hungary relations with the Rumanian state were amicable, and the ethnic Germans areas were able to develop economically almost without restriction.

In June 1941, youthful enthusiasm led 1,000 men to volunteer for the Waffen-SS. To avoid external political difficulties, the Rumanian government approved their departure as workers for Germany! At the end of April 1941, during the fighting in the Balkans, another 600 ethnic Germans seized the opportunity to avoid Rumanian military service and spontaneously attached themselves to the SS Division "Reich." They were taken by truck to the SS Barracks "Schönbrunn" in Vienna and there formed into a battalion.

Draft-age ethnic Germans had little enthusiasm for joining the Rumanian Army because of harassment they faced there, and many wished to serve in German units. Rumanian Minister-President Antonescu had no interest in transferring ethnic Germans serving in the Rumanian Army to the Wehrmacht, but at the beginning of 1943 he gave in to Hitler's urgings. On 13 May 1943 the two nations reached an agreement on the recruiting of ethnic Germans by the Waffen-SS.

47,580 volunteers had already been recruited by 2 June 1943, though it is safe to assume that not all joined up because of a desire to serve in the Waffen-SS. Instead, the majority of the men opted to serve in the German Armed Forces, which included the air force and navy. The following lines, which appeared in the "*Völkische Beobachter*" on 22 May 1943, offer a different point of view:

"Ethnic Germans from Rumania in the Waffen-SS

Everywhere in the German-settled regions of Rumania, of Transylvania, the Banat, and the Bergland, men of the ethnic group are enthusiastically volunteering to serve in the Waffen-SS.

National Minority leader Andreas Schmitt already bade farewell to the first transport of SS recruits at a station near Kronstadt. In his speech he made reference to the fact that the Rumanian Germans had previously fulfilled their duty to the utmost in service with the Rumanian Army, and that most of them wore Rumanian decorations for valor on their field-gray tunics."

Following the imposition of an age restriction of 18 to 30 years, these volunteers were mustered as follows:

17,748 fit for service in the SS
12,743 fit for combat service in the army
2,031 fit for service as garrison troops[22]
1,429 fit for labor service

And so approximately 33,800 ethnic Germans from Rumania initially joined the Waffen-SS. After the mustering of an additional five age classes (31-35 years of age) an additional 16,000 men were inducted, and thus approximately 52,000 ethnic Germans[23] had joined the Waffen-SS by the end of 1943. This was equivalent to about 10% of the national minority. Of these, about 12,000 men classified as fit for combat service in the army were assigned to the new III SS Panzer Corps then being activated. The volunteers who met SS requirements were, as a rule, assigned to core units, for example to the SS Panzer Grenadier Division "Leibstandarte SS Adolf Hitler."

Unlike the national minority in Hungary, in Rumania there was no general mobilization in the spring of 1944, with the drafting of men up to the age of 60! Nevertheless, another approximately 8,000 ethnic Germans were called to arms until the summer of 1944. A total of approximately 60,000 men from the national minority served in the Waffen-SS. This was equivalent to about 11% of the foreign Germans living in Rumania.

Hans Hedrich was one of the first SS volunteers:

"I was born in Mediasch (Transylvania) in 1924, and in 1943 I volunteered to serve in the Waffen-SS. I believed that I was obliged to make my contribution to the German people's struggle for existence—which is how the war was described to us in those days. There was also morale pressure from the organization of the "German National Minority in Rumania" and society as a whole!"

Hungary

Approximately 845,000 persons of German descent lived in Hungary, the majority of whom were organized into a national minority under Dr. Franz Basch.

In contrast to Rumania, for example, the Hungarian government pursued a chauvinistic policy when it came to minorities. For the ethnic Germans this included the Magyarization of first, and in some cases last names, and the general suppression of German culture and education. The National Minority Treaty of 30 August 1940 between Germany and Hungary did nothing to change this. Because of this suppression and discrimination, ethnic Germans of draft age had little motivation to serve in the Hungarian armed forces. After the Balkans Campaign of 1941 approximately 1,000 young men from Hungary joined the Waffen-SS in an action that, technically at least, was illegal.

The Hungarian government under Minister President Bárdossy was essentially unopposed to the growing interest of the Waffen-SS in ethnic German volunteers. It saw this as an opportunity to weaken the German national minority, and an agreement reached on 1 February 1942 declared that the SS volunteers would be deprived of their Hungarian citizenship. All ethnic Germans from the 1912 to 1925 age classes (17 to 30 years of age) were called up, provided they were not already serving in the Hungarian army.

With a total of about 6,000 ethnic Germans from each age class eligible for military service, the theoretical total of potential recruits was 84,000 men. The actual number who volunteered was 25,709. Of these, 17,860 were found fit for service. If one subtracts the approximately 30,000 ethnic Germans serving in the Hungarian military from the equation, the result is that about every second man eligible volunteered!

Between 22 March and 3 May 1942, 16,527 men left their homes for SS Training Camp "Heidelager," which functioned as a so-called recruit depot. The majority of the men were used in the formation of the SS Cavalry Division and SS Mountain Division "Nord." Volunteers who met SS requirements were assigned to core divisions of the Waffen-SS. The recruiting effort had been a major success—within a period of five weeks the Waffen-SS had gained approximately 17,000 new recruits, sufficient personnel for an entire division.

One year later an effort was made to repeat this success. With the addition of just one age class (1926), with about potentially 6,000 men of draft age, in the second agreement signed on 1 June 1943 the age was extended to 35 years. Theoretically this added six more age classes with a total of about 36,000 potential volunteers. As some of these were already serving in the Hungarian army, the new Hungarian Minister President Kallay approved their release if they wished to volunteer! The first trains left Hungary on 7 September 1943. In an action that continued until 8 February 1944, approximately 20,000 men were recruited by the Waffen-SS, though by then not entirely voluntarily.

On 28 December 1943 there were 62,845 ethnic Germans from Hungary in military service. This was equal to about 7% of the national minority. They were distributed as follows:

35,000 in the Hungarian Army
22,125 in the Waffen-SS[24]
3,500 working in Germany
1,729 in the German armed forces (Wehrmacht)
459 in paramilitary units
32 in the Labor Service

In the spring of 1944 approximately 35,000 ethnic Germans were serving in the Waffen-SS. Including losses to date, just under 40,000 members of the national minority had served in the ranks of the Waffen-SS by that date. Just a few weeks later, on 14 April 1944, a third agreement was reached with the now Minister President Sztójay, which introduced compulsory military service in the Waffen-SS for ethnic Germans living in Hungary. Through this agreement, every man between the ages of 17 and 60 had become eligible for military service! The former Senior SS and Police Commander in Hungary, *SS-Gruppenführer und Generalleutnant der Polizei* Winkelmann, recalled after the war:

"In the spring of 1944—I don't know precisely if it was April—I heard that negotiations were under way in the German legation for an interstate agreement with respect to ethnic Germans serving in the Waffen-SS. The negotiations were being conducted by the commander of the Waffen-SS in Hungary, SS-Gruppenführer Keppler, and the head of the recruiting detachment in Hungary, Heermann. I learned the following: Himmler had directed the SS Operational Headquarters (Berger) to conclude an agreement between Hungary and Germany that would allow the ethnic Germans in Hungary to be drafted into the Waffen-SS. I pointed out that there had already been two recruiting drives—prior to 19 March 1944—aimed at attracting ethnic Germans in Hungary to the Waffen-SS. These recruited volunteers, however. The SS-FHA passed the above order on to the SS Recruiting Detachment in Hungary and turned to Keppler with the request that he support the order. Keppler subsequently spoke to the Honvéd Minister Csatay and received the Hungarian government's agreement in principle. After several changes to the text, service in the Waffen-SS became mandatory for all of those who were ethnic Germans by birth and way of life. It was not envisaged that those affected would have to reaffirm that they were ethnic Germans. The Hungarian War Ministry and the SS Recruiting Detachment in Hungary agreed on the following procedure: the local organs of the German Volksbund would compile local registers of eligible ethnic Germans. These registers would be submitted to the SS Recruiting Detachment for forwarding to the recruiting department of the War Ministry.

The latter presented the registers to local notaries for examination. The notaries removed the names of those who no longer considered themselves ethnic Germans. They also suggested names in some cases. The registers were returned to the War Ministry, which passed the results to the SS Recruiting Detachment. Heermann was complaining almost daily that the notaries were clearly removing German men from the lists and that the War

Ministry was not addressing the matter. In response I told him that for the time being he should be satisfied with those who had been approved. We would be able to negotiate over the rest later. And that is what happened. Meanwhile Himmler directed me to do everything I could to accelerate the reaching of an agreement. I tried to straighten things out: the Hungarians had their responsibilities, and so it is natural that there were differences of opinion. These had to be clarified after the treaty was signed through mutual agreement. As well, the process was tied to a complicated process which could not be abbreviated. I said that it would probably take another 4 to 6 months before medical examinations could take place. Only afterwards did the Hungarian war ministry begin conscription. The SS recruiting detachment, which was responsible to the SS-FHA,[25] assigned those draftees up to 45 years of age to the Waffen-SS and those who were older to the Ordnungspolizei."

With those age 17 to 35 and fit for active duty already serving in the military, there were still about 350,000 men in the German national minority in Hungary. Now those 36 to 45 years of age were to be drafted into the Waffen-SS and those 46 to 50 into the *Ordnungspolizei*. Of the approximately 50,000 mustered from the first group, roughly 35,000 were drafted into the Waffen-SS, while of the 30,000 men from the older age classes about 15,000 joined the *Ordnungspolizei*.

More than 10,000 of these were used in the formation of the 22nd SS Volunteer Cavalry Division. In October 1944 15,000 formed the 31st SS Volunteer Grenadier Division, and approximately 5,000 were used in the formation of the 37th SS Volunteer Cavalry Division. Approximately 5,000 men reached the 6th SS Mountain Division "Nord" in the first half of 1944. Large contingents also helped form the 11th SS Volunteer Panzer Grenadier Division "Nordland," or were sent to SS panzer divisions to help make good the losses suffered in Normandy.

Altogether 75,000 ethnic Germans from Hungary served in the Waffen-SS, roughly 9% of the Hungarian foreign Germans.

Wearers of the Knight's Cross of the Iron Cross

29/12/42	SS-Hauptsturmführer von Charpentier
02/03/43	SS-Standartenführer Fegelein, Hermann
30/07/44 (Swords)	SS-Gruppenführer Fegelein, Hermann
10/03/43	SS-Obersturmbannführer Lombard
10/03/43	SS-Obersturmbannführer Zehender
17/09/43	SS-Obersturmführer Göhler
01/11/43 (posthumous)	SS-Oberscharführer Nowak
16/12/43	SS-Sturmbannführer Fegelein, Waldemar
16/01/44	SS-Obersturmbannführer Rumohr
21/04/44 (Oak Leaves)	SS-Brigadeführer Rumohr
16/01/44	SS-Sturmbannführer Diergarten
21/04/44	SS-Untersturmführer Kirchner
14/05/44	SS-Obersturmführer Schachner
16/10/44	SS-Obersturmführer Klett
01/11/44	SS-Sturmbannführer Ameiser
11/12/44	SS-Sturmbannführer Drexler
26/12/44	SS-Hauptsturmführer Vandieken
17/01/45	SS-Untersturmführer Dallmann
29/01/45	SS-Oberscharführer Buck
27/01/45	SS-Hauptscharführer Wendrinsky
04/02/45 (Oak Leaves)	SS-Brigadeführer Zehender
09/02/45	SS-Obersturmführer Mösslacher
15/02/45 (posthumous)	SS-Oberscharführer Reissmann
20/02/45	SS-Sturmbannführer Krauss
20/02/45	SS-Obersturmführer Boosfeld
21/02/45	SS-Hauptsturmführer Maringgele
21/02/45	SS-Hauptsturmführer Phönix

Wearers of the German Cross in Gold

24/05/42	SS-Obersturmführer Maeker
25/05/42	SS-Sturmbannführer Gesele
16/10/42	SS-Sturmbannführer Zehender
07/02/43	SS-Sturmbannführer von Zastrow
11/02/43	SS-Obersturmbannführer Lombard
23/02/43	SS-Obersturmbannführer Rumohr
06/03/43	SS-Brigadeführer Bittrich
17/04/43	SS-Oberscharführer Brennenstuhl
17/04/43	SS-Hauptsturmführer Kessler
17/04/43	SS-Untersturmführer Luyken
21/05/43	SS-Oberscharführer Muscheid
26/05/43	SS-Obersturmführer Weeke
22/09/43	SS-Untersturmführer Korth
22/09/43	SS-Hauptsturmführer Löschnigg
22/09/43	SS-Hauptsturmführer Schultes
22/09/43	SS-Obersturmführer Vandieken
22/09/43	SS-Obersturmführer Weckmann
26/09/43	SS-Obersturmführer Göhler
26/09/43	SS-Obersturmführer Möslacher
26/09/43	SS-Sturmbannführer Weiss
01/11/43	SS-Brigadeführer Fegelein, Hermann
26/11/43	SS-Hauptscharführer Bohnenberger
26/11/43	SS-Oberscharführer Otto
26/11/43	SS-Hauptscharführer Stieler
15/12/43	SS-Standartenführer Streckenbach
31/01/44	SS-Untersturmführer Heuer
13/02/44	SS-Untersturmführer Thamm
11/05/44	SS-Hauptsturmführer Geier
14/11/44	SS-Untersturmführer Mehles
14/11/44	SS-Hauptsturmführer Scheufele

02/12/44	SS-Sturmbannführer Fegelein, Waldemar
30/12/44	SS-Oberscharführer Steinberger
30/12/44	SS-Hauptsturmführer Wacker
06/01/45	Leutnant Georgs
06/01/45	SS-Obersturmführer Portugall
06/01/45	SS-Hauptsturmführer Schaffner
07/01/45	SS-Obersturmführer Möller
27/01/45	SS-Obersturmführer Buttkereit
27/01/45	SS-Oberscharführer Finger
27/01/45	SS-Obersturmführer Flügel
27/01/45	SS-Hauptscharführer Kerkan
27/01/45	SS-Obersturmführer Klauss
27/01/45	SS-Hauptscharführer Maringgele
27/01/45	SS-Oberscharführer Mazurek
27/01/45	SS-Hauptscharführer Meissner
27/01/45	Major von Mitzlaff
27/01/45	SS-Sturmbannführer Plänk
27/01/45	Hauptmann Reinhardt
27/01/45	SS-Untersturmführer Rosenfelder
27/01/45	SS-Obersturmführer Stahlberg
06/02/45	SS-Sturmbannführer Bartsch
06/02/45	SS-Hauptscharführer Bresinski
06/02/45	SS-Untersturmführer Dallmann
06/02/45	SS-Sturmbannführer Keitel
06/02/45	SS-Hauptsturmführer Meiert
06/02/45	SS-Oberscharführer Reinhard
08/02/45	SS-Oberscharführer Thoma
10/02/45	SS-Hauptsturmführer Pleschinger
10/02/45	Leutnant Schrader
10/02/45	SS-Oberscharführer Tappeiner
14/02/45	Oberleutnant Panck
10/03/45	SS-Hauptsturmführer Greger
10/03/45	SS-Oberscharführer Paul

Military Postal Numbers and Division Commanders

8th SS Cavalry Division "Florian Geyer"

Military Postal Numbers:

Division Headquarters	17 771
SS Cavalry Regiment 15	22 771
SS Cavalry Regiment 16	40 144
SS Cavalry Regiment 17	16 148
SS Cavalry Regiment 18	36 846
SS Artillery Regiment 8 (motorized)	23 886
SS Armored Reconnaissance Battalion 8	45 637
SS Pioneer Battalion 8	28 406
SS Anti-Tank Battalion 8	48 646
SS Assault Gun Battalion 8	48 288
SS Signals Battalion (motorized) 8	32 270
SS Flak Battalion 8	27 532
SS Field Replacement Battalion 8	59 980
SS Medical Battalion 8	43 008
SS Economic Battalion 8	42 301

Commanding Officers:

09/39 – 04/42	SS-Standartenführer Fegelein
05/42 – 01/43	SS-Brigadeführer Bittrich
01/43 – 04/43	SS-Oberführer Freitag
04/43 – 09/43	SS-Oberführer Fegelein
09/43 – 04/44	SS-Oberführer Streckenbach
04/44 – 06/44	SS-Oberführer Lombard
07/44 – 02/45	SS-Brigadeführer Rumohr

22nd SS Volunteer Cavalry Division

Military Postal Numbers:

Division Headquarters	16 360
SS Volunteer Cavalry Regiment 52	25 212
SS Volunteer Cavalry Regiment 53	17 376
SS Cavalry Regiment 17	16 148
SS Artillery Regiment 22	36 965
I Battalion	40 729
II Battalion	17 955
III Battalion	37 876
SS Armored Reconnaissance Battalion 8	45 637
SS Pioneer Battalion 22	43 338
SS Anti-Tank Battalion 8	48 646
SS Signals Battalion 22	21 359
SS Flak Battalion 22	19 168
SS Field Replacement Battalion 22	22 928
SS Medical Battalion 22	27 104
SS Economic Battalion 22	28 572

Commanding Officer:

05/44 – 02/45 SS-Brigadeführer Zehender

37th SS Volunteer Cavalry Division

Military Postal Numbers:

Division Headquarters	45 725
SS Volunteer Cavalry Regiment 92	46 450
I Battalion	47 056
II Battalion	76 195
SS Volunteer Cavalry Regiment 93	45 757
I Battalion	65 297
II Battalion	66 631
SS Artillery Battalion 37	64 669
SS Reconnaissance Battalion 37	45 637
SS Pioneer Battalion 37	65 125
SS Field Replacement Battalion 37	66 993
SS Supply Battalion 37	67 956

Organization of a Cavalry Division 44

Division Headquarters
3 Cavalry Regiments each of 6 Troops
Artillery Regiment (motorized)
- I Battalion (towed) with 1st – 3rd Batteries (105-mm howitzer)
- II Battalion (towed) with 4th – 5th Batteries (150-mm howitzer)
  6th Battery (100-mm cannon)
- III Battalion (S.P.) with 7th – 8th Batteries (105-mm howitzer) Wespe
  9th Battery (150-mm howitzer) Hummel

Armored Reconnaissance Battalion
- 1 armored car company
- 2 Volkswagen companies
- 1 heavy company

Assault Gun Battalion (3 companies)

Anti-Tank Battalion
- 1 company (14 75-mm or 76.2 mm anti-tank guns) (S.P.)
- 1 company (12 75-mm anti-tank guns) (towed)

Flak Battalion (towed)
- 1 battery (12 20-mm anti-aircraft guns)
- 1 battery (9 37-mm anti-aircraft guns)
- 1 battery (4 88-mm anti-aircraft guns)

Pioneer Battalion (3 companies)

Signals Battalion (motorized)
- 1 company (telephone)
- 1 company (radio)

Supply Services (motorized)
- 3 workshop companies
- 1 supply company
- 9 small supply columns
- 3 large fuel columns

Administration Services
- 1 rations office
- 1 bakery company
- 1 butcher company

Medical Battalion (motorized)
- 2 first-aid companies
- 2 ambulance platoons

Rank Comparisons

German SS Rank	Foreign People's SS Rank	Army
SS-Grenadier	Waffen-Grenadier	Grenadier
SS-Sturmmann	Waffen-Sturmmann	Gefreiter
SS-Rottenführer	Waffen-Rottenführer	Obergefreiter
SS-Unterscharführer	Waffen-Unterscharführer	Unteroffizier
SS-Scharführer	Waffen-Scharführer	Unterfeldwebel
SS-Oberscharführer	Waffen-Oberscharführer	Feldwebel
SS-Hauptscharführer	Waffen-Hauptscharführer	Oberfeldwebel
SS-Untersturmführer	Waffen-Untersturmführer	Leutnant
SS-Obersturmführer	Waffen-Obersturmführer	Oberleutnant
SS-Hauptsturmführer	Waffen-Hauptsturmführer	Hauptmann
SS-Sturmbannführer	Waffen-Sturmbannführer	Major
SS-Obersturmbannführer	Waffen-Obersturmbannführer	Oberstleutnant
SS-Standartenführer	Waffen-Standartenführer	Oberst
SS-Oberführer	Waffen-Oberführer	kein vgl. Rang
SS-Brigadeführer	Waffen-Brigadeführer	Generalmajor
SS-Gruppenführer	Waffen-Gruppenführer	Generalleutnant
SS-Obergruppenführer	Waffen-Obergruppenführer	General
SS-Oberstgruppenführer	---	Generaloberst

Bibliography

Bundesarchiv Berlin:	diverse Personalakten
Bundesarchiv/ Militärarchiv Freiburg:	Aktenbestände der Heeresgruppen, Armeen sowie über die 8., 22. und 37. SS-Kavallerie-Division
Bundesarchiv Koblenz:	Aktenbestand Reichsführer-SS
Bayer, Hanns:	Die Kavallerie-Divisionen der Waffen-SS, Heidelberg 1980
Dallin, Alexander:	Deutsche Herrschaft in Russland, Düsseldorf 1958
Europa Verlag GmbH (Hrsg.)	Kriegstagebuch des Kommandostabes „Reichsführer-SS" und Tätigkeitsberichte der SS-Kavallerie-Brigade in: Unsere Ehre heißt Treue, Wien 1984
Frießner, Hans:	Verratene Schlachten, Hamburg 1956
Gosztony, Peter:	Endkampf an der Donau 1944/45, Wien 1969
Haupt, Werner:	Heeresgruppe „Mitte", Dorheim 1968
Hausser, Paul:	Waffen-SS im Einsatz, Preußisch Oldendorf 1953
Hesse, Erich:	Der sowjetruss. Partisanenkrieg 1941-44, Göttingen 1993
Internationaler Gerichtshof in Nürnberg (Hrsg.)	Das Urteil von Nürnberg, München 1946
Manstein von, Erich:	Verlorene Siege, München 1979
Melcher, Hermann:	Die Gezeichneten, Leoni am Starnberger See, 1987
Michaelis, Rolf:	Die Kavallerie-Divisionen der Waffen-SS, Erlangen 1993
Michaelis, Rolf:	Die Waffen-SS: Mythos und Wirklichkeit, Berlin 2006
Schramm, Percy (Hrsg.):	Kriegstagebuch des OKW, München 1982
Wagner, Carl:	Heeresgruppe „Süd", Bad Nauheim o. J.
Wegner, Bernd:	Hitlers Politische Soldaten, Paderborn 1982
ohne	Die Wehrmachtberichte 1939-1945, München 1985

Notes

1 Not only was the age limit lowered to 17, but the strength of 25,000 men was exceeded as well. When the reinforced SS Death's Head Regiments were incorporated into the Waffen-SS on 1 August 1940 they numbered about 35,000 men.
2 This had been formed for "*special missions on behalf of the Führer arising from the final struggle between two opposing political systems.*" These included the systematic hunting down and liquidation of certain groups in the rear army area.
3 These were the former 8th Batteries of the two SS Cavalry Regiments.
4 On 10 April 1943 *SS-Brigadeführer* Gottberg reported on the effort against partisans in White Russia. The following is an excerpt from that report: "*If one moves in with an advance guard, liaison men and a point, and then the rear guard comes marching in, those who actively prosecute the partisan struggle are miles away and all one finds are old men, women, and children. If one kills them and burns down the village, then the people say that the Germans are mad dogs, even worse than the Bolsheviks, and the women run to the partisans' female battalions.*"
5 *SS-Gruppenführer* von dem Bach noted in his war diary on 14 August 1941: "*The cavalry corps actions cost the brigade just two men, killed by a mine. But if one listens to Fegelein's reports, one would think that he was fighting the Russian campaign alone. [...] The continual self-praise, the general exaggeration, and the steadfast beating of the publicity drum should disgust professional officers, whose "old Prussian tradition" is: "be, rather than appear to be.*"
6 *SS-Standartenführer* Fegelein, commander of the SS Cavalry Brigade, was awarded the Knight's Cross of the Iron Cross for this action.
7 In April 1942 the titles of the SS cavalry regiments were changed from "SS-Kavallerie-Regimenter" to "SS-Reiter-Regimenter."
8 Placed in command of the division on 4 January 1943, on 8 March *SS-Oberführer* Freitag received a written warning from Himmler because of his lack of success in combating the partisan threat.
9 The title was changed from "Reiter-Regiment" back to "Kavallerie-Regiment."
10 Florian Geyer was a low-ranking Franconian knight who, during the Peasant's War (1525), took up the cause of the peasants and demanded equality for all. This included easing the burdens and duties of the peasants and the elimination of serfdom. He led the "Black Company," whose discipline and unity distinguished it from the marauding bands. During the bloody suppression of the Peasant's Revolt Florian Geyer, who always stood for restraint and unity, was murdered near Würzburg on the night of 8-9 June 1525.

11 Several were even awarded the German Cross in Gold in the spring of 1945 for their actions with the 8th SS Cavalry Division "Florian Geyer."
12 There is no record of the title "Maria Theresia" in official documents.
13 Initially designated SS Cavalry Regiment 1, in July 1944 the division and its regiments were assigned sequential Waffen-SS numbers. SS Cavalry Regiment 17 retained its designation.
14 When it was attached to the 22nd SS Volunteer Cavalry Division, the regiment also received the designation "Volunteer Cavalry Regiment."
15 Of the just under 12,500 division members (September 1944), approximately 6,000 men had just been inducted in August-September 1944. Most of these were not sent in the coming combat deployment. Instead, together with all the horses, they remained in the formation area, and in February 1945 formed the basis of the 37th SS Volunteer Cavalry Division.
16 SS Artillery Battalion 37 was formed in Beneschau.
17 The SS Pioneer Battalion—formation of which began in September 1944, originally for the 22nd SS Volunteer Cavalry Division—was moved to Mischdorf (area SE of Bratislava) at the end of February 1945.
18 Formed with elements of SS Signals Battalion 109 of IX SS Waffen Mountain Corps (Croatian).
19 For the story of this battle group see the chapter SS Battle Group "Ameiser."
20 For the story of this battle group see the chapter SS Battle Group "Keitel."
21 The son of *Generalfeldmarschall* Keitel, he was awarded the German Cross in Gold on 6 February 1945 while serving as commander of SS Volunteer Cavalry Regiment 17 of the 22nd SS Volunteer Cavalry Division.
22 Most of the men classified as fit for garrison or labor duty were assigned to the Sturmbanne of the concentration camps, especially Auschwitz.
23 Including those inducted in 1940 and 1941.
24 The small number of about 22,000 ethnic Germans from Hungary in the Waffen-SS on 28 December 1943 was calculated as follows: approximately 17,000 men were inducted in 1942. About 4,000 were released from service (killed or wounded) during the roughly one-and-a-half years of operational service until the end of 1943. From September to December 1943 approximately 10,000 new recruits were inducted into the Waffen-SS. The remaining approximately 12,000 men followed in January-February 1944.
25 In contrast to the so-called "Germanic" nations, there recruiting was carried out within the SS Operational Headquarters (Dept VI), the former "Germanic Volunteers Central Office."